Blake's *Four Zoas*

Blake's *Four Zoas*
The Design of a Dream

Brian Wilkie and Mary Lynn Johnson

Harvard University Press
Cambridge, Massachusetts,
and London, England 1978

Publication of this book has been aided by a grant from the Andrew W. Mellon Foundation.

Printed in the United States of America

Library of Congress Cataloging in Publication Data

Wilkie, Brian, 1929-
  Blake's *Four Zoas*.

  Bibliography: p.
  Includes index.
  1. Blake, William, 1757-1827. Vala. I. Johnson,
Mary Lynn, date,   joint author. II. Title.
PR4144.V33W5   821'.7   77-26738
ISBN 0-674-07645-1

For Ann *and* for Jack

Preface This book is addressed both to readers newly acquainted with *The Four Zoas* and to those who have studied the work often and closely. We hope to smooth the way for the first group and to intensify the effect of the poem for all readers.

There is more than one right way to read *The Four Zoas*; the work communicates not only on several levels (as almost all great poems do) but in several ways. It is one of the most encyclopedic works of the last three centuries, a deeply considered critique of the public values—in religion, economics, politics, philosophy, and science—that have governed our world since the Enlightenment; at the same time, it is an intensely personal work, touching the very quick of feelings and experiences that many readers consider so intimate as to be nearly inexpressible, even to themselves.

In order to encourage the wide variety of responses that this poem can legitimately claim, we have tried to present it in four ways: as an allegory (in the honorific sense Blake sometimes gave the word) of the way the four primal human faculties work, in the psyche and in the world; as an intricate structure, articulated with an elegance obscured for many readers by the poem's unorthodox narrative method and, more generally, its difficulty; as a highly moving story that can engross us in its characters and situations much as a good novel does (oddly enough, this aspect of the *Zoas* is one of the last things many readers come to appreciate) ; and as a strangely potent kind of myth that, like dreams, can penetrate the hiding places of our weakness and our power in ways that sometimes resist even the most rigorous analysis.

The first three of these modes can be demonstrated by fairly traditional methods of literary interpretation; the fourth dictates a mildly experimental approach: the adducing of analogies from personal and familiar experience, which, it is important to understand, are not intended as glosses on the objective meaning of the passages to which they are attached but rather as stimuli that implicitly invite readers to supply other analogies that may be more helpful to them in bringing the poem alive. This analogical method was of great importance to us in our earlier essay, "On Reading *The Four Zoas*: Inscape and Analogy," in *Blake's Sublime Allegory*, edited by Stuart Curran and Joseph Anthony Wittreich, Jr. (Madison: University of Wisconsin Press, 1973); a few passages from that essay reappear here. Our earlier reading, which examined briefly the first six Nights, was primarily an aid to college course-work in Blake. The present book continues to use such analogies but more sparingly, in keeping with our intention to treat the poem more comprehensively.

We continue to feel that *The Four Zoas* can communicate much of its meaning clearly, though inwardly, before readers are confident of their own understanding of the poem. Readers of our book, then, should not expect either a totally new reading of the *Zoas* or a highly eccentric one. Most of Blake's basic ideas are now fairly well understood and agreed upon; indeed, his leading ideas have always been clear to those who read him carefully without being distracted by the old slander that he was mad. Although much that we say in our book is new and, we hope, both valid and important, we expect it fundamentally to reinforce the consensus of Blakeans; if we were to arrive at an interpretation that radically contradicted those of John Middleton Murry or Northrop Frye or the early Harold Bloom, we would belie

---

Preface

our basic premise about the poem's firmness of meaning and its subtle but demonstrable coherence.

Books by more than one author often prompt curiosity about which author did what. For us that question is not neatly answerable. Some years ago we were colleagues at the University of Illinois; through coincidence and mutual influence, each of us was beginning to do serious and intensive work on Blake. During hundreds of hours of conversation we got into the habit of explicating Blake to each other through analogies and illustrations from personal experience as well as through more objective analysis. That experience helped persuade us that *The Four Zoas* could be reliably interpreted both analytically and intuitively. Later, when we thought of writing this book, the fact that our ideas so often converged or coincided when we tried independently to elucidate passages we had never discussed together reinforced even more strongly our confidence in both modes of understanding the poem.

In writing, our typical practice was as follows: Both of us made notes; then A (played by one or the other at different points) sent some notes to B, who drafted a chapter synthesizing the two sets of notes, whereupon A took over, with complete freedom to add to, subtract from, or revise the content and revamp the style. Each chapter then shuttled between A and B until both were satisfied. Thus few passages are mainly attributable to one or the other. At no time, except in relatively small chores, was there a critical or scholarly or stylistic division of labor; almost every idea and sentence of the book is the product of collaboration.

For financial and other practical assistance we are indebted to the American Philosophical Society and to the University of Illinois Graduate College Research Board. Mary Lynn Johnson was able to begin advanced work on Blake in 1968 with the support of a summer research grant from the University of Illinois and to continue in 1972 with released time from teaching duties at Georgia State University. Especially helpful was the appointment in 1973 of Brian Wilkie as an associate in the University of Illinois Center for Advanced Study. We thank the British Library, especially its Department of Manuscripts, for the opportunity to examine in some detail the manuscript of *The Four Zoas.* We have profited also from the resources of the following institutions and their rare-book librarians: the British Museum Department of Prints and Drawings, the Fitzwilliam Museum, Harvard University Library, the Huntington Library, the Rosenwald Collection of the Library of Congress, the Berg Collection and Rare Book Room of the New York Public Library, the Newberry Library, Yale University Library, and the University of Illinois Library. We are grateful for the advice of Norman Thurston and of Stuart Curran and Joseph Anthony Wittreich, Jr., who helped initiate this book by soliciting an article on *The Four Zoas* for their collection *Blake's Sublime Allegory.* As he has done for so many students of Blake, David V. Erdman has guided us into several paths we found it valuable to explore. Deborah Holdstein and David H. Duke performed valuable research. The manuscript was typed, at various stages, by Brenda Azurmendi, Donna Bradford, Brenda J. Coker, Bonita Higgerson, Mary Kay Peer, and Irene Wahlfeldt; other aid was provided by Marjorie Beasley, Katherine Brown, Marlyn Ehlers, and Mary Knight.

We owe a large debt to Joyce Backman, who gave both warm encouragement and sound advice about the strategy of our book, and Katherine Miller, who helped us to shape the book as a whole and to tighten and clarify innumerable passages.

Our spouses, John E. Grant and Ann J. Wilkie, contributed not only encouragement but, in different degrees and propor-

Preface

tions, priceless help with matters of style, tone, clarity, information, and scholarly judgment. As our dedication suggests, we thank them most of all.

Our most general debt is to the community of Blake scholars, present and past, and to our students at Georgia State and Illinois, who have contributed more than they can possibly realize.

Brian Wilkie
Mary Lynn Johnson

The Manuscript of *The Four Zoas*

Most of Blake's poems exist as illuminated etchings, fusions of text and pictures, invented and physically executed by Blake himself. These works were meant to reach a public, either the public at large or individual patrons for whom Blake made individual copies. The last two of his three long epics, *Milton* and *Jerusalem*, exist in this finished form. *The Four Zoas*, the earliest of the epics (though it overlaps in date of composition one or both of the others), was not published in this way. It exists as a unique manuscript, located in the Department of Manuscripts of the British Library.

The document poses enormously complex questions, not only about its format, its history, and the intended sequence of parts, but also about its fundamental purpose. Whether Blake intended at some time to make it public is uncertain; one assumes that he did, since he expended vast efforts on it. But for whom, no one can say. Much of the manuscript was written in ink on fresh sheets of high-quality paper in painstaking engraver's script; we can therefore infer that during some stage or stages of the poem's gestation the manuscript was meant to be a finished product in itself and not merely a workbook. On the other hand, the latter parts of the poem were written in ordinary handwriting, often hasty and difficult to decipher, mainly in the blank spaces on proof sheets of Blake's engravings illustrating Young's poem *Night Thoughts*. (It is possible that Blake chose these proof sheets for their pictorial relevance to *The Four Zoas*.) Moreover, many even of the earlier pages, originally so elegant in their

calligraphy, have been written over with revisions, sometimes extensively and messily. It is also certain, then, that
at some point the manuscript did become a workbook.

Most of the pages contain drawings by Blake, some carefully finished, some redrawn several times, some only roughly
sketched. These pictures are unquestionably related to the
text of the *Zoas,* often in the ironic or otherwise indirect way
used in many of the illuminated poems. A number of the
pages have been erased—by whom is uncertain; they are what
many people would call pornographic. It seems impossible
that Blake could have intended them as part of a final version to be widely distributed.

The date of composition is likewise a problem. Most
scholars agree that the poem, or most of it, was written over
approximately the decade beginning around 1796, but for
how much longer before his death in 1827 Blake continued
to tinker with it one cannot be sure.

In short, despite some valuable discoveries and detective
work on the manuscript, many urgent questions about the
Zoas remain open, answerable only by educated guesses. For
concise summaries both of what we know and of what we do
not know, the reader can consult the introductory remarks in
the textual notes by Erdman and Keynes (E737-39, K897-98);
lengthier discussion can be found in the Bentley facsimile
edition and in H. M. Margoliouth, *Vala: Blake's Numbered
Text* (Oxford: Clarendon Press, 1956); but even these extended studies, redoubtable as they are, are open to challenge
in some of their conclusions. (At present a lively debate is
in progress about how the two versions of Night VII fit into
the poem; for further information on this matter, see the
notes to Night VII.)

Since the present book considers among other things the
mode through which Blake wished to communicate with
the reader, it would be helpful to know just what the *Zoas*
manuscript is. Did Blake finish the poem in the **sense** that he

The Manuscript

brought it to a stage where he was satisfied with it, or at least with its text? If not, did he ever decide definitely to abandon it? Some day we may know for sure; at present we do not. The evidence from the physical text is too plentiful and complex to have been thoroughly analyzed yet; on the other hand, definitive external evidence such as letters might provide is sadly lacking. Our case for *The Four Zoas* as a successfully coherent work rests mainly on internal evidence: the pattern of meaning, imagery, structure, and story that emerges when one reads the poem closely.

Contents

Blake's *Four Zoas*

Albion, the Zoas, and the Emanations

The principal characters in *The Four Zoas* personify the whole human being, who is also mankind, and man's four constituent faculties or forces; these are called Zoas and are portrayed as males. Each of them has an Emanation, portrayed as female, who represents the distinctive product, activity, or external manifestation of the Zoa who is her counterpart.

Albion is the whole person and mankind. His Emanation is Jerusalem, who represents the perfect freedom enjoyed by man in the unfallen state (called by Blake Eden or Eternity) where he is in harmony with himself and with the world. The fallen state is a condition in which each of the four primal powers betrays what is best in itself and wars with the others.

Urizen is reason or intellect. In his worst state of fallenness he becomes Satan. Urizen's Emanation is Ahania.

Luvah is passion. In the unfallen state his identity blends with that of Jesus; fallen, Luvah becomes Orc and in that character represents the violent libidinal and revolutionary forces. Luvah's Emanation is Vala. She has a double role, as both the outward manifestation of passion and the natural world. In her lowest state of fallenness she becomes Rahab and Tirzah.

Urthona is imagination or the creative faculty. In the fallen world he is named Los. His Emanation is Enitharmon.

Tharmas is instinct, the innocent and reflexive sense of wholeness that makes the person or mankind a harmonious unity. His Emanation is Enion.

Introduction

> Four Mighty Ones are in every Man: a Perfect Unity
> Cannot Exist. but from the Universal Brotherhood of Eden
> The Universal Man. To Whom be Glory Evermore Amen

Any attempt to say what *The Four Zoas* means hinges on the even more fundamental question *how* it means.[1] The problematical vehicle through which the work has come down to us is partly a cause, partly an apt reflection, of the challenge it presents. Almost all new readers of the poem and even some more experienced ones find it distressingly difficult. Anyone who has taught the *Zoas* knows that this is true even when students appreciate, in some sense, or at least respect the poem.

Someone once remarked that grasping its meaning is like trying to pick up a bowling ball that has no finger holes. The complaint corroborates in a homely way some points that Helen T. McNeil has made about the poem: unlike most of Blake's works, the poem seems to exist without a context, even such a personally Blakean one as that given in the expository parts of *Milton*; the mythology of the poem is offered to the reader bluntly, as a fait accompli without explanation or justification; the meanings of the poem can be derived only from its hectic and disruptive scenes themselves; the nonmimetic form of *The Four Zoas* offers either a return to pre-Homeric primitivism or an advance in literary form;

the poem has some affinity with dream narrative.[2] (This last point is particularly instructive, and we shall return to it.) All these facts suggest the personal demands, far greater than most literary works exact, that the *Zoas* makes on the reader.

Contrary to the now discredited myth that at some time in the 1790s Blake lost or renounced his ability to say things clearly, he retained to the end of his life the ability to write lucidly, indeed pellucidly, when he wanted to make forceful statements even on difficult and elusive subjects. Why then should *The Four Zoas* present to readers so forbidding a verbal texture? Surely because Blake was trying something more than either ordinary discursive communication or (which is less obvious) other kinds of mythic or allegorical narrative. The most impressive proof of this fact, if proof is needed, is that the *story* of the poem, including the development of the Zoas and Emanations as characters and of their relations to one another, is often one of the last things readers come to discern clearly. This reverses the normal psychological process of understanding narrative, a process in which far-reaching or universal implications occur to us only after we have first understood what is literally happening.

Although Blake canceled the original subtitle, which described the poem as a dream, that term remains a helpful key to the way in which the *Zoas* communicates. A powerful dream energizes a strong emotion, even in those first moments after waking when it is no more than a mood, and we ordinarily understand in some depth of ourselves why the dream has frightened or exhilarated or otherwise moved us before its details have been analyzed or even fully recalled and sorted out. *The Four Zoas* often works in much the same way, for beginners and for veteran readers when a heretofore recalcitrant passage or incident suddenly becomes excitingly clear. Readers encountering the poem for the first time frequently experience utter bewilderment; yet when they risk a bold

Introduction

surmise in considering the meaning of a specific episode, they often find themselves in agreement with other readers, including experts on Blake. This fact ought to govern the way in which new readers of the *Zoas* use the present book. It is assumed, of course, that they will read it concurrently with the text of the poem. But it is important that they allow the poem to exert its own full force before they turn prematurely, on faith, to this commentary—or to any other, for that matter. What new readers of the *Zoas* need most is not the guidance of authority but the communal reinforcement of their insights and help in clarifying them.

Mythographers of Blake, particularly Northrop Frye in *Fearful Symmetry,* have helped considerably to explain just how Blake achieves this uncanny, apparently telepathic, communication. Yet a great deal remains unexplained. A thorough explanation would probably require major new discoveries about the psychology of artistic creation, perhaps about psychology in general. Our purpose in this book does not extend so far, though we hope our discussion of certain passages will throw some light on the subject. Certainly we do not believe that any single currently existing psychological system, model of the mind, or theory of the human personality can adequately explain Blake's myth and method. Our analogy with dream-communication is merely an analogy and is not meant to suggest that the poem should be read, say, psychoanalytically. Our occasional use of Freudian terms like "libidinal" simply recognizes that such words have entered the common vocabulary of English; our meaning will usually be clearer if the terms are taken in the popular rather than technical senses.

The first requirement for reading *The Four Zoas,* then, is confidence in one's intuitions. Yet, in the light of internal evidence and of what we know about Blake's deliberate habits of thinking and creating, it would be absurd to regard the poem as an inexplicably successful attempt at automatic writing. Although the work goes beyond the normal methods of allegory and myth, it does include these. It can be read meaningfully in a way S. Foster Damon pioneered, as an allegory in which Albion, the Zoas, and their Emanations represent deliberate and conscious personifications by Blake of forces in the human psyche and in the world. Our own basic understanding of what the Zoas stand for agrees with the nearly unanimous consensus of Blakeans: Urizen is reason, Urthona or Los is imagination, Luvah or Orc is passion, Tharmas is instinct. We also recognize that the basic psychodramatic method of the poem often expands to include political, social, and religious commentary, especially in the last Nights. *The Four Zoas* is, among other things, an epic, and although Blake shares with his brother Romantics and with Milton the goal of internalizing epic heroism, he never forgot, any more than Wordsworth, Milton, or Virgil did, that epic is also a mode of therapeutic public statement. Though the *Zoas* begins as though it had no external context, by the end it has established a number of contacts with the world everyone knows.

The Four Zoas is also, as we shall try to show, an intricately structured poem, in its overall design and in the sometimes astonishing craftsmanship of its minuter details. The sheer complexity of its surface, along with its unorthodox narrative method, has obscured its structure for most readers. Yet the structure is unquestionably present and describable with confidence, even when its meaning is not beyond dispute. For example, the poem not only divides into three sections describing the fall, fallenness, and recovery of man, as Harold Bloom and others have noticed, but it traces within each of these movements basically similar progressions. Phrases and images planted early in the poem germinate gradually until their full import is revealed in the last Nights. In the richness of its structural, dictional, and imagistic patterns *The Four Zoas* is a magnificent imaginative edifice.

Introduction

And finally, *The Four Zoas* is a story. Its characters are complex but highly individualized, the nuances of their motives are subtle but realistically understandable, and their climactic conversions to evil and to good can grip us as such things do in the best novels and plays.

The ultimate pleasure in reading the poem is, of course, to experience it on all these levels. The term "levels," though hackneyed in critical jargon, can be renovated if we take it rather literally, as a recognition that Blake deals illuminatingly both with the observable world and with the nearly inscrutable depths within us of fear, despair, elation. The full and empathic identification we have urged is not counsel aimed, condescendingly, at new readers who need a crutch; on the contrary, the capacity to respond to the poem with one's whole nature, unguardedly, ought to increase, the more one knows about Blake and about the poem. Those who are willing to bring the poem alive to themselves, and to bring themselves alive through the poem, may share in the awakening of Albion, building up and living in a fully human community.

As with many of his illuminated poems, Blake's title page and frontispiece for *The Four Zoas* adumbrate central themes and ideas in the work. This front matter is, in effect, Blake's own Introduction to his poem, providing to viewers of his manuscript, if not a context for what follows, a resonant symbolic keynote.

A strategy of double, often multiple, focus is used throughout the *Zoas*, superimposing public and personal meanings, heroic grandeur and stabbing poignancy, distant panorama and close-up. The multiple layers of revision on the title page intensify this double focus; the inked title gives one impression, penciled additions and cancellations a very different one. The alterations indicate significant changes in Blake's central theme and his conception of the whole poem at various times during the decade when he worked on the manuscript. Yet the relation between earlier and later versions is not simply that of rejected and accepted alternatives. The revised, expanded title reflects some things that were in the poem from the beginning; conversely, canceled words in the title, especially "DREAM," describe important elements that remained in the poem as Blake finally completed or at least left it. The two titles differ in their emphases, but each is a guide to the meaning of the poem at all stages of its composition. The alternatives they urge on us are alternatives of perspective. For Blake such changes in perspective, whether brought out pictorially or verbally, are of enormous importance. One of the radical messages of *The Four Zoas* is that to look at things in a new way makes all the difference.

The inked title *VALA, Or the Death and Judgement of the Ancient Man: a DREAM of Nine Nights*, dated 1797, prepares the reader who knows the books of *Urizen, Ahania,* and *Los* for yet another version of the Fall of Man. This one will center on a new character named Vala, who will be revealed in the poem as the female principle in the personification of passion and the personification of the illusive beauties of nature. The title of *Vala* suggests that, despite the obvious difference in format and scale between the epic and the three earlier works, Blake was continuing to build a series of poems on the fall, each emphasizing one of the human faculties at fault while at the same time revealing peripherally the consequences for the other damaged elements of humanity. The revised title, *The Four Zoas: The torments of Love & Jealousy in The Death and Judgement of Albion the Ancient Man,* suggests a new plan which will abandon the sequential for the simultaneous and comprehensive, a poem centering not upon a single figure but on four "lifes" or living creatures who struggle with one another, singly or in complex alliances, in divided England, divided humankind, and each divided individual.

Introduction

Though Blake's revisions do not move consistently in one direction, the overall movement is toward affirmation. The inked words "Ancient Man" in the title overlie an even earlier reference, barely discernible, to the "Eternal Man"; the inked title confines him to history and deprives him of his association with eternity. But in the otherwise wholly grim context of the inked title, focusing on death and judgment, the final phrase is tentatively hopeful: perhaps this death and judgment are a mere dream, an illusion holding sway for a limited time. By the time Blake has reworked the total poem, the equivocal optimism of "DREAM" in the first title will be strengthened by a more positive sense of "dream" as vision; the more hopeful emphasis is reflected in penciled changes on the title page and an added frontispiece consisting of a figure-drawing and a motto. The phrase about the "DREAM" is eliminated, but the design added on the title page is a much more positive indication that Albion is not to remain dead. A Gabriel-like figure blows his trumpet and the dead awaken, raising their heads up through the earth that has covered them.[3] The theme of resurrection in the design balances—perhaps overbalances—the themes of death, torment, jealousy, and judgment in the words of the title.

The impression of muted optimism is confirmed as one turns the manuscript page to the enigmatic motto and design of the frontispiece. The scrawled motto "Rest before Labour" reverses the expected order of labor and rest as understood in mundane actuality, in convention, and in the Bible. The Creator's resting after his six-day labor sets the pattern for most later biblical metaphors for the relation between cause and effect, duty and reward, life and afterlife.[4] Blake's motto, in connection with the resurrection scene on the preceding page, invites us to reconsider the usual relation between labor and rest, activity and stasis, time and eternity. Sorely afflicted humanity tends to see present sufferings as

---

laborious strife whose alternative is rest, understood as peace or as an achieved goal or even simply as inactivity. These are at best dim intuitions, at worst perverse distortions, of the true form of happiness. In the motto, then, "Rest" is a euphemism for the sleep of death which immobilizes Albion throughout most of the poem before he rises in the last Nights to oversee the productive agricultural work that not only ushers in the state of salvation but is identical with it. Or we can hear the tone as reassurance: Albion's sleep, or rest, however troubled, ought not to be mistaken for genuine death; he is preserved until his awakening to the vigorous "Intellectual Battle" or "intellectual War" (ix 854; 139:9 E392) that is man's proper activity, his only true goal or resting place.

This kind of paradoxical epigram, reminiscent of Blake's Proverbs of Hell, occurs more often in *The Four Zoas* than one might expect in a work so grand in scale, and it is much more than verbal wit; it epitomizes several things in the poem's total strategy. It evokes the quietude demanded of the epic poet and prophet if he is to hear accurately his divinely inspired message and—since the four Zoas are in every man—it hints at the psychological readiness needed by readers, who should empty themselves and throw off their defenses in order to receive and participate in the poem. In addition, the rest-labor paradox exemplifies the larger paradox that is Blake's task: to bend definitions into their true form, to set straight by inverting it a world that is upside down, to restore to spiritual health through high parody the low parody of good that passes as reality.

The ambiguous design for the frontispiece suggests still another tension between time and eternity, rest and labor. We see a male nude who resembles Blake's soaring figures, but he does not look energetic enough to have broken his bonds; if we imagine ourselves looking at him not from the front but from above we catch an aerial view of a sleeper lying on his unquiet bed. He is radiating light, the Divine Vision, but his eyes are closed to it.[5] Both perspectives on Albion are true: fallen, he is asleep, but his full human potential remains, ready for the awakening that is true self-recognition.[6] Then he will be freed from the devastating external contradictions that make eighteenth-century England a nightmare, freed from such schizoid internal divisions as the wars between male and female principles and between mind and nature. Chastened, admonished, but not without hope, the reader is prepared to enter into Albion's—and therefore his own—disturbing but clarifying experience of self-examination and rectification. And then, as Blake promised, he will "be happy."[7]

Night I.

After its opening lines, which apply to the whole poem, the narrative of Night I dramatizes and is intended to inspire in readers almost primitive forms of terror and pathos. The Night has to do with the crippling of instinct and imagination, which are fundamentally signs rather than causes of human fragmentation. In the positivist world we live in, we have come to think of symptoms as superficial and of causes as more real. Yet when we are ill, in mind or body, it is pain and helplessness that most vividly distress us, not the technical facts about our malfunctioning or the clinical data reflecting it. In Night II, Blake will emphasize the ultimate cause of human fallenness, namely, the conflict between emotion and reason. But first, in the opening Night, he conveys the impact that this conflict has on instinct and imagination, the two faculties through which we most immediately recognize the world, our capacity to function in it, and our very identities. The personifications of reason and passion, Urizen and Luvah, will move through this poem like generals, commanding respectively armies of the right and left. But the human devastation of the fall will be revealed most poignantly on the front lines, where the relatively innocent victims of psychic war, imagination and instinct, feel its effects in their nerve ends. The victimization and degradation of Los is tragic, since the imagination he personifies is the only dynamic of salvation; the victimization of Tharmas is pathetic, since instinct is the most childlike and vulnerable of our faculties.

A second major function of Night I is to anticipate, usually in demonic inversions, both the imagery and the saving message of the last Nights. This technique of anticipation is one that Blake will use on a smaller scale in many individual parts of the *Zoas,* most notably in Nights VII and VIII. Not until one has read the entire poem at least once can this method of delayed resolution be fully appreciated. The spasmodic, often transitionless movement, especially in the first Night, is partly an objective correlative of the protagonists' state of panicky desperation, which leads them to disastrously ill-considered acts of sadism and self-injury. But the structural vehicle, with all its abrupt and seemingly arbitrary shifts, belies the thematic coherence of the work and its tightness of weave. The opening sections of the poem seem to scatter the portions of the psyche with brutal randomness, but in the end we shall be able to see that psychic disintegration and reintegration have proceeded with as much intricate clarity of purpose as in the disassembly and reassembly work of a watch repair shop. In the meantime, though, the poem will make demands on readers that are almost unparalleled in literature; they are expected to keep suspended in their minds, for hundreds or even thousands of lines, motifs and images that will not be resolved or entirely clarified until near the very end.

A third keynote of Night I, sounded for the first of many times, is a reminder of the ever-present possibility of redemption. Such reminders raise fundamental issues not only about Blake's notion of epic prophecy but about his whole vision of life. In some ways Blake follows the traditional felix culpa model; we are to understand that at the conclusion of the poem man has reached a state better than what was lost. In other ways he departs from this tradition, for the processes of fall, growth, and regeneration will include a great deal that is sheer waste and thus more tragic than in most theodicies. His task is the mind-bending one of combining timeless myth with the traditional epic emphasis on time and

history. Since either the acceptance or rejection of a fortu-
nate-fall archetype usually posits a view of time as an irreversible unique series of events, the very question whether
or not the fall is fortunate in *The Four Zoas* is misleading,
whether one is thinking about history or about the growth of
an individual person. Though Blake is often a Christian
literalist, he is not a fundamentalist who can arrive at a facile
formula because salvation took place centuries ago and needs
now only to be recognized and embraced after the fact or
imitated on a smaller scale, within the severe restrictions of
our merely human nature. On the other hand, Blake is no
Eastern mystic living in a world where time, space, and circumstance are simply an illusory facade that disguises a reality made up of the general and archetypal.

Thus the moments of hope with which the darker Nights
of the poem are punctuated serve two purposes. They remove
us from time in one way, by reminding us that we are free
at all stages of our lives to reject mind-forged manacles; the
Circle of Destiny, our entrapment in hours, days, and years,
is largely an illusion. But paradoxically, by the same token,
time and space can be friendly environments if we accept
every moment and every place as the material for imaginative
transformation by ourselves. Thus Blake's personifications
of hope—usually called the Daughters of Beulah—characteristically *create* times and spaces, which are the mercy of eternity, for however constricting time and space may be at their
worst, the alternative to their existing is the total loss of our
identity as human beings. It is better to live in Afghanistan
or in the ninth century than in Nirvana. What all this means
in *The Four Zoas* is that in it we can find patterns of despair
and of happiness that we share with other human beings,
while at the same time we can and should replay the drama of
the poem in terms of our unique selves and the unique events
of our lives.

Before the action proper begins, we encounter Blake's detailed reworking of the traditional epic opening. An epigraph from Ephesians 6:12, describing the conduct of mental warfare against spiritual evils, helps to interpret both the "Labour" of the frontispiece and the "Intellectual Battle" mentioned in the third line of the poem: we wrestle not against physical enemies but against the powers of darkness. Thus at the outset Blake distinguishes his heroic subject from the physical warfare celebrated in the classics, by implication allying himself with Milton in this break with the heroic tradition. Then:

> The Song of the Aged Mother which shook the heavens
>   with wrath
> Hearing the march of long resounding strong heroic Verse
> Marshalld in order for the day of Intellectual Battle
>
> Four Mighty Ones are in every Man: a Perfect Unity
> Cannot Exist. but from the Universal Brotherhood of Eden
> The Universal Man. To Whom be Glory Evermore Amen
> [What] are the Natures of those Living Creatures the
>   Heavenly Father only
> [Knoweth] no Individual [Knoweth nor] Can know in
>   all Eternity.
>
> (I 2-13; 3:1-8 E297)

Here, the first three lines are not syntactically related to anything that follows. Although they could be taken as a subtitle they are more probably part of the text proper, their syntactic independence contributing to the special effect of dislocation and uneasiness with which the poem begins.[1] The "Aged Mother" is presumably the Eno mentioned in a deleted line. Her "Song" can hardly be the poem as a whole, since she appears as a character later in Night I; what she sings would seem to be the immediately ensuing three-line chant describing the brotherhood of the Zoas in Eden.[2] But the mention of the Aged Mother in the very first line of the poem must mean that she is important; she is almost surely some kind of primal state of consciousness to which the poet has privileged access. Her three lines about the brotherhood of the Zoas sound the keynote for the poet's nine-book epic about the disintegration and recovery of this brotherhood. The Aged Mother provides the centering intuition of human unity from which the poet's perception of the fall starts. Like other Muses, she is an ancestral feminine consciousness, awake more than ever during the sleep of the mankind personified in Albion; within her consciousness the nightmarishly contradictory and overlapping flashback accounts of the fall are unified. She is also a peculiarly Miltonic and especially Romantic development of the Muse-figure: like Keats's Mnemosyne or Moneta, she is the collective memory of the human race; like Milton's, Wordsworth's, and especially Shelley's Urania, she is a maternal source of sublime inspiration as well.

Although the poem opens in a world of epic superhumanity, we are reminded immediately that this cosmic superstructure is to be internalized in our understanding of our individual human selves. As though Blake were taking special pains not to be mistaken for a creator of mere heroic fantasy, he reminds us that the heroic verse is being prepared for "the day of Intellectual Battle"; the poem we are reading will itself help to bring about the return to "intellectual War" prophesied as the culmination of apocalypse in the second-last line of Night IX. According to a deleted passage, if "Whosoever reads" comprehends "with his Intellect . . . the terrible Sentence" (i 3-4; E739), the universe will quake in fear of the mental warfare to come. The entire opening passage implies Blake's concern with the psychology of the reader and perhaps an earlier intention to address a wider audience than a unique private manuscript could reach. The Four Mighty Ones are in every man, and the refocusing of the original subtitle, "The Death and Judgement" of the Ancient

Night I

Man, as "The torments of Love & Jealousy" in his death and judgment, also implies a turn to the familiar, the troubled heart and psyche. Marginal references to the Gospel of John further emphasize oneness, incarnation, the recovery of lost unity between man and God in the universal brotherhood of Jesus. Though the "Natures"of the Zoas are known to the "Heavenly Father only"—according to a later penciled addition—the remoteness so suggested is dispelled not only by the marginal gloss and the fact that the whole poem reveals the Zoas' natures, but also in the way the "Father" directs us ahead to the first Zoa whose plight is described, the "Parent power" Tharmas who paradoxically is also the most childlike of the personified powers of humanity. One implication here is that unless we become as children (who could elucidate Blake's visions easily, as he wrote in his 1799 letter to Dr. Trusler) we shall not understand this poem. We must trust our intuitions.

But before Tharmas's first speech the Zoa called Los is introduced:

> Los was the fourth immortal starry one, & in the Earth
> Of a bright Universe Empery attended day & night
> Days & nights of revolving joy, Urthona was his name
> In Eden; in the Auricular Nerves of Human life
> Which is the Earth of Eden, he his Emanations propagated
> Fairies of Albion afterwards Gods of the Heathen,
>   Daughter of Beulah Sing
> His fall into Division & his Resurrection to Unity
> His fall into the Generation of Decay & Death & his
>   Regeneration by the Resurrection from the dead
>   (I 14-23; 3:9-4:5 E297)

This is the point in the formulaic opening at which we expect to meet the epic hero. According to the title page the hero is mankind, all of us, and our four primary faculties; but as the main agent of salvation, Los is prominently fea-

tured here even though it is only in the last three sections
of the poem that he will be capable of heroic action. This
apparent false start is necessary to give due recognition to
the Zoa on whom the action of the poem will pivot: Los is
the imaginative faculty, among the last to fall and the first to
work toward recovery. The lines on death, fragmentation,
and resurrection are appropriate for the beginning of the epic
because they apply to Albion as well as to Los; what is true of
Albion, the total human being, is true also of his subdivisions.
Each of the Zoas will split away from his brothers and from
his own female counterpart, or Emanation. Each will undergo a death and a complex fragmentation before his final
awakening into unity with his Emanation, with the other
Zoas, and with the fully human Albion. Pictorially, the first
split is anticipated in the ambiguous male figure on the
verso leaf containing the frontispiece; on the facing recto
where the text begins, the result of the split of female from
male receives complementary attention, as the females, or
Emanations, are shown in both their fallen and resurrected
states.[3]

The introductory lines on Los accomplish three other purposes besides signaling his heroic status. They identify Earth
as an element in the unfallen state as well as in the fallen,
"vegetated" world: it is the soil of imagination. The tenor
and vehicle of this metaphor are so nearly indissociable that
in Nights VIII and IX human rebirth will be symbolized in
a vast, long-sustained agricultural metaphor that is virtually
a practical handbook of farming, like Virgil's *Georgics*. Further, they reveal a permanent continuity between fallen and
unfallen states of consciousness: our own auditory power,
"the Auricular Nerves of Human Life," makes up the fertile
soil of Eden wherein Los's work bears fruit. The most universal and ancient metaphors for the poet's own inspiration
draw on the sense of hearing, his response to a Muse who
does not write but dictates. Similarly, the prophetic tradi-

tion, especially in the Bible, provides a model for the relation between poet and audience in which the audience, suffering from faulty vision, is admonished to "Hear."[4] Finally, though Los is able to propagate emanations (his delights and fancies) in our imaginations, these English fairies follow the process of deterioration traced in *The Marriage of Heaven and Hell* in that they are "afterwards" corrupted into heathen gods. Historical accuracy is not important in this Anglo-centric myth of the derivation of pagan gods from English fairies; the point is that whenever poets in the fallen world create a myth, it is preempted by the established powers and made over into a religion, a pattern repeated microcosmically and psychologically when any human being gives up his childlike inventive exuberance and adopts inhibiting rules of creativity like realistic representation and parallel perspective. The artist Los will adopt several modes of creativity in the poem; his choice of wrong and right ones, with all that that implies about the imaginative activity of any human being, will determine whether Albion is to recover or remain ill.

Blake's daring attempt to combine myth and history is reflected in the very grammar of the opening lines, with their bold linguistic dislocations. Tension of language dramatizes a chronic tension between the fallen world that is and the unfallen world that was or could be or shall be (unless we are determinists, the distinctions between tenses and modes hardly matter). In his juxtapositions of verb tenses Blake realizes for us an eternal present glimpsed in vision, a fallen present dominating ordinary consciousness, a half-remembered ideal past, and an even less localized time (scattered pieces of it, so to speak) conveyed by a free-floating present participle. After the narrative has been launched in medias res, flashbacks by different characters will hint at a single traumatic event that precipitated the fall, only parts of which are recoverable at the levels of consciousness voiced by the

various characters. This knowing in part and seeing by
glimpses, which explains why all accounts of the fall in the
Zoas are in conflict while sharing certain details, is identified
grimly by Wordsworth with a present half-blindness inferior
to the clear-sightedness of lost childhood, and disparagingly
by St. Paul with a present vision that is faulty *because* it is
childlike (*Prelude,* xii 281 ff.; 1 Cor. 13:9-12). For Wordsworth the implication is a temporal decline from vision, for
Paul an ascent to vision in the future. In accepting time as
a constricting linear corridor with doorways to the light only
at the extremes of distant past and future, both visions block
out Blakean windows to Eternity, the state of human wholeness and fulfillment. Perhaps one of the reasons Blake loved
Wordsworth's Intimations Ode is that in it Wordsworth does
allow for a season of calm in which our inland souls travel
"in a moment" to the immortal sea; these glimpses of eternity
through the loops of time are moments of grace in our fallen
experience.

Within the narrative of postlapsarian events, three addi-
tional time orientations are introduced in the future tense
alone: an obsessive preoccupation with futurity as an alternative to a loathed present, a fretful forecasting of feared and
desired outcomes as inevitable results of present acts, and a
comforting promise—usually voiced by the Daughters of
Beulah—that humanity can or will (again, to insist on the
difference is an error) recover Edenic life. Both Eternity
and fallen time can be expressed in all three of the standard
grammatical tenses, though each must do double duty in
order to express the six times represented in the poem. When
the false forms of time divisions are destroyed at the very
end of the poem, Los's role as prophet (in the sense of one
who forecasts) is no longer meaningful and all time schemes
and tenses collapse into the present. (Our fallen view of the
present as both the most inescapable of all things and an in-
finitesimal, durationless, and therefore nonexistent point is

a tragically ironic parody of Blake's view.) At the end Los, the personification of time as his counterpart Enitharmon is of space, is reabsorbed into his eternal identity as Urthona, who busies himself in the eternal-present tense of the concluding lines with his altruistic work as an artificer of equipment for mental warfare.

From the very outset of the poem Blake requires his reader to master these ambiguous verb tenses. The maternal Muse, the poet, and the reader must share a language of reversible time references without becoming enmeshed in merely linear time as the characters are. The Aged Mother's song, for example, "shook" the heavens in the remote past; yet the poet invokes her (if she is the "Daughter of Beulah") in the present to "Sing" what appears to be this same song. The participle "Hearing" modifies "the heavens," which apparently are enraged at the sound of the Mother's song, yet because there is no verb for "Song," the participle also dangles in a yet-unfulfilled limbo of the historical present and "Hearing" remains with the reader as a signal that he too should heighten his attentiveness to this momentously heralded poem. Blake's wordplay on the verb "to be" in its temporal and eternal applications forces the reader to adjust to rapid shifts between states of being: Four Mighty Ones "are" (eternal present and historical present) in every Man, but only the Heavenly Father knows what the natures of these living creatures "are" (eternal present) ; Los "was" (historical past) the "fourth immortal starry one" who "was" (eternal past) named Urthona in Eden; human hearing "is" the Earth of Eden (either temporal or eternal, depending on one's attunement to Eden) in whose soil Los once propagated his emanations.

After the overture the curtain rises with an abrupt line hardly longer than a dialogue tag: "Begin with Tharmas Parent power. darkning in the West." This can be read as a continuation of the gentler invocation of the Daughter of

Beulah, as an appeal to the "Mother" mentioned in the opening line, or as a directive aimed at the reader by Blake or by
some universalized and unidentified prophetic voice. In the
Songs of Innocence a darkening in the west prefigures the loss
of innocence; here, because Tharmas is not only an innocent
but innocence itself, it is he and not the sun or sky that
darkens. Following as it does the high magniloquence and
ceremony of the preceding seventeen lines, Tharmas's cry
is a sudden knife-stab, piercing in its immediacy:

> Lost! Lost! Lost! are my Emanations Enion O Enion
> We are become a Victim to the Living.

There is nothing remote or Olympian in this pain; it is
frighteningly human.

Tharmas has been described as innocence, instinct, the
binding force of the human personality, and the body. All
these are valid identifications, except that in the present
context the "body" must not be understood as that of sexual
maturity, which is closer to Blake's Luvah. Tharmas is the
body as a child knows it, unselfconsciously and without question—the body of Wordsworth's child that feels its life in
every limb—which is why his pain is so naked and terrible.
Tharmas is the "Parent" power in the sense that the child
is father of the man. He is the innocent's trust, his sense of
wholeness, and more than any other Zoa he has an affinity
with that pastoral mood and state that Blake calls Beulah.
Just as children are uncannily alert to indefinable atmospheres long before either mind or emotion can identify them,
so Tharmas and his Emanation Enion show throughout the
poem a primitive, instinctual awareness of the fall and, conversely, the possibility of reintegration before any of the other
Zoas does. Tharmas is the personality's unconscious knowledge of its own intactness. Thus the fall of Tharmas, which
implies the fall of all the Zoas, is described first.

What Tharmas has sensed is the generic human fall, considered either as that mysterious historical and evolutionary leap that awakened humanity simultaneously to its unique gifts and its unique capacity for evil or as the more individual lapse that caused each of us to be divided from others and against ourselves. This is the leap from simple to complex, from spontaneity to self-consciousness. The most salient symptom and cost are sexual, the torments of love and jealousy; therefore we can all recognize the transformation through what we underwent at adolescence and to some extent at that even earlier climacteric called the age of reason.

We encounter Tharmas and Enion in the middle of a shattering quarrel reminiscent of that between Milton's Adam and Eve, their heretofore unitary consciousness riddled with contradictory feelings of sinfulness and victimization. Some of the confusion may result from Blake's incomplete alterations in the manuscript, but most of it seems to be a deliberate picture of panic. Tharmas says that his emanations are lost, then that he has hidden Jerusalem, then that Enion has abducted her, then that he has taken Enitharmon in and cannot cast her out, then that he has accepted as refugees the Emanations of the other Zoas who have been stricken dead.[5] The occasion for the quarrel is sexual jealousy, but the vector lines of attraction and repulsion are not clearly drawn; Blake is representing a blurred emotional state especially characteristic of confused instinct. Since Jerusalem is the communal Emanation of all mankind, it is appropriate and ironic that both Tharmas and Enion should, in different ways, protect or hide her (I 27-30, 69-70; 4:9-12, 5:6-7 E297, 298). That Enion should be accused of jealousy, rightly or wrongly, is also ironic, since even the bitterest enmities among the females in the poem are ultimately superficial, less important than their fundamental unity as sisters.

But we must not expect even sense, much less logic, from the instinctual powers at this point; we are observing in them not causes but effects, a disorientation like that of experimental animals whose primary impulses have been scrambled by contradictory rewards and punishments. In the dialogue, or rather their obliquely parallel monologues, neither Tharmas nor Enion listens to or responds to the other's comments, questions, and accusations; his key word is "pity," hers "terror." The sexual attraction-repulsion familiar in adolescence has been awakened; Tharmas sees Enion alternately as a root growing in hell to draw him to destruction and as a celestially beautiful, expanding flower (I 57-59; 4:39-41 E298).

Themes and images closely associated with the other three Zoas in the rest of the poem make their first appearance in embryonic form in this quarrel between the Parent powers. Each of the four Zoas epitomizes the fate of the others and of the whole man; this fact is especially clear in episodes involving Tharmas, the bonding instinct. Tharmas's words "victim" and "contrition" (I 26-27; 4:8-9 E297) foreshadow the persistent issue of atonement in the poem, which is destructive until it begins to be understood as Christ-like self-sacrifice in the last two Nights. Tharmas's lament over his lost, stolen, or hidden emanations contrasts directly with Los's free propagation of emanations in Eden. When a Zoa has many emanations, they seem to be "secret loves & Graces," as Enion jealously calls them in canceled lines (I 164; E742). Used in the singular, as an appellation identifying the four female counterparts of the Zoas, an Emanation is something both better and worse than these undifferentiated loves and graces. The Emanations—Ahania, Vala, Enitharmon, Enion—have individual identities and names because each is the perfect mate for her Zoa, the expression of what is best and most distinctive in him. But in the fallen condition typified by jealousy, the four individualized Emanations are symbols of exclusiveness—the fallen way of understanding monogamy, as it were. In this more sinister context an Emanation is the estranged but greedily hoarded projection of what one loves or creates, both the object of desire and the focus of sexual antagonism. Such ambivalence makes no logical sense, even to human faculties more complex than instinct, but anyone who has ever felt the insecurities of jealousy need only recall them to recognize the truthfulness of Blake's psychology.

The idea of unfallen emanations implied in Los's Adam-like cultivation of them in the earth of Eden is reinforced by a comparison between the eternal cyclical movement of male/female contraries and seasonal metamorphoses in nature. Emanations are like self-sacrificing butterflies or Psyches:

> In Eden Females sleep the winter in soft silken veils
> Woven by their own hands to hide them in the darksom grave
> But Males immortal live renewd by female deaths. in soft
> Delight they die & they revive in spring with music & songs.
>
> (I 64-67; 5:1-4 E298)

This seasonal rhythm, like everything else that is natural in the wholesome and innocent sense of the word "natural," has been disrupted in Tharmas's constricted relation with his emanations. Instead of enjoying his many loves and graces, formerly taken for granted and in no way opposed to a single allegiance, Tharmas now concentrates his loyalty on Enion, in a paradoxical response to their identification of the other emanations as her rivals. (Precisely the same psychology underlies the confused motives of the speaker in *My Pretty Rose Tree*.) Instead of sending his emanations out and recalling them like breaths of air, Tharmas feels that they are now lost within him. The new, unknown space within, an innermost secret soul, appears to Tharmas to be a protective "Labyrinth" and a "Soft recess" and to Enion to be "mazes of delusive beauty" and "Dark recesses" where sin lurks (I 28-45; 4:10-27 E297-98). Both Tharmas and Enion are bewildered by a newly sensed need to conceal: his desire for privacy becomes (and is perceived by Enion as) a morbid compulsion for hiding; her forthrightness becomes (and is perceived by Tharmas as) cold-blooded prying. The psychopathology of secrecy is another of the larger themes of *The Four Zoas* which is anticipated in this opening dialogue.

During the past two centuries there has been a fundamental mutation in the meaning of guilt. Before the Romantics the idea that guilt had both moral and psychological dimensions had been anticipated in a few great works like *Oedipus Rex* and *Macbeth*; in the latter, for example, Lady Macbeth's compulsive hand-washing is a sign not merely of her evil but also of disabling illness. But these works are exceptional; whether guilt was treated as a quasi-objective condition (to *be* guilty) or as an emotional condition (to *feel* guilty), the defining criteria were good and evil. It was the Romantics' achievement (for better or worse), in works like *The Borderers, The Ancient Mariner, Christabel, The Cenci, Manfred,* and many others, to portray guilt as both the symptom of moral evil and a pathological condition in which moral culpability is essentially the subjectively experienced symbol of mental illness. Whether the Romantics should be held accountable for certain more recent extrapolations of this shift of attitude, which have drained guilt of almost all its moral content, is a controversial and perhaps unanswerable question. At any rate, it is necessary in understanding many great Romantic works to distinguish between moral and psychological guilt (what Robert F. Gleckner, in discussing Byron, calls the guilt of the "sinful" and the guilt of the "inadequate"[6]) while recognizing that the *feeling* of guilt remains the same for people experiencing it, whether their actions are truly blamable or just sick in the literal sense of the word.

The Four Zoas is a pioneer work in exploring this psychic territory. In the opening quarrel Tharmas reveals a sense of his own inadequacy in relation to Enion's independence, which is repeated in later quarrels between the other Zoas and their Emanations. Though in eternity Los propagates

Night I

his emanations in Edenic soil, in the fallen world Tharmas complains that Enion's new growth leaves him an empty shell. Virtually identifying himself with the seed hull from which she has sprung, he sees her as a root, flower, or fruit, vigorously "growing," "expanding," or "breaking from [her] bud" while he without her is "an atom / A Nothing left in darkness yet I am an identity" (I 57-62; 4:39-44 E298). Here too Tharmas anticipates a dominant imagistic and thematic pattern. Throughout the poem vegetation imagery can express either of two things: a condition of merely biological existence without spiritual meaning or on the other hand the principle of growth and renewal in the life of the imagination.

As the primeval relation between Tharmas and Enion disintegrates, the couple reassess each other and create a new emotional dynamic through which each reunites with the now debased image of the other. The pattern will become familiar: a character projects a diminished sense of himself upon his spouse or partner, then hates himself because he has diminished his partner and also hates his partner because she is now small or base; at the same time the characters are drawn together in a panicky pseudolove out of the need each has for a companion at least as low and mean as he is. (The gender of the pronouns in these statements can, of course, be reversed.) Milton's Adam and Eve again provide an analogue, and so does the pattern in familiar life which makes a weak person (or one who feels weak) marry an even weaker one who can be controlled and contemned. Tharmas as prime mover sets in motion the Circle of Destiny, a desperate alternative to the chaos that threatens the fallen world (it is typical of the poem's scrambling of times that this act is described before Enion's creation of the Circle), resigns his "pale white corse" to the sea, and gives over his miserable being to his consort (I 73-90; 5:10-27 E298-99). This pattern too is repeated throughout the early Nights of the poem, as one after another of man's fallen faculties abdicates and leaves behind a smaller residue of human nature to re-create the world in a yet narrower form.

Enion's method of creation is weaving, another recurrent image in the *Zoas*; throughout, it has both positive and negative associations. Females in both unfallen and fallen states weave cocoonlike structures symbolizing the human body or some other mundane enclosure, which can be either a suffocating prison for the human spirit or the tomb of a dead personality from which regenerated humanity arises. Enion begins weaving as if she were still one of the unfallen Emanations, or the Daughters of Beulah who periodically accommodate potentially dangerous elements. But since Enion has now fallen into contention with Tharmas, this activity goes awry and her creation takes on an independent life, "not / As Garments woven subservient to her hands but having a will / Of its own perverse & wayward" (i 83-85; 5:20-22 E299). It is characteristic of both Enion and Tharmas in the fallen state that they begin reflex actions that produce unintended results; because the signals of instinctive communication, which should be reflexive, have been jammed, their behavior has become irrelevant to their situations. The result is pathos and absurdity; Enion's persistence is as wasted as that of the giant sea turtle who, confused by radioactive fallout, lays her eggs on the beach and then heads in the wrong direction, plodding inland until she collapses. Enion's nine-day task of weaving creates both the world as she sees it and her fallen counterpart as he appears to her—and as she half wants him to be.

The Circle of Destiny is a time-space continuum that operates like the primum mobile of the Ptolemaic system; it is an outer limit containing the worlds-within-worlds constructed by the other Zoas: the Mundane Shell built by Urizen in Night II, the sensorium for Urizen's brain built by Los in Night IV, and that better edifice the Golgonooza or city of art built by Los and his Spectre in Night VII. All that remains of these elaborately constructed universes—even that of art itself, conceived of in a narrow and literalist sense—is finally rent asunder in the apocalypse of Night IX. In Night I, Enion's Circle of Destiny is a vague and primitive world view, little more than an enveloping atmosphere of determinism (illustrated, very probably, in drawings later in the manuscript).[7]

Enion draws out from Tharmas his "Spectre," the male version of the sexual and personal possessiveness that in Blake balances the shadowy "Female Will." The drawing-out (I 78-79; 5:15-16 E298) is a kind of suspended pun: in the long run of the poem such drainings-off of the essential evil in a character will serve a constructive purpose of defining and clarifying, but at present it has the same force as in the expression "to bring out the worst" in someone. The Spectre of Tharmas emerges as a golden idol, narcissist and megalomaniac (though the designs, once again, provide an alternative view).[8] Filled with desire and contempt, the Spectre calls the cowering Enion—in a deleted passage—a "Diminutive husk & shell / Broke from my bonds" (I 149-50; E741). The male has become a tyrant, partly through female encouragement. Enion meanwhile becomes a crystallized phantasm, the essence of adored female mystery, "Half Woman & half Spectre" (I 184; 7:4 E299),[9] as narcissistic as her male counterpart—though Blake's usual practice is to reserve "Spectre" for the male half of the divided personality. Enion's delights are imagistically related to those described in *The Crystal Cabinet,* a poem that exposes an intoxicating sexual paradise as no more real than a house of mirrors. In deleted lines, recently recognized as having been restored by Blake, Tharmas is called Enion's "own Created Phantasm" (I 118; E741); a "self enjoying wonder" wandering in "sweet solitude," Enion rejoices to find "mild Eternity shut in a three-fold shape delightful" (7:9-14 E300).[10]

The word "threefold" is repeatedly associated with the

state of Beulah, a soft paradise of sexual delights superior to ordinary consciousness but inferior to Eden, the ideal four-fold state of heightened imaginative activity. In Beulah weary spirits seek rest from Eden. Enion seems to be at the lowest level of this state, but two passages of authorial exposition interrupt the narrative to present Beulah at its best. The first, already quoted, describes the winter sleep of the females "in soft silken veils," and the second, in which Beulah is mentioned by name, explains its function as a guarded place of repose mercifully created by the Lamb "around / On all sides within & without the Universal Man." The idea that Beulah is a protective cushion, a buffer zone allowing a margin of error or diminished vision from which one may easily recover after a period of rest, is particularly vivid in the statement that the Daughters of Beulah "follow sleepers in all their Dreams / Creating Spaces lest they fall into Eternal Death" (ɪ 97-100; 5:32-35 ᴇ299), for the dream of falling is the most primitive of all nightmares. With the fall of Tharmas and Enion, the accommodating capacity of the Daughters is strained to its limit: when they create a space for the Circle of Destiny it becomes a new state named Ulro.

Ulro will be Blake's lowest state of existence, a world of pure unreality where all things are reduced to their lowest common denominator of spiritless physical matter. Brooding with nurselike solicitude over this ultimate home of the spectrous, the Daughters of Beulah condemn the corrupted sexuality of Tharmas and Enion, exposing the Spectre, or shadow personality in every man, for what it is in relation to full humanity: "insane & most / Deformd." Accustomed to meeting each fallen spirit "with our Songs & loving blandishments" and giving to it "a form of vegetation" to protect it until it can return to Edenic reality, they are at a loss to help Tharmas recover from his new spectrous state of "Eternal Death." Praying for help, they sadly close "the Gate of the

Night I

Tongue," the organ through which Tharmas's primitive senses of touch and taste operate (I 103-08; 5:38-43 E299).

The action and prayer of the Daughters is the first of several hints in the poem of an elusive-to-define providence, an economy of preservation for man, that operates almost independent of his will. The same motif occurs later in Night I in the description of the Council of God in Eternity (I 469 ff.; 21:1ff. E306). Perhaps the Daughters of Beulah are Blake's personification of hope; certainly it would be anomalous if so profoundly Christian a poet as Blake did not give a large place in his scheme to what is sometimes considered the most distinctively Christian virtue. Like hope, the Daughters see, however imperfectly, a way out of the deepest distress—as parents do who, for little or no apparent reason, trust that their confused and dislocated child will come through the ordeal of growth, or indeed as any person does who refuses to see a dark night of unhappiness as permanent.

After their mutually infecting quarrel, Tharmas and Enion copulate in anguish and generate Los and Enitharmon. The two new characters, as Zoas of the imagination, will eventually be the agents of redemption in the poem. For a long time, however, they are repellent figures, as they are in their earlier appearances in the Lambeth books. Since these embodiments of man's power to see and shape are the offspring of the instinctive powers, Blake's point seems to be that the first panicky impulse after the instinctive recognition that a fall has occurred is to evoke, just as instinctively, the power to do something—anything—about it; for the action of Los and Enitharmon, though misguided, is a dynamic, a potential for change that makes redemption possible. Like Shelley, Blake sees the regenerating spark in man not as mind or even heart in itself but as an imaginative, creative force arising from instinctive sources.

There follows for the human imagination an interval of

heady though ill-founded bliss; the youthful couple reenact their parents' decline, living at first happy and naked in Beulah ("the Moony spaces of Eno") but soon falling into contentious shame and jealousy: "Alternate Love & Hate his breast; hers Scorn & Jealousy / In embryon passions" (I 232-38; 9:19-25 E300-301). In the world of Tharmas, now fallen into Generation, they delight in the suffering of their parents and eventually come into Urizen's sphere of influence. With the nasty elusiveness that will later half madden Los, Enitharmon recommends ingratitude and scorn toward their parents as a means of insuring their continued attention. On the dramatic level, the tensions between generations have seldom been better delineated, but the point goes deeper. In their rejection of instinct, the primitive parent, and in their allegiance to fallen reason, Los and Enitharmon show what is all too likely to happen to imagination in man's confused condition: it loses touch with basic human needs. It becomes elitist, irresponsible, governed by its own whim; it is encouraged in this irresponsibility by a rationalist intellectual Establishment that seeks to corrupt art and imagination by enshrining them, so that rationalism can pursue unchecked the "real" business of the world in such activities as scientific research, commerce, and war. (This elitist isolationism is perhaps the most fundamental charge brought by the Romantics, explicitly or implicitly, against eighteenth-century art and eighteenth-century definitions of the imagination.[11]) Los will never be entirely happy in this role of privileged and pampered child, but there are times in the poem—especially at the banquet later in Night I and in Night IV—when he will prefer it to more honest activity.

The process of degeneration, as well as the attempt of Beulah to arrest and contain it, continues in a chain reaction: the children begotten by the Spectre-Tharmas create a further division within their mother. Because of her maternal suffering, Enion begins "Rehumanizing from the Spectre in

pangs of maternal love" (I 216; 9:3 E300) ; at the same time
the children repeat the act of drawing-out and draining-off
that Enion had performed for Tharmas:

> drawing her Spectrous Life
> Repelling her away & away by a dread repulsive power
> Into Non Entity revolving round in dark despair.
> And drawing in the Spectrous life in pride and haughty joy.
>
> (I 217-20; 9:4-7 E300)

(This transformation too is visually illustrated in the designs.[12]) The result is both to make manifest what is evil in
Enion by isolating it and to purify her. The children are
entirely happy to imbibe this demonic version of mother's
milk. They prefer the spectrous mother to the human one
because that preference conveniently reinforces their cynical
view of what they owe their parents. A depraved creativity
can thus have it both ways: it can blithely rationalize bo-
hemian irresponsibility by attributing it to its origin in an
equally selfish instinct, but it can also scorn basic instinctual
human needs as beneath the high dignity of art. Art can
thus be both amoral and highbrow.

Mercifully, however, Eno, a Daughter of Beulah, attempts
to meet even this new development; it would seem that the
protective capacity of Beulah deepens with each new demand
placed upon it. Eno opens time and space "& in Every year
made windows into Eden," while her sisters "Alternate kept
watch over the Youthful terrors." Perhaps the greatest tribute
Blake pays these Daughters is to say that they do what they
can to meet this emergency through their own resources,
without any assurance that their earlier prayer for help has
been heard: "They saw not yet the Hand Divine for it was
not yet reveald / But they went on in Silent Hope &
Feminine repose" (I 222-31; 9:9-18 E300) .

Apart from her role as Los's counterpart, Enitharmon may

be defined in relation to her mother Enion, in that Enitharmon enacts a later chapter in the story of the fall of woman.
Enitharmon and Los enter the plot of Night I as mortals
born into a state of supratemporal beings. Despite the
"glories from their heads out beaming" (ɪ 196; 8:6 ᴇ300),
Enitharmon and Los are greedy brats; after sucking their
mother dry they turn next on each other, with Enitharmon
always in the lead in suggesting new forms of cruelty. At
a much younger stage of sexual maturity than their parents,
"they kiss'd not nor embrac'd for shame & fear"; yet "She
drave the Females all away from Los / And Los drave all the
Males from her away" (ɪ 238-44; 9:25-31 ᴇ301). (Interest-
ingly, Tharmas and Enion had been introduced as physical
adults, but their behavior had been childlike; Los and
Enitharmon are disturbingly adultlike in behavior though
still children or adolescents.) Feeling restrained by Los,
Enitharmon urges him to plunge more deeply into the fallen
world, where "warlike charions" sound, by forcing him to
listen to her fantasies of dalliance with Albion in "a Song
of Death! it is a Song of Vala!"

Enitharmon's song (ɪ 260ff.; 10:9ff. ᴇ301-302), the first of
at least fourteen references in the poem to the circumstances
of Albion's Fall (see Appendix B), introduces in a garbled
form three of the four main motifs in that story: Luvah's
seizure of Urizen's horses of light, Vala's seduction of Albion,
and Albion's refusal to look upon the Divine Vision. (The
fourth motif is Urizen's usurpation—with or without Luvah's
help—of Albion's place as ruler of the Zoas.) Enitharmon
prefers the female version of the story, in which Vala seduces Albion. Laughing in her sleep as she does in *Europe*,
Enitharmon projects herself into the fantasy, modeling her
role after Vala. When Albion finds that Enitharmon has
slipped into his "night-repose" in the guise of Vala (ɪ 272;
10:21 ᴇ301), he reproaches her for tormenting her own mate,
but Enitharmon unheedingly quotes these reproaches in

her "Song of Vala" as one more way to show Los the impotence of men and the power of women.

Los has not yet lost all of the visionary faculty as Enitharmon has; "in his vigorous voice was prophecy" (I 239; 9:26 E301). After knocking her to the ground, he resists her "Song of Death" by revealing his own visions of Albion and Vala, which differ from Enitharmon's partly in the account of events but mainly by prophetically going beyond the history of the fall and adumbrating what can be done to remedy it (I 281ff.; 11:3ff. E302). In his fallen condition, Los believes punishment is necessary, and he has an inkling that Luvah is to offer a vicarious atonement. A deleted passage prophesies the incarnation and sacrifice of the Lamb of God (I 290-98; E745), but apparently Blake decided to depict Los as not yet capable of this perception, reserving it for Night VII, after Los has matured through his own suffering. Los is also aware that Tharmas's "cold expanse" is not his and Enitharmon's true home; his description of their original life within Albion, however, errs in centering on the brain—Urizen's domain—rather than on the imagination or the laboring hands (I 302-305; 11:15-18 E302).

In an ominous, almost too broad parody of the sennet heralding a royal entrance, the "warlike clarions ceast" and instead "A Groan was heard on high" as Urizen makes his entrance. The first of the two primal powers, or faculties, that had warred in heaven is ready to appear in the fallen world, leaving his antagonist Luvah, along with Vala, still standing for a time in the sky. The first confrontation between Urizen as false god, or Satan, and Los as potential visonary of Jesus is accompanied by an echo of Jesus' response (John 11:33) to the news of Lazarus's death; Eternity "groand & was troubled at the Image of Eternal Death" (I 313-15; 12: 2-4 E302). In what is clearly an effort to get Los to fight his battles for him, Urizen, "prince of Light" (or reason), offers **Los power** over Luvah, "prince of Love," who is charged with the murder of Albion. Aware that Urizen, like Satan in *Milton*, is "one of those who when most complacent / Mean mischief most," Los refuses to recognize Urizen's authority, accept his bribes, bend to his law, or negotiate with him in any way: "One must be master. try thy Arts I also will try mine" (I 321-33; 12:10-20 E302-303). Urizen's reply is in Blakean terms the ultimate blasphemy, since it negates a precisely accurate definition of the true path to human integration:

> Art thou a visionary of Jesus the soft delusion of Eternity
> Lo I am God the terrible destroyer & not the Saviour
> Why should the Divine Vision compell the sons of Eden
> to forego each his own delight to war against his Spectre
> The Spectre is the Man the rest is only delusion & fancy.
> (I 337-41; 12:25-29 E303)

The imaginative power is seriously ill, too ill to combat even this blatant error. Los humbles himself before Enitharmon, and their travesty of marriage is celebrated at a feast at which Urizen presides. The banquet scene is one of the great set pieces in Blake, a kind of Black Mass solemnizing the total denial of the human and imaginative, a blasphemy that will be directly reversed in the poem's last Nights. Urizen's hosts sing to the sulky newlyweds a terrible song of Experience (I 386-433; 14:7-16:12 E304-305) in which the humane labors of harvest and vintage are despised and replaced by bloodshed. The utilitarian triumphs over the human; in wartime the horse is of more value than the man. The enemy is declared to be the fallen incarnation of passion, who is to be chained by imaginative power—a foretelling of the most shameful episode in Los's earthly life, the jealous binding down of his son Orc in Night V. Blake's lament at this triumph of genteel and academic art over the vigor of passion and its replacement by the sham aesthetic vigor of warfare is powerful. Like much epic poetry it exemplifies the imagina-

Night I

tive fascination of the horrific—all the more horrific here in that the demonic hymn is directed at the imaginative powers, potential agents of salvation now reduced to torpid conformity.

The touching antiphon is sung by Enion, the now weakened and distant shadow of human instinct (I 445-460; 17: 2-18:7 E305-306). She mourns tenderly over the animal victims of the very blood-sacrifice that Urizen's hosts have just celebrated so gleefully. Feebly, the instinctual warning system in man, despite the depraved form of imagination it has produced without so intending, tells us that there is something dreadfully wrong in a world where creatures survive only by preying on others and, by extension, a world where the psyche preys on itself. Her lament is a refutation of all complacent rationalizations about chains of being and ecological life cycles which would render meaningless the subtle terrors of Frost's poem *Design* or Tennyson's outcry against nature's waste and bloodiness (*In Memoriam,* lvi).

The last movement of Night I returns to Blake's hopeful theme of a salutary providence. Albion, deathly sick, has struggled to the edge of Beulah, which is marked by "the Palm tree" and "the Oak of Weeping" (I 464; 18:11 E306). These trees, which will be mentioned together at intervals throughout the poem, are complementary: the palm is representative of the Holy Land and the oak tree of Britain; further, the palm tree probably signifies life and longevity, the oak Druid sacrifice. At this boundary of Beulah, Albion sinks into sleep or death and is carefully laid out by the Savior upon the Rock of Ages. The Eternals of Eden meet in a Council of God, personified in Jesus.[13] Assembled above Mount Snowdon, the Council hears the frightened report of the fall (I 477-549; 21:9-19:5 E306-08) from Beulah's messengers, gentle, pacific spirits who may be thought of as personifications of the prayer sent up by the guardian Daughters of Beulah earlier in this Night.

Heretofore we have had the fall presented as it appears to the human being actually undergoing its horrors; now the story is told almost from an omniscient point of view by those who love and protect mankind and intercede for it in Eternity. The innocence of Beulah is to the state of Eternity as Tharmas, whose distress we observed at first, is to Albion. The messengers sense the fall in terms not of its symptoms but of its causes, not in terms of stunned instinct or confused imagination but as a conspiracy and power struggle between Luvah and Urizen, desire and restraint, the two ultimate powermongers in man. They also see the total picture of devastation—and how far it exceeds Beulah's ability to cope with it—which has not been clear to any single entity involved in the story: "Sudden down fell they all together into an unknown Space / Deep horrible without End. Separated from Beulah far beneath" (I 541-42; 22:38-39 E308). Like Tharmas, the messengers represent the bewilderment of the innocent psyche at the new turmoil that afflicts it. Unlike Tharmas, however, they have a clear reference point in Eternity; their account of the fall is fairly consecutive and coherent. Their awareness of complex causes and motivations goes much deeper than Enitharmon's; they explain Urizen's responsibility as instigator and organizer of revolt and Luvah's as furious smiter of Albion. Other pieces of the puzzle fall into place: in the primal conflict Urthona was an innocent bystander, working at his anvil on spades and coulters (plowshares), but the war of titans tore him asunder and sent his Emanation fleeing to Tharmas for refuge—which is where we came in at the beginning of the quarrel between Tharmas and Enion.

The messengers want the Savior to act directly, violently, by cutting this Gordian knot (I 548-49; 19:4-5 E308). But the Savior is not a deus ex machina. Instead, Seven Eyes of God—who are not fully identified until Night VIII—are elected to watch over fallen man, suggesting that he will be able to

Night I

recover when he is ready, in the fullness of time. Jesus, the seventh of the Eyes, watches with particular solicitude while the Daughters of Beulah guard Albion's Emanation, Jerusalem, who was also a point of contention between Tharmas and Enion and is now debarred from Beulah by the jealous Enitharmon. The salvation of man must be achieved by a spiritual and internal effort during a terrible sojourn in the darkest and lowest states of Albion's being, as later Nights will show.

Night II.

At some stage in the composition of *The Four Zoas* Night II was intended to be the first.[1] This plan would have been logically sound, for Nights II and III focus on Urizen and Luvah, who as reason and passion are the primary causes of action in man, the *fuel* of his psyche, while Night I focuses on Tharmas and Los, man's instinctive and imaginative faculties, the *instruments* of or ways of dealing with the two primary powers. Though the Zoas are often thought of as four different but coordinate cardinal faculties, they actually function as two pairs: a primary system of antagonistic opposites and a secondary or responsive system of compatible potential allies. Urizen and Luvah-Orc set things in motion by confrontation, one attacking or restraining the other; Tharmas and Urthona-Los, responding independently to the disharmony caused by the other pair, are sometimes capable of cooperation. Urizen and Luvah are like negative and positive poles generating an electrical current; Tharmas and Los are more like circuitry. Blake's decision in the later version to postpone his detailed description of the Urizen-Luvah conflict until Night II and to open the poem with episodes featuring Tharmas and Los reflects a change in his narrative strategy from logical to psychological development. After opening, in medias res, with man's recognition of and response to his fallen situation, Blake is ready in Night II to depict the underlying causes of the fall.

The thematic and strategic differences between the first Night and the two succeeding ones explain, among other things, their differences in tone and emotional effect. Night I derives much of its power from shock; its pathos is of a peculiarly frightening kind because its arena is an instinctual and imaginative depth in our minds that is close to the unconscious essence of our human nature. As Tharmas and Enion grope to find out who and where they are and what has happened to them, the reader too struggles to locate himself in the strange cosmos of a strange poem; indeed the reader's sense of disorientation contributes to the atmosphere of bewildered panic that characterizes Night I. Moving into more familiar territory, Blake concentrates in Nights II and III on passion and reason, the elemental faculties that we are used to confronting more overtly and consciously in personal conflicts between desire and restraint; accordingly, in these sections the action becomes more smoothly consecutive. Except for a few abrupt leaps, the transitions in Nights II and III are more fluid than in the rapid cuts or lightning flashes between scenes in Night I. And the mood of Nights II and III is not primitive terror but clearly understood sadness and frustration.

In the opening lines of Night II readers are given their first level look at the situation of the fall from the present or real-time perspective of Albion, humanity as a whole, rather than in confused flashbacks from below, the partial and distorted points of view of man's separated faculties, or from above, the timeless reassurances of providence. The equivocations of time, place, and perspective in the opening scene convey vividly some of the central insights of *The Four Zoas*: the simultaneity and interconnectedness of apparently unrelated events, the ambiguity of causes and effects, and the interlocking of responsibilities in relation to the fall—all of which are aspects of Blake's gigantic correction of the tendency in traditional interpretations of the biblical account to fix blame upon all of mankind as a result of one foolish action at the beginning of time. Everything Albion does in recognizing and attempting to arrest his fall is, however, certain to be self-defeating. Unable to see through the paralyzing fog of his diseased consciousness, he blurs—rather than seeing the relations between—symptoms and causes, fate and free will, past and present, appearance and reality:

> Rising upon his Couch of Death Albion beheld his Sons
> Turning his Eyes outward to Self. losing the Divine Vision
> Albion calld Urizen & said. Behold these sickning Spheres
> Whence is this Voice of Enion that soundeth in my Porches
> Take thou possession! take this Scepter! go forth in my might
> For I am weary, & must sleep in the dark sleep of Death
> Thy brother Luvah hath smitten me but pity thou his youth
> Tho thou hast not pitid my Age   O Urizen Prince of Light.
> (II 1-8; 23:1-8 E309)

As the consciousness of his full humanity slips away, Albion tries to strengthen his specialized rational powers, partly in order to dull his awareness of the deeply buried instinctual sense of loss and despair heard in Enion's faint voice "that soundeth in my Porches." According to narrative chronology, Enion's lamentation in Night I causes Albion to become aware of his illness in Night II, but according to the mythic scheme of the poem, her despair results from Albion's fall. That is, Enion had begun to drift into non-entity in Night I after Tharmas had accepted the outcast Emanations of the other Zoas, who—in a conflict that was not described until the ambassadors of Beulah reported to the Universal Family near the end of that Night—had already "recieved their death wounds" (I 33; 4:15 E297) ; her wail from non-entity actually is Albion's dim consciousness of the fall, even though his having already fallen into intellectual and emotional conflict is what has caused the weakening of his instinctive integrity.

The place of Enion's lament is as equivocal as its cause and timing. Albion's porches, where Enion's voice is heard, are the portals of his conscious mind, one of the main arenas of conflict in the poem; at the same time there is perhaps a verbal echo of the "porches" of the ear of Hamlet's father, into which Claudius poured his poison. The ambassadors from Beulah have already noted in Night I Urizen's determination to control the porches while Albion is asleep, but in the opening scene of Night II, it is Albion who summons Urizen to take possession of his porches. At this point Urizen is appalled at his first clear view—by daylight, as it were—of the void within Albion, which is the same space as the nonentity of Night I from which arises Enion's lament. Ironically, Urizen does not seem aware that it is his own presence, the glare of his cold rationality, that in part has caused the dimming of Albion's consciousness; upon Urizen's arrival in the human brain "all its golden porches grew pale with his sickening light" (II 13; 23:13 E309).

In a state of uncertainty about the priority of cause, effect, and perspective in the analysis of the fall, the reader is led further into Albion's mental universe. Albion, for his part, begins to externalize both his senses and their objects in order to distract himself from his inner conflict. In bringing about the primal subject-object split he succeeds only in blotting out the Divine Vision and deepening the void within. The statement that Albion turns "his Eyes outward to Self," an image repeated later when the sense organs of Reuben and Levi "roll outward" so that "What is within" is "now seen without" (II 54-55; 25:22-23 E310), expresses a fundamental idea in the *Zoas* and a paradox characteristic of Romanticism. The phrases emphasize the oxymoronic nature of the very act and word "introspection," in that the attempt to isolate consciously the subjective "I" in ourselves requires an objectivity that can dehumanize. Tharmas and Enion in Night I are self-conscious in something like the ordinary sense of that word—that is, ill at ease and therefore unable to act spontaneously. The self-consciousness of Albion in Night II is a more literal, radical, and even philosophical kind suggestive of the torturous self-examinations of

Descartes and Hume. It is felt as that new awareness of inner space which, according to Lionel Trilling, has been an important human attitude only since the Renaissance.[2]

Albion, fearing these inner spaces as Pascal did the outer ones, feels helpless to govern them. He reacts to psychological crisis as most people do, by summoning the policeman Urizen, the enforcer of mental rigidity, though he is aware that not only Luvah but Urizen too has wounded him (II 7-8; 23:7-8 E309). In this emergency Albion is concerned not with justice but with what will work; he needs a vicegerent who will be able to function while humanity shuts down most of its systems to preserve itself at a basal level until it can recover. Instead of comprehensive self-knowledge, tolerance of all that is human within him, his only goal in his diminished condition is total self-control; he wills himself to be what is often called, euphemistically, reasonable.

Urizen accepts only too eagerly his "assum'd" power (as Blake puns in the first line of *Urizen*): rising "from the bright Feast like a star thro' the evening sky / Exulting at the voice." But almost immediately he sees how impossible his position is: "No more Exulting . . . Pale he beheld futurity" (II 9-15; 23:9-15 E309). Though humanity is perverse enough to enthrone the very power of rationalism that had helped subvert him, rationality is capable on its own of recognizing its inadequacy. Yet Urizen is so horrified by the other human faculties (as the supergo is horrified by the id in Freudian myth) that he accepts his quixotic solo mission in a mood of gloomy fatalism that we shall come to associate with him in his fallen state.

It is generally agreed that Night II portrays the fall of passion, Night III the fall of reason. But "fall" seems not to mean the same thing for passion that it does for reason. The most active figures in narrative present-time in both Nights are Urizen, Los, and their Emanations; the primeval crimes committed by Luvah are treated only briefly and indirectly, primarily through flashbacks. It seems that the fall of passion means its defeat or victimization, not—as with the fall of reason seen in Urizen—its inherent or self-willed deterioration. Although Blake's theoretical paradigm calls for an equal division of blame between Urizen and Luvah, the *Zoas* retains from the earlier Lambeth poems an insistence that passion is a victim whose errors and excesses are partially justified by what it suffers. Blake redresses the imbalance caused by Urizen's performance of most of the overtly evil acts in the poem, however, by establishing parallels between the victim Luvah and his archenemy Urizen. Their reflections of each other, which are explored more fully later in the poem, are anticipated through brief allusions in Night II.

Luvah's passivity toward Urizen is related to his virtual absence from the poem as a character in his own right. We see very little of the Zoa of passion in his true identity as love rather than lust and violence. The main exceptions occur in brief and scattered passages of Night II and one extended pastoral scene in Night IX. The unfallen aspect of Luvah is almost wholly absorbed in the figure of Jesus, the fallen aspect in Orc.

Two explanations for Luvah's lack of definition as a character suggest themselves. One is the obvious artistic problem of presenting love in a way that will appear neither too ethereally sacred nor too earthily profane to a fallen audience. When our loving impulses transcend the carnal we too often suspect a self-deceiving sublimation; yet we are equally wrong to explain away our physical desire for the beloved as a hormonal necessity. The problem of imagining concretely a love that is both whole and human may simply have defied Blake as it has defied other artists. The second explanation has to do with the relation between energy and love in Blake's evolving mythology. His first reference to Luvah, a brief allusion to the renewal of his horses in *Thel* (1789), suggests a life-affirming force but not a fully developed mythic being. Luvah is not otherwise mentioned before *The Four Zoas*, though his alter ego Orc appears in *America* and *Europe* (1793, 1794) as a militant insurgent whose mission is to "scatter religion abroad / To the four winds as a torn book" (*America* 8:5-6). An Orc much like this survives in the *Zoas* and will appear prominently in later Nights, for the first time identified as the debased form of Luvah. But in the *Zoas* Orc is a fallen parody of what is best in Christianity, not, as in *Europe,* the essential revolutionary reality of which a fallen Christianity is the parody. Whether Blake intended all along to identify Luvah with Orc or whether in reconsidering his own view of Christianity he came to see hatred and lust as perverted forms of love, Blake makes Orc a vivid personage but keeps Luvah's character shadowy, implying that there is something inexplicable about the redemptive action of love. Urizen and Los, as persons and as psychic forces, make much sharper impressions on the reader than does Luvah.

To clarify the new character of Luvah and to achieve a portrait of unfallen love in the *Zoas*, Blake makes room within his own myth for a revitalized Christian myth; he names Jesus directly but introduces him into history (and the poem) as one wearing Luvah's robes of blood. This complex recurring symbol of Incarnation and Crucifixion, already present in Night I, will be explored in Night VIII, where it underlies Blake's transformation of the Christian doctrine of Atonement. In the very incongruity of the symbol, with its suggestion of duplicity and disguise, Blake acknowledges the paradox of associating the saving power of Christian self-sacrifice with his own Zoa of passion—who even in his unfallen state is as strongly erotic and Dionysiac as he is Franciscan or Gandhian. Thus the other characters in the poem have difficulty in recognizing Luvah either as the bodily form of Jesus or as the alter ego of Orc. They are especially dismayed by their vision of Jesus in Luvah's robes and regard this figure as an anomaly or even an impostor.

An equally intriguing interpretative problem is posed by Vala, Luvah's female counterpart. She retains in *The Four Zoas* much of the overwhelming presence she has in the earlier version of the poem, which was named for her, though in theory she is only one of four Emanations and in reality appears no more often than, for example, Enitharmon. Unlike Luvah, however, she regularly appears under her own name as well as in various disguises. In Night II we see her, like Luvah, mainly as a victim of oppression; in Night IX she is the leading character in an idyllic interlude immediately preceding her bacchanalian participation with Luvah in the great vintage of the apocalypse. Yet she is more often a villainess, whether in her own identity or in the guise of the nefarious females who spring from her in Night VIII.

In both early and late versions of the poem Vala is important in relation to Albion and Luvah as well as in her own right. She is one of the principal figures in Blake's first anatomy of a distinctive feminine element, operating for good and ill, in the human psyche.[3] Blake's earlier depictions of female characters are narrower in scope. The protagonists of both *Thel* and *Visions of the Daughters of Albion* can be placed within conventions of fantasy or allegory (as seen in Shelley's *The Witch of Atlas,* for example, or *The Sensitive Plant*). But the techniques of characterization in *Thel* and *Visions* are as much dramatic as mythic. In *Urizen* and *Europe* Blake develops a mythic female in Enitharmon, but only in her sinister aspects. The Shadowy Female of *America* and *Europe* is too vague to be called a character until in Night VII of *The Four Zoas* she is identified as a manifestation of Vala. The title character of *The Book of Ahania* is similarly vague, having only a choral function, in her plangent complaint near the end of the poem.

The Four Zoas uses all these views of the feminine and methods of treating it—allegorical, symbolic, dramatic, choral —but adds a new and comprehensive view of the feminine as an indispensable element, both divisive and saving, in cosmic and psychological reality. As nature and the feminine side of passion, Vala was originally conceived as the seductive illusion that blocks the Divine Vision and is solely responsible for Albion's fall into error. Rather than following the precedents of biblical and classical myth and allowing Jerusalem, Albion's true Emanation, to fall or cause the fall, Blake hides her away and gives the role of temptress to Vala; in biblical tradition, this would be like preserving Eve's innocence by exposing Lilith as the guilty female. Jerusalem remains uncorrupted as the spiritual side of Albion's feminine being, separated from him by the fall; Vala, the physical side of femininity, is ambitious to usurp the whole of humanity and is therefore in herself a sufficient cause—but not the only cause—of the fall. At the same time, through Vala's lesser role as Luvah's fallen Emanation, Blake presents passion as an active feminine force who dominates the passional life while her male counterpart, the erotic-altruistic principle, is incapacitated.

To recapitulate the main point about Blake's presentation of passion's participation in the fall before tracing its consequences for fallen humanity: Luvah's covert attack on Albion—though described by the ambassadors from Beulah in Night I and referred to by Albion in the abdication scene that opens Night II—is not stressed as a primary cause of the fall. Rather, Luvah is himself a victim. The fall of the passions occurs simultaneously with, and seems contingent upon, the rise of the intellect. Immediately after Albion's abdication, Urizen as "great Work master" stands upon the "verge of Non Existence" where the "Abyss" begins and utters the fiat that, in the "indefinite space" within Albion, is the psychological equivalent of God's first act of creation in Genesis (II 15-22; 23:15-24:5 E309). At this stage of events, Luvah and Vala are described as if they are still partly unfallen. In Night I, "standing in the bloody sky . . . above the heavens forsaken desolate suspended in .blood," they remain in some indeterminate state between "Eternity . . . above them" and the "misty earth" beneath: "Descend they could not. nor from Each other avert their eyes" (I 359-65; 13:4-10 E303). But they are gradually drawn down into Enion's void; when they hear Urizen decree the building of the Mundane Shell, the rationally ordered universe, they tremble and shrink (II 22; 24:5 E309) and soon find themselves under his power, estranged from each other. In the narrative sequence, all this—the suspension in limbo, Urizen's fiat, and the descent of Luvah and Vala—takes place just as Albion summons Urizen in Night II from the wedding feast described in Night I (I 371-73; 13:16-18 E303-04; II 9; 23:9 E309).

Between two extended descriptions of the building of Urizen's world, Blake inserts a dramatic scene depicting Luvah's imprisonment in Urizen's "Furnaces of affliction" (II 72; 25:40 E310; cf. Isa. 48:10). Luvah's suffering is caused not only by his imprisonment under Urizen but also by Vala's sadistic firing of the furnaces. Her inability to recognize in Luvah's howlings the voice of her once-innocent lover with whom "she walkd in bliss, in times of innocence & youth" (II 79; 26:3 E311) links her with Enion as a female now out of touch with her male counterpart. Under the control of fallen reason, humanity now perceives sexual desire as destructive and guilt-producing. Urizen's furnaces of affliction imprison Luvah's passionate energy in the fig leaf, the chaperone system, Victorian sexual ethics; whereas Vala's stoking the fires in "cruel delight" is the provocative withholding of sexual gratification which so inflames the passions as to obliterate their origin in love. In the psychological allegory of individual development, Luvah's sufferings depict

the rational-emotional conflict that is especially acute in early
adolescence, when an exaggerated cerebralism often masks
and suppresses the sexual aspect of youthful energy. Luvah
finally melts with woe, leaving Vala to collapse into ashes
beneath the furnaces; her ashes are later mingled with mor-
tar to bind together the stones of Urizen's temple (II 171;
30:13 E313). Now the furnaces can be tapped:

> Then were the furnaces unseald with spades & pickaxes
> Roaring let out the fluid, the molten metal ran in channels
> Cut by the plow of ages held in Urizens strong hand
> In many a valley, for the Bulls of Luvah dragd the Plow.
>
> (II 117-20; 28:7-10 E312)

Urizen holds the plow but the motive energy is Luvah's;
the manipulation is reason's but the power is passion's. We
have a succinct verbal emblem not only of repression, in both
technical and popular senses of the word, but also of psychological sublimation. We have moreover an image of the
venting of passionate energy into socially acceptable intellectual competition.

During his sufferings Luvah utters a fervid lament from
inside Urizen's furnaces (II 80-112; 26:4-28:2 E311). Ironically, the poet's exhortation "Hear ye the voice of Luvah"
can apply only to the reader, since the other characters are
oblivious to his voice. Luvah's speech, a mixture of truth
and ghastly error, describes and typifies the affliction of all
the Zoas in Nights II and III, a psychological instance of
the random collision of atoms in the Lucretian universe.

> we all go to Eternal Death
> To our Primeval Chaos in fortuitous concourse of incoherent
> Discordant principles of Love & Hate.
>
> (II 101-03; 27:11-13 E311)

The passage applies to both Luvah himself and Urizen if the
emphasis falls on "Discordant principles," for their dishar-

mony results from principled opposition. The words "fortuitous" and "incoherent" are a good description of Tharmas's condition, and perhaps of Los's. In contrast to Tharmas, Luvah is admirably percipient in both his self-diagnosis and his analysis of his chief antagonist; he continues: "I was love but hatred awakes in me / And Urizen who was Faith & Certainty is changd to Doubt." Luvah's next remark, however, is as flatly erroneous as Urizen's blasphemous attack on the Divine Vision in Night I (I 337-41; 12:25-29 E303):

> The hand of Urizen is upon me because I blotted out
> That Human delusion to deliver all the sons of God
> From bondage of the Human form.
>
> (II 106-08; 27:16-18 E311)

As is often the case, we cannot be entirely sure whose error is described here; if the infinitive phrase beginning "to deliver" is in apposition with "delusion," the error is one Urizen made and Luvah opposed; more probably, though, "to deliver" means in order to deliver, and the error is a fundamental one made by Luvah himself. The fallen libido, it appears, would also make a good tyrant, especially when it makes the mistake of "Reasoning from the loins" (II 112; 28:2 E311). And the similarity in the kinds of error Luvah and Urizen make sustains the theme of ironic kinship between these polarized antagonists.

The account given by Luvah of his nurturing of Vala from an earthworm, through a serpent, through a bright and poisonous dragon, makes specific and personal the theme of fallen sexuality. The serpentine imagery reflects Luvah's perception of the development of his own phallus as well as the emergence in his mind of the female genitalia as a horror and threat; the new mental image is reflected in the grotesquerie of the drawing on the facing MS page 26. The synopsis is embryological, probably because Blake wishes to

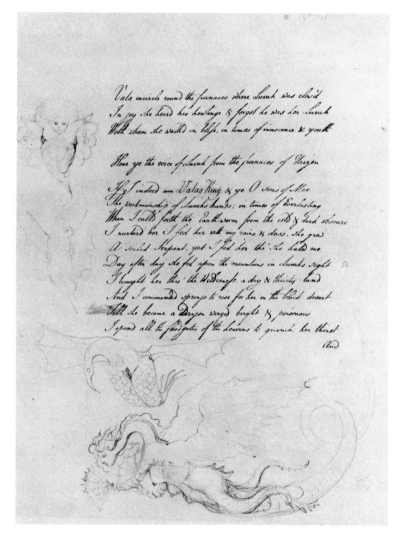

Transformations of Vala: sexuality seen as horror. MS page 26 (Night II). Reproduced by permission of the British Library Board.

show that the view of sex as evil is a development, not a sudden trauma.

After the interpolated account of Luvah's tortured perceptions, Blake returns to his description of the world Urizen is creating—his Mundane Shell, a construct of pure reason. The interruption of the narrative, pointed up by a contrast between imagery of the organic and of rigid geometrical shapes, strengthens the central idea in Night II that Luvah must be rationally contained and restricted in order for Urizen's purely mental world to exist at all. Urizen's is the second comprehensive world view to appear in the poem; his is the intellectual cosmos that supersedes Enion's primitive Circle of Destiny. The Mundane Shell, though beautifully ornamented, eventually leads to the utterly bleak mechanistic perception of the universe, depicted in the "dens" of Night VI. Even at its best, the only vision of the world of which Urizen is capable sets nature up as recalcitrant matter apart from and in opposition to the human mind. Just as a child loses the desire to hug or kick objects that please or injure him, in this stage of the fall the mind ceases to share its life with the inanimate universe. In the unfallen state, every object would be a "thou" instead of an "it" in response to a greeting of the human spirit. As Coleridge speculates in *The Eolian Harp,* man and nature together would vibrate to the movement of "one Life"; in the fallen state, the effect of Urizenic rationalism is to make man feel ashamed of such exuberant animism, as Coleridge's Sara does in his poem.

At first Urizen acts through his agents to fill the void not with stars but with pyramids and cubes. The ironic point that the cubes are weighed on scales "That Luvah rent from the faint Heart of the Fallen Man" (II 143; 29:1 E312) is another indication that the ascendency of abstract reason is made both necessary and possible by the emotional disequilibrium accompanying Luvah's fall. Each step in Urizen's ascendency, however, marks a further decline in the whole of humanity.

The weaving that is usually associated with the female powers becomes the making of "Atmospheres" of nets and traps, which "condens[e] the strong energies into little compass" (II 145-65; 29:3-30:7 E312-13). Finally with the creation of the stars a limit to this stage of man's fall is reached. Acting as a "golden chain / To bind the Body of Man to heaven from falling into the Abyss" (II 266-67; 33:16-17 E315), the stars resemble the absolute limits of Opacity and Contraction discovered in Night IV. Both the stars and the limits have positive and negative implications: though they bind humanity, they simultaneously arrest the fall—temporarily in Night II, absolutely in Night IV.

The Mundane Shell is not yet the world of Newtonian mechanics, or its Lockean correlative, the world of absolute imaginative death we would inhabit if we believed with Gradgrind that "Quadruped. Graminivorous" is an adequate definition of a horse. Urizen's is an earlier model, the system of Ptolemy and Dante, highly intellectualized but made splendid by a blend of poetic precision and mathematic elegance, a fragile construct from which may be viewed the oceanic chaos of the unorganized instinctual reality represented by Tharmas:

> But infinitely beautiful the wondrous work arose
> In sorrow and care. a Golden World whose porches
>   round the heavens
> And pillard halls & rooms recievd the eternal wandering stars
> A wondrous golden Building; many a window many a door
> And many a division let in & out into the vast unknown
>
> .   .   .   .
>
> For many a window ornamented with sweet ornaments
> Lookd out into the World of Tharmas, where in
>   ceaseless torrents
> His billows roll where monsters wander in the foamy paths.
>
> (II 240-57; 32:7-33:7 E315)

Night II

Urizen's Pythagorean or Rosicrucian numerology, Masonic tools of plumbline and square, title of "Architect divine," and esoteric design—all playing upon arcane interpretations of biblical directions for the building of Solomon's temple— breathes the Renaissance spirit of humanistic science, the mystical intellectual atmosphere of Mozart's *Magic Flute*:

> First the Architect divine his plan
> Unfolds, The wondrous scaffold reard all round the infinite
> Quadrangular the building rose the heavens squared by a line.
>
> .   .   .   .
>
> Twelve halls after the names of his twelve sons composd
> The wondrous building & three Central Domes after
> the Names
> Of his three daughters were encompassd by the twelve
> bright halls
>
> .   .   .   .
>
> Each Dome opend toward four halls & the Three Domes
> Encompassd
> The Golden Hall of Urizen
>
> (II 166-79; 30:8-21 E313)

His palace includes chambers for his spouse Ahania; the sumptuous appointments, which one associates with Keats's "Chamber of Maiden-Thought" and, more ominously, with the precariously surviving palace of Hyperion, recall the medieval stage of the history of ideas when *sophia* was a divinity worthy of elaborate ceremony and nearly literal worship; perhaps they also allude slyly to the enthronement of the goddess Reason in Notre Dame in 1793:

> Urizen formd
> A recess in the wall for fires to glow upon the pale
> Females limbs in his absence & her Daughters oft upon
> A Golden Altar burnt perfumes with Art Celestial formd
> Foursquare sculpturd & sweetly Engravd to please their
> shadowy mother.
>
> (II 187-91; 30:29-33 E313)

The stars now move in the measured courses of rationalism, with absurdly exaggerated precision in angular orbits "obtuse / Acute Scalene" or "intricate ways biquadrate. Trapeziums Rhombs Rhomboids / Paralellograms." Yet even in "their amazing hard subdued course in the vast deep" they are seen poetically as animated creatures renewing their wasted strength in winter and reappearing in the summer skies "fired with ardour fresh recruited" (II 279-86; 33:29-36 E315-16). Some capacity to humanize his vision of the sky—though it will shortly be exhausted—still remains for man; conversely the humanized vision of the heavens regained in Night VII will signal the return of true imagination, the beginning of man's regeneration.

A brief passage at the height of the Urizen-Luvah conflict describes the reaction of the "Children of Man" to the titanic struggle. Though some are aghast and attempt to rally their brethren, others "stood silent & busied in their families" and still others are willfully oblivious:

> We see no Visions in the darksom air
> Measure the course of that sulphur orb that lights
>   the darksom day
> Set stations on this breeding Earth & let us buy & sell
> Others arose & schools Erected forming Instruments
> To measure out the course of heaven.
>
> (II 121-31; 28:11-21 E312)

The first two of these states of error correspond to those that Bunyan attacks, for his purposes, in Pliable (after he returns home to the City of Destruction) and Mr. Worldly Wiseman; Blake's third group epitomizes the new threat represented by the natural scientist. All three groups have something better to do than become visionaries; being too "sensible" even to recognize their distress, theirs are perhaps the most seriously endangered attitudes of mind that Blake considers. By applying the anodyne rationalism that Coleridge describes in the sixth stanza of the *Dejection* ode and inducing a dissociation of sensibility, they keep themselves going, in a limited way, in families, businesses, and laboratories. Blake is also satirizing, with laconic grimness, the assumption that the inner life as revealed in art, literature, dreams, and spiritual experience is less real than, say, the fluctuations of bonds or the latest findings in celestial spectroscopy. What happens to these self-blinded ones we never find out; Blake does not follow up on them any more than does Bunyan. But we have seen enough to recognize an essential experiential fact: the conviction of sin or danger or fallenness does not strike home equally to everyone; some people are incapable of recognizing that humanity is in any trouble at all. Blake's nonvisionaries are not really characters in the poem but rather reflections of a certain part of his potential audience, those who, as in the parable of the sower, cannot receive the seed, cannot listen even to the voices of conflict within themselves, and therefore would find a visionary epic irrelevant.

Throughout Night II both Urizen and Luvah exhibit a mixture of sorrow over new evils and determination to impose them on the world; for example, in "woe" and "lamenting," Urizen goes on "Commanding all the work with care & power & severity" (II 132-34; 28:22-24 E312). Both recognize the existence or threat of chaos, but they feel obligated—Urizen especially—to make their gloomy visions and predictions come true. Like Thel or like the speaker of Wordsworth's *Resolution and Independence,* who experiences "hope that is unwilling to be fed," they nurture their despair. Their psychology is like that of Jonah or any prophet of doom who ought to want to be proved wrong but in fact wants, egocentrically and irrationally, his prescience to be vindicated; the result is a dynamic of self-fulfilling prediction. Reason takes this perverse path because of its proverbial admiration for foolish consistency, but it shares with the more rebellious aspect of the personality an even darker and more mysterious need to hypostasize evil in order to achieve self-definition as its suppressor (Urizen) or resister (Luvah). Much as adolescents create caricatures of their parents, rabid partisans in the camps of tyrant and rebel define the opposition so as to create an antagonism that will eventually feed on itself, without regard to actual issues.

The most striking dramatization of such perverseness in the early Nights is in the separation of Urizen from Ahania; this is an especially radical kind of irrationality because, although Luvah is in some sense a true antagonist, Ahania is at first a near-caricature of docility, a patient Griselda who brightens when Urizen smiles and weeps when he frowns (II 182-83; 30:24-25 E313). Even before she takes the extraordinary liberty of presenting, through gentle hints, a well-meant warning in the form of a contrary opinion, Urizen feels a rift has occurred: "Astonishd & Confounded he beheld / Her shadowy form now Separate . . . Two wills they had two intellects & not as in times of old."[4] The estrangement, essentially willed by Urizen, soon develops its own momentum: "He drave the Male Spirits all away from Ahania / And she drave all the Females from him away" (II 203-10; 30: 45-52 E314). The now familiar pattern of jealousy, possessiveness, and—as will become clear in Night III—guilt is repeated once more. In quarreling with the inoffensive Ahania, Urizen demonstrates that reason's megalomania is not only aggressive toward the other faculties but self-destructive, attacking what is loveliest and gentlest in reason itself.

In what seems a deliberate parallel, Blake at this point interpolates a lament by Vala for her vanished Luvah (II 218-30; 31:4-16 E314); she too assumes an exaggeratedly lowly position toward her "Lord" (it is not clear to us, perhaps not to Vala either, whether this "Lord" is Luvah, Urizen, or Albion). The similarity between Vala's abjectness and Ahania's is a reminder not only of the parallel between Luvah and Urizen but also of the interconnections between

Night II

Emanations, despite the obvious distance between Ahania the queen and Vala the slave working for Urizen. Vala's lament that the beloved is judged by merely utilitarian standards might serve as a warning to all the Emanations. Ahania, however, is still able to communicate with her spouse; Vala, despite her professed love for Luvah, is never aware of his presence and in some respects even despises him (II 231-35; 31:17-32:2 E314).

At this moment, in the image of Jesus garbed in Luvah's robes, we are given a timely reminder that love will survive (II 263-65; 33:13-15 E315), though the sexes are sorely embattled and love has assumed its sick and fallen form. What a person suffers, he imposes on others; what he imposes, he also suffers. These cardinal laws in the *Zoas* are illustrated in the cruel game that Los and Enitharmon invent and then cannot stop playing. They are "drawn down" by their desires —a recurrent figure of eduction marking successive stages of the fall—and are now bent on a plot to divide Urizen and Ahania by bringing to Ahania an awareness of the outcast Enion. In Night I the imaginative power had pitted itself against instinct; earlier in Night II reason had repressed passion. Since psychic conflict is a war of all against all, we now see another permutation: it is reason's turn to be victim of imagination.

The methods imagination uses against reason are as demonic as those directed against instinct in the preceding Night. Los, who feels more threatened than Enitharmon, is the more active conspirator. But however repellent it may seem, Blake probably means to show the plot against reason, or fallen reason, as salutary in the long run. If creativity is ever to perform its saving work, it must abjure the cold rationalism it has heretofore obeyed. But that is not an easy task, as we now discover. Most of the remainder of Night II is an especially detailed and horrible account of the imagination's destruction not just of rationality but also of itself. In

keeping with the theme of Luvah's fall and its effects on the
other Zoas, the central motif of Night II, the vehicle for
the corruption of Los and Enitharmon is guilty and posses-
sive love. The third side of the triangle is Urizen, whom
Enitharmon plays off against Los with consummate skill at
amatory strategy.

In much fuller psychological detail than in Night I, Blake
describes the couple's fall from power and sensory flexibility
to the torments of jealous division (II 295ff.; 34:9ff. E316).
Expressing a direct inversion of Oothoon's rhapsody on free
love in *Visions of the Daughters of Albion*, Enitharmon boasts
of her success in withering Los by instilling in him a sense
of sin so deep that even when she is not watching him he can
delight neither in other loves nor in any form of the world's
beauty:

> I have seen thee sleep & turn thy cheek delighted
> Upon the rose or lilly pale. or on a bank where sleep
> The beamy daughters of the light starting they rise they flee
> From thy fierce love for tho I am dissolvd in the bright God
> My spirit still pursues thy false love over rocks & valleys.
>
> (II 313-17; 34:27-31 E316)

Los now can be trusted contemptuously to monitor himself—
he is somewhat like the degraded Winston Smith at the end
of Orwell's *1984*—at the very times when Enitharmon, by her
own taunting admission, is dallying with Urizen, "the bright
God." Enitharmon's viciousness is explicit and brazen: "for
thou art mine," she tells Los, "Created for my will my slave
tho strong tho I am weak" (II 331-32; 34:45-46, E317). Such
cruelty is the more horrendous because it is a reply to Los's
touching and vulnerable appeal: "I know thee not as once
I knew thee in those blessed fields / Where memory wishes
to repose among the flocks of Tharmas."

After her recitative, Enitharmon sings a radiantly beautiful but sinister anthem of female domination, one of the most metrically elaborate passages in the *Zoas* (II 343-78; 34:57-92 E317-18). Delivered with sensuous languor, the canticle is the definitive prescription of how to tame men by alluring and emasculating them at the same time (and is thus, among other things, both an exposition and an exposé of the tradition of courtly love):

> The joy of woman is the Death of her most best beloved
> Who dies for Love of her
> In torments of fierce jealousy & pangs of adoration.
> The Lovers night bears on my song
> And the nine Spheres rejoice beneath my powerful controll.

Part of the fascination of Enitharmon's song lies in her bland self-satisfaction in cruelty and the juxtaposition of her malevolence with placid joy:

> Now my left hand I stretch to earth beneath
> And strike the terrible string
> I wake sweet joy in dens of sorrow & I plant a smile
> In forests of affliction
> And wake the bubbling springs of life in regions of
>   dark death.

These images of regeneration, together with Blake's beautiful proverb "every thing that lives is holy"—the words of Oothoon's credo—find a chilling new context in Enitharmon's song. The strange tonal contrasts and combinations are paradoxical only on the level of logic; experientially Enitharmon's hymn expresses perfectly the heady exhilaration of winning in the adversary form of the game of love. Such victories, Blake reminds us, are sham ones, deceptions not only of one's lover-opponent but of oneself. Enitharmon entices Los to approach her, only to flee when he takes the bait. It is easy to understand, then, why his "hopes" are "delusive"; but

Enitharmon herself sings "in Rapturous delusive trance" (II 379-80; 34:93-94 E318).[5]

This entire episode would seem to reflect the so-called antifeminine side of Blake, the strain in him that many readers are at a loss to reconcile with the ardent feminism of works like *Visions of the Daughters of Albion.* Such comparisons are not very helpful, however; *Visions* is drama and sociological commentary; *The Four Zoas,* though it too is drama, is mainly myth. Night II of the myth is concerned with spoiled love; in such a context a literal indictment of either sex exclusively would be a falsification of reality. That the portrait of Enitharmon as a virtuoso of sadism is not a gratuitous indictment of women is proved by its careful placement in the poem, juxtaposed immediately with Urizen's brutal treatment of Ahania as an inferior, in this Night and especially in Night III.

Los has fallen victim to a combination of sensuality and celestial otherworldliness, the confusion that drives and derides the young boy in Joyce's *Araby.* Since Enitharmon's ability to unman Los is made possible by her allegiance to her "God" Urizen, who is something between her protector and her lover, Los decides to attack Urizen in Urizen's own most vulnerable spot, his attachment to Ahania. Los's plan of revenge is to "draw" Ahania into the vacuum of exile where Enion now exists (II 383-84; 34:97-98 E318). One of the more grimly comic of the many ironies here is that Urizen needs no provocation to jealousy; the demented compulsions of rationality, like Satan's envy and ire, operate not only independent of but in spite of real circumstances. Urizen feels jealous over Ahania when she is most devoted to him; similarly, even before the long scene in which Enitharmon boasts of her dalliance with him, we read that "Urizen saw & envied." Envied whom? Most immediately, Los and Enitharmon, but Urizen also suffers from a generalized, detached anxiety over "the visions of futurity / That his dread fancy

Night II

formd before him in the unformd void" (ii 291-94; 34:5-8
e316).

A Night that had begun in heroic solemnity and sadness
has very nearly turned into farce, revealing in rapid succession almost every conceivable permutation of love gone wrong
through misunderstanding, mistaken identity, and misalli-
ance. We are lifted above these degrading entanglements by
Enion's second great dirge (ii 387-418; 35:1-36:13 e318-19).
She reproaches herself for having ruined or rejected everything that had been valuable to her. After so many unedify-
ing recriminations, naked threats, and sleazy self-justifica-
tions, Enion's mea culpa brings back dignity and nobility
to the narrative:

> I have planted a false oath in the earth, it has brought
> forth a poison tree
> I have chosen the serpent for a councellor & the dog
> For a schoolmaster to my children.

Though she is too harsh to herself, Enion's words contain
this much truth: the human psyche and its separate elements
are not mere victims; they destroy themselves. Thus, beneath
the surface of the lament—its agonized emphasis on what is
lost—lies a deeply buried seed of hope, which will spring
forth in Night VIII; for if man bears the responsibility for
his downfall, he has also some power to redeem himself.

Instinct too has learned the high price of experience:

> What is the price of Experience do men buy it for a song
> Or wisdom for a dance in the street? No it is bought
> with the price
> Of all that a man hath his house his wife his children
> Wisdom is sold in the desolate market where none come
> to buy
> And in the witherd field where the farmer plows for
> bread in vain.

The emphasis is on waste, on the exorbitant price of experience and wisdom. There is again, however, a latent though highly muted hopefulness: the price—house, wife, children, "all that a man hath"—is exchanged for wisdom, which like the pearl of great price is invaluable once acquired, whatever the cost.

Enion's saddest insight is that ease of mind is possible only for those who live in comfort, only so long as the universal misery surrounding them does not touch them personally. "It is an easy thing to rejoice in the tents of prosperity / Thus could I sing & thus rejoice, but it is not so with me!" Enion's shock may be compared to the fallen Titans' bewildering discovery of pain in the primeval world of Keats's *Hyperion* or to the traumatic initiation of a Dickensian waif. The pointedness of her lament comes also from its juxtaposition with the cruelty of Enitharmon and Los, for Enion is their mother. In responding to the fall by generating imagination, instinct seems to have ruined both love and imagination itself, with reason soon to follow.

Enion's inability to remain callous in the face of suffering reaches to Ahania's voluptuary palace and bed, awakening her to insomniac sympathy. The medium of communication is mysteriously indirect and intuitive: "Ahania heard the Lamentation & a swift Vibration / Spread thro her Golden frame" (II 419-20; 36:14-15 E319). Ironically, Enion is unaware that Los's plot against Ahania, who is "drawn thro unbounded space," will drive Enion herself further into nonentity; what happens to one Emanation affects them all. Ahania's uneasiness is like what happens to intellectuals when their delight in knowledge is soured by awareness of the world's ills, when they reject the life of the mind as socially self-indulgent and irresponsible. In Night III Ahania, the mind's delight in its activity, will bow before a colder notion of reason, which holds that the pleasurable element in thought is merely a coddling of that dilettante, imagination. To enjoy learning will no longer be an innocent activity.

Night II, and especially the latter half of it, is so impressive, dramatically and lyrically, that it seems to be a direct depiction of human behavior. But Blake is still drawing a map of the mind. The repression of desire already portrayed will produce an intolerable strain on the imaginative powers, disrupting their half-willing, half-uneasy subjection to rationality. The product of creativity, Enitharmon, is still in the service of Urizen; but that a revolt has taken place on a deep level is shown by Los's stirring up of Enion, the voice of instinctual innocence, just as earlier Los himself had been called into action by the Parent power, instinct. The subversion of Urizen is highly disturbing but it has to happen, and the alliance of imagination with instinct will survive, though not without strain at times, until it begins to work toward reunification and renewal in Night VIIA.

Night III.

The third Night, as drama, exerts a powerful forward thrust. It combines economy of episode with detailed narrative and psychological exposition. Night III is shorter than Night II, which in turn is shorter than Night I, roughly in the proportion of 3:2:1. Furthermore, Night III consists of only two scenes, the first involving Urizen and Ahania, the second Tharmas and Enion; even these are linked by a narrative bridge so that one gets the sense of a single continuous action. The poem acquires momentum that can be felt almost physically, as if Blake had imaginatively realized the fall in the literalizing spirit that he brought to so many exhausted metaphors,[1] suggesting here an almost gravitational acceleration. The disorientation felt by Tharmas and Enion at the opening of the poem, particularly as they float in their waterlike element, is a kind of weightlessness; by the end of Night III, with the precipitant crash of Urizen and his world, the descent of man has become headlong, rapid, apparently irreversible. Each of the three triads of Nights is a movement, not only in the figurative musical sense but almost literally, as kinesthesia: the fall, the hitting bottom, and the rebound. As we come to the end of Night III, completing the first triad, virtually all elements of the poem reach a climax. The devastation of human faculties comes as close to being total as is possible, while expressions of emotion—cries of anger, suffering, despair—reach a piercing high pitch and fortissimo volume.

Thematically, the leading motif of Night III is the suicide of reason, whose tenure as regent of the psyche has been

Night III

short-lived. In order to appreciate properly the self-destructiveness of reason here, its utter unreasonableness, we must be aware of the beauty, the sensuality even, that Blake attributes to the unfallen mind of certainty and faith. That condition is evoked nostalgically by Ahania in the last chapter of the book named for her, in a description of her relation to her husband Urizen, the plowman, lover, and teacher:

Swell'd with ripeness & fat with fatness
Bursting on winds my odors,
My ripe figs and rich pomegranates
In infant joy at thy feet
O Urizen, sported and sang;

Then thou with thy lap full of seed
With thy hand full of generous fire
Walked forth from the clouds of morning
On the virgins of springing joy,
On the human soul to cast
The seed of eternal science.

(*Book of Ahania*, 5:24-34)

Ahania herself, reason's epiphany, is described in Night III as having a "bright head sweet perfumd & . . . heavenly voice" (III 26; 38:14 E320). She is the embodiment of everything graceful and urbane and human about the intellectual life, one of the loveliest and most loving female characters in Blake —ingenuous but wise, forthright but tactful, voluptuous but delicate in mind and personality. She is a combination of Desdemona and a Near Eastern princess, and in Night III Urizen is a jealous Othello, a base Indian who throws away a pearl.

Long narrative arches, fullness of dramatic detail, and subtlety of character analysis make Night III the most novelistic section of *The Four Zoas*. It makes gripping reading simply as a story, even if we ignore mythic or allegorical meaning. The first episode is both an accurate account of the buildup and release of sexual tensions in a lovers' quarrel and an anatomy of the dynamics of the sort of mental breakdown that occurs when rejected desire reasserts itself and infects the entire rational system. The allegorical meaning of the episode, the collapse of reason in the universal order, is so closely akin to the specific breakdown of Urizen as a lifelike character that the tenor and vehicle of Blake's story are almost indistinguishable. Indeed, the indissociability of fable from moral makes Night III in some ways the most mythic part of the poem as well as the most novelistic.

Blake's efforts to give the opening scene a directly understandable human urgency may be seen in his revisions of the opening lines; in an early draft Ahania refers to herself regally in the third person ("look on thy Wife"), but in the revision she uses the more intimate first person:

> O Urizen look on Me. like a mournful stream
> I Embrace round thy knees & wet My bright hair with
>   my tears:
> Why sighs my Lord! are not the morning stars thy
>   obedient Sons
> Do they not bow their bright heads at thy voice?
>   at thy command
> Do they not fly into their stations & return their light to thee
> The immortal Atmospheres are thine, there thou art seen
>   in glory
> Surrounded by the ever changing Daughters of the Light
> Why wilt thou look upon futurity darkning present joy.
>   (III 3-11; 37:3-10 E319; cf. E750)

Ahania's words are illustrated graphically in Blake's drawing on MS page 37, from which these lines are quoted. She concedes to Urizen more power than he really has, but that is the kind of loyal and dedicated wife she is. Later we learn that she is aware that he is by no means in firm control. Her

Night III

Ahania abases herself before Urizen. MS page 37 (Night III).
Reproduced by permission of the British Library Board.

misgivings at the end of Night II are not the explicit source
of this awareness; Blake is presenting not a conscious thought
but an intuition, strong though not fully shaped, that the
whole human being cannot be sustained by mathematic cere-
bration alone. This intuition has reached Ahania through
untraceable channels; now it enters the mind of Urizen just
as obliquely, through a gentle warning from his consort, the
side door of his psyche.

All Urizen's responses to Ahania are perverse. To her
initial assurances of his successful regency he replies that he
is, on the contrary, "a King of trouble" with cause enough to
fear futurity, which will one day find him subservient to
"that Prophetic boy." Under this epithet he subsumes all
that he fears in both Los and Luvah.[2] According to his "determind Decree"—both willed and fated—Vala and Luvah
"shall" descend into the womb and loins of Enitharmon and
Los. He wants to punish his immediate rivals with the ordeal
of rearing these unruly personifications of the passions, yet
he fears the reappearance of his formerly defeated enemy
Luvah in an unknown—and youthfully energetic—new form:
"Alas for me! what will become of me at that dread time?"
(III 14-23; 38:2-11 E319-20).

His "determind" decree, which in its fear and fatalism
recalls Herod's reaction to the Nativity, is part of the whole
motif of suicide that Urizen sustains in his every thought
and action throughout the Night. To Ahania's encouraging
and well-meant half-truth he responds with a gloomy emphasis on his impotence; yet he responds to her better-
founded (though still sympathetic) regret over his loss of
power with the megalomaniac insistence that he is supreme,
is "God." His earlier reaction, however perversely motivated,
is the truer one: what he predicts and causes to occur is the
union of imaginative power, which until now has been an
at least occasional ally, with the libidinal or emotional powers
to which in his fallen state he is invariably opposed. He

feels uneasily that he has been set on a spurious throne for the real purpose of serving, not ruling, the human imagination. He suffers from the prurient conviction that art, if it is not restrained, will be lascivious and will rip the fabric of the social order. Understood more generally, his fear is the familiar one that the exuberance which is beauty will turn into lust, that if a man lets his feelings go he may lose the anchor of his religious beliefs or his political tenets.

After weeping for seven days Ahania changes her tack, trying dutifully to accommodate herself to Urizen's irrationality. Her basic purpose is the same as in her first speech, to urge Urizen to be his best self; now, however, her approach is to agree that much is amiss but to avoid putting the primary blame on Urizen. The parallel with Desdemona is close: Ahania is gifted with the woman's gentle touch but every attempt she makes to use it turns out to be a barb tearing at the ulcerated part of Urizen's mind:

> O Prince the Eternal One hath set thee leader of his hosts
> Leave all futurity to him Resume thy fields of Light
> Why didst thou listen to the voice of Luvah that dread morn
> To give the immortal steeds of light to his deceitful hands
> No longer now obedient to thy will thou art compell'd
> To forge the curbs of iron & brass to build the iron mangers
> To feed them with intoxication from the wine presses
>   of Luvah
> Till the Divine Vision & Fruition is quite obliterated
> They call thy lions to the fields of blood, they rowze
>   thy tygers
> Out of the halls of justice, till these dens thy wisdom framd
> Golden & beautiful but O how unlike those sweet fields
>   of bliss
> Where liberty was justice & eternal science was mercy.
>
> (III 27-40; 38:15-39:11 E320)

Several things in this love-inspired speech jar with what

Urizen in his dementia wants to hear, even though they would assuage a sane form of grief. A person whose uppermost thought is "what will become of me?" is incapable of accepting an admonition to "Leave all futurity" to someone else. On the simplest level of story, it is maddening to Urizen that his wife should prefer a pastoral life to the palace he has been at such pains to build. Even her choice of the word "dens" for their new home prefigures Blake's word for the barren material world left for Urizen to explore in Night VI after his golden system has broken down. Ahania unwittingly rubs salt into Urizen's wounds by pointing out that his own tools and his laborers are recalcitrant or unwilling instruments; though he has overcome Luvah, Urizen has not overcome the passions he represents. Ahania further diminishes Urizen's self-importance by attributing to Luvah the initiative in the plot against Albion. And she reminds him that he is a deputy—a point that Urizen apparently allows only himself to make. We know from Blake's work as a whole that the Divine Vision is the highest good, and we know from Night II of the *Zoas* that Urizen's rule has been commissioned by Albion, the whole that subsumes reason as a part; in his public and official role, however, Urizen refuses to acknowledge this fact.

But the worst is yet to come. In the "vision" Ahania now narrates, her account of the fall as she remembers it (III 41-104; 39:12-42:18 E320-22), there will emerge still another implication, one that despite her loyal desire to exculpate her spouse touches the sorest spot of all and brings on Urizen's final frenzy.

As the Emanations generally do, Ahania remembers the fall mainly as a sexual seduction. (The male Zoas tend to recall it primarily as warfare and political conspiracy.) The accompanying designs for her speech, especially during her vision, depict numerous sexual acts of surprising variety and inventiveness (MS pages 38-42).[3] From the more reliable narrative of the messengers of Beulah in Night I, we know that Ahania's account is not entirely accurate in placing most of the blame for the fall on Vala and Luvah; she seems to be indulging her wifely bias toward Urizen. The second line of Ahania's account suggests that her vision may be seen as an expression of Urizen's own dream, "the vision of Ahania in the slumbers of Urizen"; her dramatization of Urizen's hidden thoughts, memories, dreams, and feelings helps to explain the violence of his rejection of her at the end of her speech. Furthermore, her vision serves as an oblique response to and interpretation of Urizen's fatalistic query about his future relationship with Los and Luvah, for in recounting the disastrous separation of the Zoas she is also reminding Urizen of their original unity and brotherhood.

In Ahania's vision, Albion, walking with Vala, looks up and sees "thee Prince of Light thy splendor faded" and shortly afterwards becomes captivated by "a Shadow from his wearied intellect"; Ahania seems unaware, however, of the connection between these apparitions: that the shadow is Urizen himself, in his present decline. The shadow is

Of living gold, pure, perfect, holy; in white linen pure
   he hover'd
A sweet entrancing self delusion, a watry vision of Man
Soft exulting in existence all the Man absorbing.

(III 51-53; 40:4-6 E320)

This pure and perfect golden monster is the embodiment of holiness in the negative sense that Blake detests so heartily and that Orc excoriates so wrathfully in plate 8 of *America*. Caught in flagrante delicto, Vala and Albion prostrate themselves; Albion, "Idolatrous to his own Shadow," delivers himself of a groveling prayer in which the thrice-repeated refrain is "I am nothing" (III 54-65; 40:7-18, E320-21). Ahania's inappropriate term for this speech, "words of Eternity," along with Albion's ironic allusions to Job and Genesis, suggests that Blake may have intended an ironic glance at right and wrong ways of interpreting the Bible. Ahania too trembles, more in astonishment at the entire scene than in fear of the shadow; her ability to identify Albion's error indicates that the best side of the human intelligence disavows this sham deity on purely intellectual grounds.

This healthy intellectual reflex, however, counts for nothing; we are now in a world of mental sickness where puritanical conscience exerts absolute tyranny, as in the excruciating struggles of someone trying to cling to a rigidly orthodox faith even when his highest understanding rejects it. It is the world where, as Shelley puts it, "the loftiest fear / All that they would disdain to think were true" (*Prometheus Unbound,* I 619-20). Though Albion's dalliance with Vala has distracted his attention from the Divine Vision to the charms of the illusory material world, the true blocking agent is the guilt-inducing conception of God caused by Urizen's perverted mind, and Albion now shares Urizen's obsessions: "futurity is before me / Like a dark lamp. Eternal death haunts all my expectation" (III 74-75; 41:7-8 E321).

The next development—surprising but psychologically inevitable—is that Luvah, energy and sexuality, emerges as a cloud from the shadowy idol. In deleted lines, Luvah is said to dwell in a cloud he has spread to hide Los and Enitharmon from Albion's vision; these lines would have placed Luvah in the scene all along, but Blake's cancellation has the effect of making him precipitate out of the cloud, first in "balmy drops," then in his almost Christ-like aspect as "Son of Man" (III 47-48, 67-68; 39:18-40:1, 41:1-2 E320, 321).

The sudden shift connecting the idol with Luvah instead of Urizen accords dramatically with Ahania's refusal to implicate her husband but it indicates something deeper. Perhaps in spite of herself—for she still seems to see Luvah as the aggressor against Albion—she recognizes that excessive purity is linked with the libidinous, as in Saint Anthony's temptations and the night visions of Hawthorne's young Goodman Brown; Blake calls this cast of mind "pale religious letchery" (*The Marriage of Heaven and Hell,* plate 27). Within Ahania's vision Albion is completely unmanned by the appearance of passion where he had projected stern moral condemnation. His last healthy impulse is to recognize that he has been overcome by his "dismal vision" and is dying, "Rent from Eternal Brotherhood" (III 73-76; 41:6-9 E321). At this point, dovetailing with the opening of Night II, Albion is ready to abdicate and name Urizen as his deputy, cursing and banishing both Luvah and Vala.

When Ahania comes to the part of her speech that she intends to be the most comforting to Urizen, her description of Luvah's villainy, she begins to lose her thread under the pressure of Urizen's signs of wrath and her own misgivings. Just as she is ready to describe Luvah's act of smiting Albion with sore boils, mentioned also by the ambassadors from Beulah in Night I (see Appendix B), she interrupts herself to exclaim that a voice "crying Enion" sounds in her ears (III 77; 41:11 E321). The thought of love's seeking dominion, Luvah's plot against Albion, has attuned her mind to the plight of the lovelorn Enion. She is herself becoming more susceptible to the void that will draw her into Enion's condition of nonbeing. The voice may actually be Tharmas's, calling for his missing spouse, but at any rate Enion has become a presence in Ahania's consciousness. As she proceeds with her story of Luvah's downfall, signs of Urizen's gathering rage become more and more alarming; she has to keep breaking into her narrative with soothing efforts to head off his onrushing tantrum. The moment she stops talking, his wrath explodes.

More than anything else, the revelation of the prurience at the center of his holiness—Luvah in the cloud over the golden idol—pushes Urizen over the brink of madness. An absolutely central idea in the psychodrama of the *Zoas* is that in the fallen state the rational faculty is motivated by the very force it seeks to oppose, and more generally that Luvah and Urizen very often abide by each other's rules. It is one measure of the idea's importance to Blake that Urizen's reaction is so extreme. In keeping with the awful comedy of self-contradiction, the sexual bravado of Urizen's refutation of the charge is a confirmation of the obsession with sex he is implicitly disclaiming:

> Shall the feminine indolent bliss. the indulgent self
>   of weariness
>
> .   .   .   .
>
> Set herself up to give her laws to the active masculine virtue
> Thou little diminutive portion that darst be a counterpart
> Thy passivity thy laws of obedience & insincerity
> Are my abhorrence.
>
> (III 114-19; 43:6-11 E322)

Urizen's outrage over Ahania's daring to be a "counterpart" is of a piece with his repudiation of the other Zoas' equality with him, yet ironically her offence (as Urizen sees it), her attempt to rise above her status as portion to equality with the whole, even if true would be simply a lesser form of Urizen's own crime in renouncing his true status as an aspect of Albion and claiming everlasting supremacy. "Masculine virtue" is a complex pun, "virtue" having at the same time its ordinary modern sense of morality, its archaic pharmaceutical and alchemical sense of essential active principle (the masculine is active, the feminine passive), and its etymological sense of virility. Urizen's insistence that Ahania is "diminutive" repeats the pattern of Tharmas's rejection of Enion in Night I; in both instances a domineering character projects his own smallness or sense of it onto his more passive partner.[4] Urizen's abhorrence of Ahania's alleged "laws of obedience & insincerity" is also heavily ironic: "laws" reflects Urizen's own legalistic compulsions, the taunt of "in-sincerity" reveals his discomfiture at what in fact is candor, and his scorn of her "obedience" indicates that like other tyrants such as Shelley's Count Cenci he despises the submis-siveness of those he can dominate.

The pattern of projection in *The Four Zoas* is intimately connected with that of causation; this connection too appears in Urizen's casting-out of Ahania. When Urizen attempts to evoke the memory of a bygone idyll, that time of healthy love between the mind and the thought it delighted to prop-agate, his figures of speech—in contrast to Ahania's images of luscious pleasure—turn out to be dank and stagnant. He recalls Ahania, apparently admiringly, as "A sluggish current of dim waters . . . A cavern shaggd with horrid shades. dark cool & deadly" (III 121-22; 43:13-14 E322). A mind this sick is capable of any perversion; like standing water it "breeds reptiles of the mind" (*The Marriage of Heaven and Hell*, plate 19), and Urizen accuses the loving partner who has been trying to avert his fall of causing it:

> And thou hast risen with thy moist locks into a watry image
> Reflecting all my indolence my weakness & my death
> To weigh me down beneath the grave into non Entity.
> (III 125-27; 43:17-19 E322)

In reality of course his fall is entirely his own doing, though the groundwork has been laid in the other plot line describ-ing Los's and Enitharmon's conspiracy to bring him down by separating him from Ahania. His logical fallacies are so many and tangled as to make systematic analysis of them almost impossible. Yet one premise seems to govern his twisted thinking; he believes that anyone, including himself, who mentions an evil—whether to predict it, avert it, or express fear of it—causes the evil to become real. Since he suffers from this delusion and therefore not only is incapable of hope himself but also reads that despair into Ahania's warnings, his habitual fatalism is sufficiently consistent to be understandable, though quite insane.

All in all, the casting-out of Ahania is one of Blake's most intricately ironic scenes. Urizen has done what Enion accused herself of doing at the end of Night II: he has destroyed everything that would have made him happy. When his better half (the epithet comes alive in Ahania) gives him a true insight into the deathlike nature of a lonely and false holiness, his response is to deny the truth hysterically. In this scene Blake approaches most closely a literal and clinical description of an actual nervous breakdown, though in a larger sense the entire poem reflects the universal, less strictly clinical, psychosis of mankind. In spite of warnings by both Enion and Ahania—instinct and the best surviving part of reason—that mental constructs cannot subsist in isolation from the rest of the personality, the obsessed psychotic insists on being governed by his perverted notion of pure rationality until he loses not only what is best in his psyche but even the compulsively rigid rationality that had been his last hope of self-control. Then he goes completely berserk.

In the ensuing bridge passage (III 131-61; 43:23-44:22 E322-23), disasters multiply rapidly. The fragile clockwork of the mathematic universe and psyche has been shattered, indirectly through instinct and, beyond that, through the assault from imagination originally launched by Los. Ahania falls like lightning, Urizen like its echoing thunderbolt (reason almost literally topples from its throne), their sons flee, Destiny breaks its bounds. The broken bounds of Destiny are the last traces of Enion's Circle of Destiny established in Night I in her effort to contain chaos. The collapse of the rationalistic world order and the human intelligence that supports it has apparently destroyed the very foundation and principle of order, so that even this primitive structure cannot hold together. The image of a collapsing dike, as the "swelling Sea / Burst from its bonds," is an accurate corre-

Night III

lative for the failure of Urizen's attempts to dam up energy. His fragile geometrical palace, which has looked out complacently upon the chaotic sea of Tharmas's disorganized instinct, is no longer able to withstand the deluge. Urizen falls to a world "Where the impressions of Despair & Hope enroot forever / A world of Darkness" and the insomniac Ahania to the edge of non-entity where Enion had been earlier (III 135-44; 43:27-44:5 E322-23).

As the ocean rushes in to overwhelm Urizen's order, Tharmas and Enion reappear. Now that all the Zoas have fallen and the last rational edifice (Urizen's Mundane Shell) is sunk into the original gulf of things, the "Parent power" Tharmas attempts to reassume its integrity and authority. From the perspective of Tharmas or instinct, the period of Urizen's Mundane Shell was no more than an interval between the flood of primal chaos, which Blake elsewhere calls the Sea of Time and Space (corresponding to the deluge that left Atlantis only a myth), and the second flood of vague and dim longings (corresponding to Noah's flood which in receding gave humanity promise of a second chance) which now rushes in over the fallen world. Tharmas has become merely the personification of psychic chaos out of which almost anything—or nothing—might arise; he is no more than that residual humanity which separates a comatose person from absolute nonbeing. This level of existence is reflected in an onomatopoetic interplay of floundering repetitions and a frenzied piling up of adjectives, suggesting that Tharmas is drowning, grasping at straws, yet struggling to regain his consciousness and throw off his numbness. Substanceless as a shadow of smoke, he is

                                             stamping
The nether Abyss & gnasshing in fierce despair. panting
    in sobs

Thick short incessant bursting sobbing. deep despairing
   stamping struggling
Struggling to utter the voice of Man struggling to take
   the features of Man. Struggling
To take the limbs of Man at length emerging from the smoke
Of Urizen dashed in pieces from his precipitant fall
Tharmas reard up his hands & stood on the affrighted Ocean
The dead reard up his Voice & stood on the resounding shore

Crying. Fury in my limbs. destruction in my bones & marrow
My skull riven into filaments. my eyes into sea jellies
Floating upon the tide wander bubbling & bubbling
Uttering my lamentations & begetting little monsters
Who sit mocking upon the little pebbles of the tide
In all my rivers & on dried shells that the fish
Have quite forsaken.

                     (III 154-68; 44:15-45:1 E323)

In the remainder of Night III the combination of concrete
but surreal images (such as these rudimentary or extinct
marine creatures) with entirely nebulous ones (like smoke
and showers) suggests the dissolution of instinct's fundamental binding force, even though in the vacuum left by Urizen's
fall that force is able to make its presence known. In Blake's
design for page 44, Tharmas rears up, observed by an aloof
female clothed in emblems of royalty and holiness; he is
human from the waist up, but strange, indistinct shapes like
barnacles cover his torso. On page 46, though he is fully
formed as a human being, he is separated from Enion by a
vast ocean wave. Now that "rage & mercy are alike" to him
(III 196; 45:29 E324), he is as vehement in his antagonism
toward Enion as in his longing for her. Their sado-maso-
chistic relationship in Night I seems to be slipping into absolute hatred and separation even as their mutual dependency
intensifies.

Night III

*False and destructive holiness: Tharmas struggles to survive.
MS page 44 (Night III). Reproduced by permission of the British
Library Board.*

Enion, for her part, expresses in her third great lament a simple need to exist, even in the most minimal way. Like both her earlier hymns of mourning, this third one is concerned with the survival of life; now, however, it is her own existence that is at stake. The tender specificity with which she had earlier mourned over ravens, sparrows, robins, lambs, dogs, and of course human beings, is succeeded by a blank, almost imageless terror:

> O Tharmas do not thou destroy me quite but let
> A little shadow. but a little showery form of Enion
> Be near thee loved Terror. let me still remain & then do thou
> Thy righteous doom upon me. only let me hear thy voice
> Driven by thy rage I wander like a cloud into the deep
> Where never yet Existence came, there losing all my life
> I back return weaker & weaker, consume me not away
> In thy great wrath. tho I have sinned. tho I have rebelld
> Make me not like the things forgotten as they had not been
> Make not the thing that loveth thee. a tear wiped away.
> (III 184-93; 45:17-26 E324)

Having persuaded us, through a hundred lines of shrill fortissimo, of the dreadness of this condition, Blake can afford to label it, with terse dryness, the "indefinite," or "Non Entity" (III 208,211; 46:9,12 E324). Both Tharmas and Enion have become shadows, mists, inaudible voices of chaos. The instinct for survival—what some doctors call the will to live— is very nearly gone. The fall cannot proceed further without the total decay of all human substance. It remains to be seen how the imprisoned or scattered or faded faculties will cope with what is left in Albion's, and our, grim world,

Night IV.
Nights IV through VI are the poem's middle movement. In its mood, events, and settings it is almost unrelieved gloom, the darkness of the mindscape brightened fitfully by ambiguous moments of hope. The whole man personified in the unfallen Albion sleeps a deathlike sleep, his psyche in chaos. Reason is fragmented and stupefied. Passion has sunk to its lowest forms—corporeal violence and lust. Shapeless instinct has lost most of its power of psychological bonding. The least-affected power, the imagination, is at its weakest, for Los and Enitharmon are sullen and inert, divided from the other life-forces and hostile to each other. The final three Nights will represent and attempt to foster a redemptive process, however painful; the first three Nights had at least the adrenal excitement of immediate trauma. Now, in the middle part, like an amputee no longer able to summon the emergency resources that were available at the time of trauma, humanity is threatened with a monotonous, irremediable state of deprivation that apparently must be accepted simply as the nature of things.

The first triad of Nights begins with the response to the fall by instinct and imagination, then proceeds to passion in Night II and reason in Night III. The middle Nights have a similar construction: in Night IV instinct and imagination limit the fall, after which the poem focuses on passion in Night V and reason in Night VI. In the final movement of recovery man's powers are redeemed in the same order. Imaginative impulses, set in motion by instinct, create new forms in Night VIIA; in the Lamb of God's assumption of

Luvah's robes of blood and the Crucifixion of Night VIII, love transforms violent energy; in Night IX, among other apocalyptic events, reason at last abandons all efforts to tyrannize over the other faculties and is liberated from an obsessive concern with futurity.

As in Wordsworth's Intimations Ode, the three movements of *The Four Zoas* are set off by a kind of thematic and structural punctuation;[1] for example, Nights III, VI, and IX all end with a transformation of something that can be called science. The openings of the three movements have even more, and more striking, parallels. The injunction "Begin with Tharmas Parent power" that launches the narrative proper in Night I applies equally to Night IV; here too Tharmas appears first, epitomizing the state of fallenness. He remains in character in Night IV, his speeches and emotions betraying the confused self-contradictions that Blake sees as characteristic of fallen instinct. But Night IV is the only part of the poem in which Tharmas displays in addition to his basic function as a psychological sensor an active capacity to influence the course of events, if not in his own right at least through the impulses he transmits to imagination. That he and the Urthona group of characters should dominate Nights IV and V would seem inevitable; just as in the individual mind the daytime turmoil of conscious thoughts and feelings gives place during the night to those subliminal psychic powers that never wholly sleep, so in Albion's coma, with the immobilization of Urizen and Luvah, the power of action shifts by default to Tharmas and Los.

Night IV, like the opening Night, is often difficult to follow; in several places its narrative is wrenched from clear continuity, even from elementary consistency of tone and message. The reason is that it depicts psychic confusion and realizes in its action the ambiguity inherent in the very concept of a lowest point. It is both depressing and eerily comforting to know that things cannot possibly get worse;

thus all episodes in this Night are heavily ambiguous. The principle is validated in human experience; for example, in some forms of addiction and depression a point of utter desperation is the only possible turning point. Severely ill patients often seem unable to get well until the bottom falls out and they hit a new and final low, until they deeply feel there is nowhere to go but up. Sad as it is to lie flat on the basement floor, it is reassuring to know there is a floor. Moving on a continuum between the fullest possible being and utter nonbeing, humanity in the *Zoas* is in danger of ceasing to exist, of falling into a state that, though it need not literally be permanent psychosis, can be well imagined and imaged as that. In such a state suicides, unable to believe in the possibility of change, make their irreversible decision. But the fall of man is arrested at the Ulro-point; the limits of time, space, matter, and the human body are set. The species and most individuals do survive—though just barely—through Tharmas, the vestigial voice of instinct that signals the absurdity of all this unhappiness and waste, through Los, the power that makes possible even in the fallen state moments of ecstatic vision, and through that mysterious providence or hope that Blake calls Jesus, the Council of God.

The desperate defensive processes of which Night IV will largely consist begin with Tharmas's first appearance, in the opening line. He wants to die, though his very desire for death is conditioned by an especially acute sense of what was vital and beautiful in life. His "bowels yearnd over" his offspring Los and Enitharmon, and the anguished "love & pity" he expresses toward Enion recall his cries of pain at the very beginning of the poem (IV 3-7; 47:3-7 E324-25). When Los and Enitharmon "Emerge / In strength & brightness from the Abyss," the scene is a reenactment of their birth, now into an objective external world. The cause of Tharmas's distress, the sense that no misery is greater than the memory of lost former joy, is so widely felt that it has prompted some of the most memorable passages in literature. "Ah, if it *be* passed, take away, / At least, the restlessness, the pain"—Arnold's plea in *Stanzas from the Grand Chartreuse*—expresses a historical sense of loss analogous to the vague psychological loss that Tharmas is unable to put into words. Like Byron's Manfred, Tharmas simply wants to lose consciousness, but the life-force within allows neither Tharmas nor Manfred to destroy his body or annihilate his identity. Instinct needs no logic, indeed cannot use logic, to recognize the fallacy of fleeing from death by running to embrace it:

> Deathless for ever now I wander seeking oblivion
> In torrents of despair in vain. for if I plunge beneath
> Stifling I live. If dashd in pieces from a rocky height
> I reunite in endless torment. would I had never risen
> From deaths cold sleep beneath the bottom of the
>   raging Ocean
> And cannot those who once have lovd. ever forget their Love?
> Are love & rage the same passion? they are the same in me
> Are those who love. like those who died. risen again
>   from death
> Immortal. in immortal torment. never to be deliverd
> Is it not possible that one risen again from Death
> Can die! When dark despair comes over can I not
> Flow down into the sea & slumber in oblivion.
>
> (IV 12-23; 47:12-23 E325)

Tharmas's immediate rebound from his death wish is entirely reflexive. Even at man's worst, something in him wants to be healthy again. The thought of his ungratified desire for Enion rouses Tharmas to bracing anger as he puts "The all powerful curse of an honest man . . . upon Urizen & Luvah." Such honesty is the hallmark of instinct, which cannot lie any more than the knee-jerk reflex can be faked. Tharmas's reaction against despair, in fact, becomes a kind of overreaction, moving beyond healthy anger to braggadocio. The lines that follow his curse are at the same time an echo of the birth of Los in Night I, an anticipation of one version of Night VII, a parody of Albion's delegation of power in Night II, and a more bizarre parody of Urizen's claim in Night III to be supreme God:

> But thou My Son Glorious in brightness comforter of
>   Tharmas
> Go forth Rebuild this Universe beneath my indignant power
> A Universe of Death & Decay.
>
> (IV 26-28; 48:3-5 E325)

The most richly allusive parody is of Milton. In Night VIIB two passages, one spoken by Urizen and one by Tharmas, will recall the Father's begetting of the Son in *Paradise Lost* and his commission to destroy the army of archangelic rebels.[2] The present passage parodies the Father's charge to the Son to create the universe in compensation for the damage done by Satan and his followers. With irony even more cutting, Tharmas's words, especially the phrase "Universe of Death," parody the creation of Hell, which according to Milton is ultimately God's handiwork:

> A Universe of death, which God by curse
> Created evil, for evil only good,
> Where all life dies, death lives, and Nature breeds,
> Perverse, all monstrous, all prodigious things[3]
>
> (*Paradise Lost,* II 622-25)

Enitharmon is to cooperate with Los in this negative creation, an antitype of their constructive collaboration in Nights VII and VIII:

> Let Enitharmons hands
> Weave soft delusive forms of Man above my watry world
> Renew these ruind souls of Men thro Earth Sea Air & Fire
> To waste in endless corruption. renew thou I will destroy
> Perhaps Enion may resume some little semblance
> To ease my pangs of heart & to restore some peace
> to Tharmas.
>
> (IV 28-33; 48:5-10 E325)

Tharmas's willing this universe of death into being, as well as his contradictory threat to destroy everything that Los renews, seems to annul the impulse toward life he had intended to express; on the other hand, he believes steadfastly though illogically that somehow Los's nihilist activity may, at least minimally, restore Enion.

Perhaps the best way to understand Tharmas's striking but apparently self-canceling speech is to think analogically of this Zoa as the force behind dadaist art. The only kind of making Tharmas has observed up to now is the rigid pseudo-order that was temporarily imposed by Urizen and is at the opposite pole from instinctual spontaneity. This spontaneity still cries out for expression, but through an art that is the antithesis of high or academic art. A less anachronistic analogue might be the cult of Romantic primitivism, which produced some specimens even more iconoclastic and anti-academic than its most famous succès de scandale, *Lyrical Ballads.* Tharmas will later confess explicitly that one motive in urging Los to restore Urizen in a new and bound form is a fear "Lest he should rise again from death in all his dreary power" (IV 121; 51:4 E327). Instinct, then, is torn between a need to urge doing and making and a fear of the only forms it can envisage as the result of such creation.

But the creative principle will have no part of this. Los's rejection of Tharmas parallels Luvah's rejection of Urizen's conspiracy, as well as Los's own repudiation of Urizen's in-

Night IV

fluence in Night I. Los's first response is to tell Tharmas to keep his distance and to assert his own allegiance to the fallen Urizen, a "higher" faculty than inchoate instinct. Beginning with an almost exact repetition of the lines in Job (38:11) asserting God's control of the sea, "Hitherto shalt thou come. no further. here thy proud waves cease," Los continues his scornful boasting in language specifically designed to insult the oceanic and primitive Zoa:

> We have drunk up the Eternal Man by our unbounded power
> Beware lest we also drink up thee rough demon of
>   the waters
> Our God is Urizen the King. King of the Heavenly hosts
> We have no other God but he thou father of worms & clay
> And he is falln into the Deep rough Demon of the waters
> And Los remains God over all. weak father of worms & clay
> I know I was Urthona keeper of the gates of heaven
> But now I am all powerful Los & Urthona is but my shadow.
>   (IV 35-43; 48:12-20 E325)

Los's sudden reversal of his earlier enmity toward Urizen, whom he now hails as God and king, is understandable when we remember that this oath of allegiance is not a fully considered act but in part a startled reaction to instinct's demand for total power. Imagination's first thought is to retain its autonomy; Los's resistance to dictates from "below" reflects this need for independence in much the same way that his rebellion against the "higher" power of reason did in Night II. Moreover, his acclamation of Urizen is a gesture that costs him nothing; since Urizen has been dethroned, Los can now claim the vacant throne, cynically using any title or genealogy, however spurious, to legitimate his claim. Art wishes to owe nothing to anyone; for its own purposes it may spurn one pretender by seeming to shift allegiance to another —but only for as long as is necessary to alter the balance of power. Blake is surely implying that any autonomy art achieves by such dubious means is corrupt. It is difficult to think of any passage that so clearly contradicts the notion that the Romantics deified art for its own sake.

The marked contempt in Los's words to Tharmas is also significant; it reflects not merely policy by Los but a hostility compounded of fastidiousness and fear. He is appalled by the chaotic instinctual principle, much as certain militantly cerebral poets of the 1920s and 1930s were repelled and embarrassed by overt expression of feeling. In his repeated sneers at his own father as "father of worms & clay," Los renounces the earth and what is earthy in his own personality as artist; he rejects what Yeats identified as the place from which all "ladders" to the lofty must start: "the foul rag-and-bone shop of the heart."

Still another way in which Los becomes less by claiming to be more is in his claim that, although he was once Urthona, Urthona is now nothing more than his shadow. This repudiation of his true self is Los's worst error as fallen artist. In the regained Eternity pictured at the end of Night IX the real Urthona is unobtrusive, anything but godlike; thus Blake seems to be showing here in Night IV the megalomania that afflicts the creative principle when it puts prestige above service to man and the Divine Vision (another complaint voiced by the Romantics in their attacks on neoclassical academies and schools of art).

It is uncharacteristic of instinct to persist in head-on confrontations such as this one, much less to win out. Tharmas therefore departs after one last and unconvincing assertion of his will and power. He addresses his assertion, however, not to Los but to Enitharmon (IV 53-55; 49:1-3 E326), who has expressed even more overt anger toward Tharmas than has Los, for to her the architectural world of Urizen was a "sweet world" (IV 50; 48:27 E326) symbolizing the Urizenic relationship she had tried to establish with Los. Tharmas then does something crucial. Apparently sensing from her reaction where Los is vulnerable, as Los had done with Urizen in separating him from Ahania, Tharmas carries Enitharmon away from Los—immobilizing art, rendering it a mere impotent abstraction or theory. The abduction of Enitharmon is another mark of structural punctuation; it both recalls the harboring of Enitharmon by Tharmas at the opening of Night I and foreshadows by contrast the fruitful reconciliation of Los with his Emanation in the productive tasks they undertake in Night VIIA. The separation here is an inversion of the creation of Eve; in Genesis and Milton the female torn from man's side is a completion of him, but for Los the experience is a mutilation:

> O how Los howld at the rending asunder all the fibres rent
> Where Enitharmon joind to his left side in griding pain
> He falling on the rocks bellowd his Dolor.
>
> (IV 59-61; 49:7-9 E326)

The separation, in accord with a pattern already established, coincides with the appearance of a Spectre, the third such appearance in the poem (the Spectre of Tharmas appeared in Night I, the Spectre of Urizen in Night III). In one sense the Spectre of Urthona is synonymous with the diminished Los; that Blake intends this meaning is shown by the statement, only three lines after the mention of Los's fall upon the rocks, that the Spectre "had falln." It is easy to overlook this fact, since, unlike the Shadow of Enitharmon who briefly splits off later in the poem, Urthona's Spectre is fully realized in the *Zoas* as an independent character. The loss of Enitharmon in Night IV, though, is a more nearly total destruction of Los than her wayward infidelities in Night II had been; they had brought out cruelty in Los but had not paralyzed him, reduced him to the impotence of a poet who writes no poetry. Tharmas, in his intuitive way, senses the import of what he is doing; when he presently sends Enitharmon back to Los she will be in the company of Urthona's Spectre, the agent through whom Tharmas induces Los to obey the commands of instinct. That the Spectre is in Tharmas's service is reflected not only in the narrative events but also in their mutual recognitions: "Tharmas I know thee. how are we alterd our beauty decayd"; "Art thou Urthona My friend my old companion" (iv 79,111; 49:27,50:28 e326,327).

This aspect of the imaginative power is not above acknowledging the old friend it had known in humbler days. The spectrous Tharmas of Night I and the spectrously holy Urizen-Luvah of Night III had been golden statues; Urthona's Spectre appears "like a statue of lead" (iv 65; 49:13 e326). Like all Blake's Spectres this one is a repulsive, chilling figure; the base metal suggests the defeatist dreariness of creative power in its uninspired periods of dullness. Yet his emergence, and even some aspects of his personality, are salutary; a drudging apprentice, a Caliban, he performs the lowly tasks needful in Los's creative work; moreover, through his simple-minded doggedness, he exerts a will of his own that virtually coincides with the promptings of instinct. Eventually merging with Los, in Night VII, he willingly cooperates with his Prospero. What instinct has done in Night IV is to take high art down a peg, reminding it of its dependence on craftsmanship and the unglamorous. Sir Joshua Reynolds is reminded that it is better to paint than to pontificate; novelists are reminded that they must write, not just utter opinions at symposia; all of us are reminded that we should work at improving vision rather than merely surveying the cultural wasteland in disdain. If Damon's allegorical gloss on Enitharmon as inspiration is valid, and if the Spectre is in part a personification of drudgery, their return — together — to Los implies Blake's answer to an old question: artistic genius is both inspiration and perspiration.

The Spectre's part in the dialogue with Tharmas is still

another version of the fall (IV 79-110; 49:27-50:27 E326-27;
see Appendix B). Tharmas's warm response to his old friend
"With whom I livd in happiness before that deadly night /
When Urizen gave the horses of Light into the hands of
Luvah" (IV 112-13; 50:29-30 E327) implicitly supports the
Spectre's story and helps establish him and Tharmas as the
most reliable historians among the Zoas. Their basic guilt-
lessness in the tragedy, implied earlier by Beulah's messengers, is corroborated in the Spectre's account. Neither
Urizen nor Luvah is blamed exclusively (or even named, except in lines added by Tharmas as a kind of footnote). Nevertheless, the point is confirmed that some disruption of the
primal powers of love and reason had caused the fall. Its
immediate consequence, as the Spectre remembers it, has
been the separation from Urthona of his Emanation. At
the same time, his loins broke forth into veiny pipes and
englobed; as with Luvah in Night II, the externalizing of
the sexual organs blends psychologically with the false
epiphany of woman as a separate, alien being. But just as
the Zoas' mutual recognitions—soon to be completed when
Tharmas recognizes his son in both Urthona and Los (IV 131;
51:14 E327) —foreshadow their eventual reunion as one man,
so tentative gestures toward their Emanations offer dim hope
in this dark Night that the feminine portion of the psyche
will some day be restored.

Having now proved his power either to separate or to
unite Los and his creative capacity, Tharmas too returns,
resuming his threats, his grandiose rhetoric, and his exaggerated (though in the present context not totally untrue)
claims to supreme power. Instinct has performed a saving
act, but we are in no danger of taking him as the primary
hero; not only are his claims to power ludicrous in themselves, but Tharmas cannot sustain the bravura tone. He interrupts his own Marlovian rhetoric with a passage of nostalgic wistfulness, weariness, and longing for Enion:

Yet tho I rage God over all. A portion of my Life
That in Eternal fields in comfort wanderd with my flocks
At noon & laid her head upon my wearied bosom at night
She is divided She is vanishd even like Luvah & Vala
O why did foul ambition sieze thee Urizen Prince of Light
And thee O Luvah prince of Love till Tharmas was divided
And I what can I now behold but an Eternal Death
Before my Eyes & an Eternal weary work to strive
Against the monstrous forms that breed among my
    silent waves.

(IV 137-45; 51:20-28 E328)

When he resumes his attempt at sternness after this interruption, his posturing has a touch of dignity, of convincing urgency: "Take thou the hammer of Urthona rebuild these furnaces . . . Death choose or life" (IV 149-52; 51:32-52:2 E328). The challenge of this last command, echoing Deuteronomy 30:19, indicates that Tharmas's own jammed reflexes—which had drawn him simultaneously toward death and life—have now cleared up, and instinct is once more firmly committed to life. Each of the Zoas takes his turn at playing God, but it is significant that Tharmas quickly and willingly gives up his claim without being deposed and is the first to recognize the primacy of true humanity:

Is this to be A God far rather would I be a Man
To know sweet Science & to do with simple companions.

(IV 146-47; 51:29-30 E328)

This insight and the elevation of "sweet Science," or humane knowledge, to replace ignorance and superstition anticipates the apocalyptic change in consciousness that builds up in Night IX until "sweet Science reigns" in the final line of the poem.

The furnaces that Los is to rebuild at Tharmas's behest are those belonging to him in his proper role as the blacksmith

Urthona; they are also, however, "the Ruind Furnaces / Of Urizen" (IV 165-66; 52:15-16 E328), which in Night II both imprisoned Luvah and were part of the manufactory for Urizen's own cosmos. Though Los's new use of the furnaces for the binding of Urizen will be one of the most complex mythic passages in Blake's poetry, its basic meaning can be sketched with rather simple allegorical lines. Urizen's rule in Night II had been a usurpation not only of Albion's supremacy and of Luvah's energy but also of the proper shaping role of Urthona, as represented by the furnaces. In using the furnaces to bind and humanize Urizen, Urthona-Los is reclaiming his own, rejecting mere cerebralism as the form and mode of art and of human visionary power in general. But Enitharmon, both Los's helpmeet and the product of his creative work, has been an ally of Urizen up to now; therefore Los must bind her too:

> But Enitharmon wrapd in clouds waild loud. for as Los beat
> The anvils of Urthona link by link the chains of sorrow
> Warping upon the winds & whirling round in the dark deep
> Lashd on the limbs of Enitharmon & the sulphur fires
> Belchd from the furnaces wreathd round her. chaind in
>   ceaseless fire
> The lovely female howld & Urizen beneath deep groand
>   (IV 184-89; 53:5-10 E329)

The relationship between Los and Enitharmon will be tested severely in ensuing Nights, but that they are mates for better or worse will never again be in doubt; her flirtations with Urizen are over. In binding Urizen, Los retakes lost ground; in reclaiming Enitharmon, however, he accomplishes something even more crucial: he begins to reestablish his authentic role and identity.

It is a mere beginning, though; to Los, who hates what he now has to do, the reshaping of Urizen appears to be one more form of domination by him:

> Round him Los rolld furious
> His thunderous wheels from furnace to furnace. tending
>   diligent
> The contemplative terror. frightened in his scornful sphere
> Frightend with cold infectious madness.
>
> (IV 175-78; 52:25-28 E328-29)

In the narrative context, "frightened" and "scornful" are apt terms for either Urizen or Los, and that the former's madness is "infectious" is Los's worst fear.

Los's rescue of Urizen from the indefinite, by forging a human body for him (IV 208-46; 54:1-55:9 E329-30), is a close paraphrase of the corresponding passage in *The Book of Urizen,* plates 10-13. The power of both passages arises from their making the human body seem awesomely strange by means of a visionary anatomical description, though the short nervous line of *Urizen* is more suitable for this material than the loose fourteener of the *Zoas*:

> In ghastly torment sick. within his ribs bloated round
> A craving hungry cavern. Thence arose his channeld
> Throat. then like a red flame a tongue of hunger
> And thirst appeard
>
> (IV 239-42; 55:2-5 E330)

It is characteristic of the Romantics to make us recognize, as Byron and Wordsworth often do, the utter strangeness of the sheer fact of mind or consciousness, but in the present passage Blake finds the same *unheimlich* quality in the matter-of-fact and physical.

The collaboration between Los and the Spectre and the forced or equivocal reunion with Enitharmon anticipate the critical turning point in Night VIIA, where the action will be unequivocally positive and humane. Both there and here in Night IV the creation of bodies or a body is emblematic of a whole new spiritual and perceptual cosmology. Los

Night IV

shapes on his anvil not only a body but "many a planet," and he creates time as well (IV 169,179-82; 52:19-53:3 E328-29). All this, at the present stage of psychic development, is both tragic and saving. The parallel with adolescence is clear. The child's former unselfconscious confidence in the rightness of his body is long past; his all-flexible senses had earlier rigidified into rationalism, and now that too has failed. The new body or cosmos, the new sense of the limitations of the physical and the entrapment by time and circumstance that succeeds childhood, is a terrible thing; the shades of the prison house are closing in. Life has become a dreary prospect stretching ahead into an unexciting future, like man's life after the postdiluvian covenant between God and Noah, when God promised to let life run its course without catastrophic interventions but made man settle for a limited kind of happiness (Genesis 8:21-9:17). On the other hand, what might have been a total calamity, the madness of retreat from the senses into the psychosis of pure rationality, is averted; the newly sensed body that catches colds, needs eyeglasses, and cannot fly is also the body that hears melody, inhales fragrances, and embraces its beloved. Man's limited body is the seal of his fallenness, yet it provides avenues for achieving an eternity even better than what was lost. It is important that, after the skull, skeleton, and heart have been forged on Los's anvil, "pangs of hope" begin when the first of the sensory organs take shape (IV 232; 54:24 E330).

Los is conscious of no such hope. He has been acting unwillingly, driven by an instinct he detests. Nevertheless, from outside the prison of time in which Los feels trapped there sounds, for the reader at least, Blake's note of reassurance, in the dialogue between the Daughters of Beulah and the Council of God, who is Jesus. The application to the *Zoas* of the raising of Lazarus in John 11—the passage that so moved the timid magdalen Sonia in *Crime and Punishment*—is a brilliant tour de force. But it is more: it suggests the tenderness of Blake's sympathy with fallen man. For the third time in this Night man is reminded that he need not wholly die. The Daughters appeal to Jesus in the form of a double female (counterparts to Mary and Martha), the "Feminine Emanation" (IV 263; 56:11 E331). They speak as simple, sad, trusting but troubled, women:

> Lord. Saviour if thou hadst been here our brother had
>   not died
> And now we know that whatsoever thou wilt ask of God
> He will give it thee for we are weak women & dare not lift
> Our eyes to the Divine pavilions.[4]
>
> (IV 253-56; 56:1-4 E330)

Bending over the corpse of their dead brother Albion, the Savior replies, "If ye will Believe your Brother shall rise again";

> And first he found the Limit of Opacity & namd it Satan
> In Albions bosom for in every human bosom these
>   limits stand
> And next he found the Limit of Contraction & namd it Adam
> While yet those beings were not born nor knew of good
>   or Evil
> Then wondrously the Starry Wheels felt the divine hand.
>   Limit
> Was put to Eternal Death.
>
> (IV 270-76; 56:18-24 E331)

As at the end of Night I, the Savior will be merciful but will not simply take over the redemptive task, which belongs to humanity itself; there will be no equivalent of the command "Lazarus, come forth." As Blake wrote in his annotations to Watson, "Jesus could not do miracles where unbelief hinderd . . . The manner of a miracle being performd is in modern times considerd as an arbitrary command of the agent upon the patient but this is an impossibility not a miracle neither did Jesus ever do such a miracle" (E606, K391). The first two limits, of Opacity and Contraction, are *found* by Jesus. They are in Albion's bosom; inherently the lower limits of human nature, they exist independent of Satan and Adam, after whom they are named. The third limit, to the Starry Wheels, is *put,* not found. This means first that the dreary cycles of time and nature, the "many wheels resistless" (IV 183; 53:4 E329) which Los had been rolling from furnace to furnace, will come to an end. Psychologically it means that human beings need not resign themselves to permanent fallenness but can hope for an apocalypse of vision. On both levels the apathy implied in Noah's covenant has been implicitly reversed.

The passage about Jesus' intervention separates two identical passages, which appear in different contexts: "terrified at the Shapes / Enslavd humanity put on he became what he beheld" (IV 202-03, 285-86; 53:23-24, 55:21-22 E329, 331). The relation between beholding and becoming is altered after Jesus intervenes. Before this dividing point in the poem, all the Zoas and Emanations have caused what they beheld to come into being. Their perceptions of each other have taken on objectified, externalized reality: as each Zoa has rejected his Emanation, for instance, the most intimate portion of himself has become a threatening alien. The characters in the poem have responded to others not as persons in themselves or as psychic forces that have a right to exist, but as mere projections of the beholder. After Jesus' intervention we see the reversal or reflex of such projection. The images and creations take possession of their creators. Los becomes not only what he beholds but also "what he was doing"; he is "himself transformd" (IV 287; 55:23 E331). As he limits Urizen, he is himself enslaved. The image on his anvil is so frightening that it remakes Los; his idea of Urizen becomes his idea of himself as well. Shelley's Prometheus, beholding the "execrable shapes" of the Furies,

mankind's foulest ideas, is appalled: "Methinks I grow like
what I contemplate, / And laugh and stare in loathsome sympathy" (*Prometheus Unbound*, I 449-51); just so, when Los
sees humanity distorted under the shapes he imposes, he
turns this new distortion on himself.

The first time we were told that Los became what he
beheld (before Jesus' intervention) there was nothing good
about this development:

> absorbd in dire revenge he drank with joy the cries
> Of Enitharmon & the groans of Urizen fuel for his wrath
>
> .   .   .   .
>
> terrified at the Shapes
> Enslavd humanity put on he became what he beheld
> Raging against Tharmas his God & uttering
> Ambiguous words blasphemous filld with envy firm resolvd
> On hate Eternal in his vast disdain
>
> (IV 191-206; 53:12-27 E329)

But after Los has completed his task and has become both
what he beheld *and* what he was doing (after Jesus' intervention), he suffers along with his victims and is thrown into
spasms of involuntary sympathy with them:

> he became what he beheld
> He became what he was doing he was himself transformd
> Spasms siezd his muscular fibres writhing to & fro his pallid
>   lips
> Unwilling movd as Urizen howld his loins wavd like the sea
> At Enitharmons shriek his knees each other smote & then he
>   lookd
> With stony Eyes on Urizen & then swift writhd his neck
> Involuntary to the Couch where Enitharmon lay
> The bones of Urizen hurtle on the wind the bones of Los
> Twinge & his iron sinews bend like lead & fold
> Into unusual forms dancing & howling stamping the Abyss.[5]
>
> (IV 286-95; 55:22-31 E331)

Night IV

In the manner of Coleridge's Christabel with Geraldine, Los passively imitates Urizen and Enitharmon (who significantly is the personification of, among other things, his pity). Every time Urizen howls, Los's bones twinge and his sinews bend. Every time Enitharmon shrieks, Los's knees knock. This pain in Los is a hopeful sign, despite the macabre nature of the spastic dance it occasions; it indicates that these men and women, and these fragments of the psyche, are really part of one another, whether they know it or not. Los is feeling like the legendary Siamese twin, cut apart from his brother, who still twitches when his brother is hurt. The sympathy thus born, like the limits defined in this Night, is presented negatively, but it is an augury of salvation.

Night V. Having done its one thing needful in bringing imagination to the challenge "Death choose or life," Tharmas, the personification of instinct, disappears from the poem in Night V—except for a single four-word reference (v 78; 60:5 E333). Having chosen life, the wedded personifications of imagination become the sole movers of the action. Los and Enitharmon are hardly recognizable now as the moodily impulsive youth and amateurish femme fatale of the early Nights; the fifth Night inducts them into a world of Experience. Their new roles as securely yoked mates and parents (the intimate and prosaic term "husband" is applied to Los, the only instance of the word in the entire poem—v 21; 58:1 E332) uncovers depths in them not visible before, both a new depth of evil in the enchaining of their son Orc and a new depth of sorrowful, loving sympathy in their remorse over that act and their attempt to undo it.

The style and setting of Night V are peculiarly vivid, in keeping with the paired subjects of bleak suffering maturely endured and youthful suffering experienced exuberantly. These are dramatized in imagery of terrible cold and raging fire. The supercharged language and scenic variety range from surreal, sometimes gothic, gloom to riotously gorgeous brilliance. The tonal chiaroscuro makes Night V high melodrama; it is also an inversion of apocalypse. Extreme polarizations occur, not only in the contrast between Orc and his parents but also in Orc's awakening of his archetypal opponent Urizen. Yet the violent imagery suggests not the explosive effect of true apocalypse but the implosive violence of shrinking or containment.

The opening words, "Infected Mad [Los] dancd on his mountains," establish immediate continuity with Night IV, as do the more general images, carried over from the end of that Night, of contraction, cooling, entropy. Los's features "stonify"; the sparks he had emitted earlier become "sparks of blighting." He and Enitharmon shrink "into fixed space,"

> As plants witherd by winter leaves & stems & roots decaying
> Melt into thin air while the seed drivn by the furious wind
> Rests on the distant Mountains top.

That this shrinking is a psychological and perceptual change is made more emphatically clear than usual through an explicit, almost cautionary, gloss: "Yet mighty bulk & majesty & beauty remain but unexpansive" (v 1-13; 57:1-13 E332).

Nature imagery pervades both this Night and the following one, as architectural and geometrical imagery pervades Nights II and III, the corresponding Nights in the poem's first movement. The reason is that although the whole poem expresses Blake's fundamental view of the subject–object relationship, Nights V and VI treat this relationship in specific ways, by concentrating on the two most widely prevalent views and definitions of "nature." For Blake, mind and object correspond: Orc in Night V is both an external phenomenon and the mental state that projects it. Something analogous happens in Night VI, where nature is both the world seen by Newtonian rationalism and the stuntedness of reason itself. In Orc we see both fallen passion and nature experienced as a life-force unredeemed by human vision— nature as evolutionists regard it, for example, when they feel awe and admiration for its ruthless but (in some sense) inexorably right violence. It is the fallen view of the cycle of nature, as *The Book of Thel* is the unfallen view of it.

Later this violent nature will be identified more precisely
with Vala, an Emanation and therefore an outward embodiment of the energy in nature. In the meantime, we are to
understand the Orc of Night V as fallen nature. Although
both Urizen, as incarnated in Night IV and reactivated at
the end of Night V, and the newborn Orc of this Night show
traces of their Edenic potential, neither is fully human.
Fallen sexuality, for example, is a reminder of the energy of
Eternity, but it is also the motive force for corporeal war.

Thus several especially daring confoundings of tenor and
vehicle in Blake's treatment of mind and object occur in
Nights V and VI. The psychological shrinking of imagination has been imaged in the opening lines as plants withering
in the winter. Conversely, as Enitharmon goes into labor
before the birth of Orc, Blake projects onto nature, in an
audacious sustained metaphor, her travail and that of the
psychic imaginative force she represents:

> Earth convulsd with rending pangs
> Rockd to & fro & cried sore at the groans of Enitharmon
> Still the faint harps & silver voices calm the weary couch
> But from the caves of deepest night ascending in clouds of
> mist
> The winter spread his wide black wings across from pole to
> pole
> Grim frost beneath & terrible snow linkd in a marriage chain
> Began a dismal dance. The winds around on pointed rocks
> Settled like bats innumerable ready to fly abroad.
>
> (V 28-35; 58:8-15 E332)

The "dismal dance" of the mountains glances back at Los's
mad dance; the union of frost and snow in a "marriage chain"
is at the same time an objectifying of the somber marital
bond between Enitharmon and Los and a glance ahead to the
chain of Jealousy that will plague Los, shackle Orc, and

ultimately become an indissociable part both of earth and of Orc himself, until he is all but bereft of human dignity.

The creation of the human body as we know it was the central overt act of Night IV. It is still frozen and inert, however; Urizen, "the cold / Prince of Light," is "bound in chains of intellect among the furnaces," and the furnaces themselves are extinguished (v 15-17; 57:15-17 E332). The elaborate verbal and imagistic detail that bridges Nights IV and V makes it clear that the birth of Orc is the inevitable concomitant to the earlier incarnation of Urizen. The parallel is enforced by the seemingly incongruous background music for the two embodiments. Tharmas had promised Los that if he took up again the hammer of Urthona to bind Urizen and thus chose life, "all the Elements shall serve thee to their soothing flutes / Their sweet inspiriting lyres thy labours shall administer" (IV 152-54; 52:2-4 E328). Similarly, Enitharmon's cries of pain when she is in labor with Orc are set against gentle music:

> But the soft pipe the flute the viol organ harp & cymbal
> And the sweet sound of silver voices calm the weary couch
> Of Enitharmon but her groans drown the immortal harps
> Loud & more loud the living music floats upon the air
>
> (V 23-26; 58:3-6 E332)

Both juxtapositions, like the blandly soothing music piped into factories and hospitals, can be seen either as grotesque irony or as mercy, reminders of genuine peace and hope from beyond the immediate scene of labor—a pun Blake may well have had in mind in establishing the parallel between what Los and Enitharmon bring forth in Nights IV and V respectively.[1]

An analogue in human psychological development for Blake's linking of the incarnations of Urizen and Orc can once more be found in the state of adolescence: the first

fruits of our awareness of the utter physicality of the body
are the imperatives of sexuality and of raw physical energy.
The moment of birth itself once more draws on an image
from nature, the eruption of a volcano:

> The groans of Enitharmon shake the skies the labring Earth
> Till from her heart rending his way a terrible Child sprang
>   forth
> In thunder smoke & sullen flames & howlings & fury & blood.
>
> (V 36-38; 58:16-18 E332)

The "howld" chant with which Orc is greeted (v 41-65; 58:
21-59:20 E333), sung appropriately by "Enormous Demons"
and doubtless intended as a parodic reversal of the legendary
quiet that silenced the demons when Christ was born in
midwinter,[2] is better understood as sheer sound effect than
as statement. If such roarings can be said to have a theme,
it is the celebration of energy in itself, divorced from moral,
rational, or other human controls: "Luvah King of Love
thou art the King of rage & death." The hymn is another
version of the fall, this time a seduction remembered as cataclysm: Vala "drew the body of Man from heaven into this
dark Abyss," and when "Urthona wept in torment of the
secret pain,"

> He wept & he divided & he laid his gloomy head
> Down on the Rock of Eternity on darkness of the deep
> Torn by black storms & ceaseless torrents of consuming fire
> Within his breast his fiery sons chaind down & filld with
>   cursings
> And breathing terrible blood & vengeance gnashing his teeth
>   with pain
> Let loose the Enormous Spirit in the darkness of the deep
> And his dark wife that once fair crystal form divinely clear
> Within his ribs producing serpents whose souls are flames of
>   fire.

It is difficult to keep straight the shifting addressees of this hymn (Vala, Orc, the "gloomy prophet" who is probably Los but may be Orc). The personal references are even more problematical. For example: in the portion just quoted, the words "He wept & he divided" are linked syntactically to Urthona but, from what we know of the fall, seem more applicable to Albion; the reference to chaining down and cursings best suits Urizen, though again the syntax provides no connection with him; the "Enormous Spirit" let loose in the deep could be the Urizen first invested with power by Albion in Night II or the newborn Orc; the dark wife who was once a "fair crystal form" could be any of the Emanations, including Jerusalem, the Emanation of the whole man. Vala is repeatedly mentioned or invoked, also in ambiguous ways: as both a soft-sighing seducer of Albion and a chaste warlike Amazon releasing "rage on rage . . . out of her crystal quiver"[3] in an inversion of the mental warfare that is the main activity in man's unfallen state. The core meaning of the passage is that Urthona engendered Orc and his yet unborn counterpart, respectively the fallen forms of Luvah and Vala (see Appendix B). To call this passage merely ambiguous is inadequate, since ambiguity implies a complex relationship of lines that are in themselves clearly drawn. It is, rather, a rhetorical realization of cataclysm, in which recognizable but shattered fragments of sense and of the story are hurled indiscriminately against one another, the result being less a meaning than an effect: of anarchic violence.

There follows the account, as in the *Book of Urizen* (plate 20), of the rearing of Orc, the development in Los of fear and jealousy of Orc as the love between him and his mother grows, the emergence from Los's bosom of his "uncouth plague," the chain of Jealousy, and the binding-down of their son by the "Obdurate" Los to the accompaniment of Enitharmon's weeping (v 70-113; 59:25-61:10 E333-34). At the same time that Los is trying to cope with his domestic unhappiness, he develops a fear of "Eternal Death," which motivates him to build a new structure called Golgonooza (with a mysterious gate called Luban), apparently an artist's heterocosm reared upon the basis of instinct: "Tharmas laid the Foundations & Los finishd it in howling woe" (v 78; 60:5 E333). All this is constructed upon a new limit, the limit of Translucence, apparently an upper limit opposed to the lower limit of Opacity which was providentially discovered in Night IV.[4] For the most part, however, Los misdirects his creative enterprise in oppressing his son. His use of his smithy-forged chains and the assistance provided by the Spectre of Urthona establish a clear parallel between the binding of Orc and that of Urizen in Night IV, though the effect there was to freeze Urizen while in Night V it is to set Orc aflame.

The explosive mixture in the adolescent psyche, of sexual and sensuous energy with rebelliousness against constraint, is now dramatized in a powerful passage depicting Orc as both suffering intensely and enjoying gigantic delights (v 114-36; 61:11-62:2 E334-35). He howls in flames, but at the same time spirits are ransacking the universe to bring him the most literally far-fetched joys of the senses.

> His limbs bound down mock at his chains for over them a
>   flame
> Of circling fire unceasing plays to feed them with life & bring
> The virtues of the Eternal worlds ten thousand thousand
>   spirits
> Of life lament around the Demon going forth & returning
> At his enormous call they flee into the heavens of heavens
> And back return with wine & food. Or dive into the deeps
> To bring the thrilling joys of sense

He is close to nature, to her intimate secrets as well as her grander manifestations:

His eyes the lights of his large soul contract or else expand
Contracted they behold the secrets of the infinite mountains
The veins of gold & silver & the hidden things of Vala
Whatever grows from its pure bud or breathes a fragrant soul
Expanded they behold the terrors of the Sun & Moon
The Elemental Planets & the orbs of eccentric fire.

The entire portrait is ultimately a set of variations on the central theme of sexual energy:

His loins inwove with silken fires are like a furnace fierce
As the strong Bull in summer time when bees sing round the
heath

As a portrait of adolescent energy, this passage can hardly be surpassed, except perhaps in the dialogues between Orc and Urizen in Night VIIA and in *America*.[5] Although Blake still feels much of the admiration for such Orckian energy that he had expressed in earlier works, in *The Four Zoas* he is aware of its negative implications:

Spirits of strength in Palaces rejoice in golden armour
Armed with spear & shield they drink & rejoice over the slain
Such is the Demon such his terror in the nether deep.

(V 140-42; 62:6-8 E335)

One does not have to be Urizen or Euripides' Pentheus to recognize the archetypal kinship between love and violence when neither is attuned to the needs of the whole human being. The kinship usually exists even when love is espoused as an alternative to war. Elevating love above war is a specious reform if love is no more than a bacchanal enacted in the selfish and life-denying spirit of aggressive fury. Both are merely natural, in the sense of "nature" that is opposed to a full human potential higher than nature. That is why Blake subsumes as part of this portrait of the libido Orc's inti-

mate contact with the natural world. Like other Romantics
who were sometimes realists and sometimes visionaries—
Byron and Wordsworth, to name two—Blake saw both the
positive and the negative sides of nature. When one is obsessed with man's unique capacity for evil acts that spring
from reason at its most perversely satanic, nature seems a
blessed norm. But when one considers the forms of beauty
and the acts of charity that can arise only from consciousness
and intelligence, a blind and amoral nature inclined equally
to bring forth wild flowers and tornadoes is unworthy of allegiance, much less worship.

Just as, after binding Urizen, Los had been horrified by
his handiwork, so now he and Enitharmon repent of what
they have done to Orc. They return from Golgonooza (the
scene of Los's activities which will elsewhere be identified
as the city of art) impelled by parental love to unchain their
son. But it is too late; the chain of Jealousy has taken root
in the rock, even to the earth's center. The images, organic
and inorganic, natural and artificial, external and psychological, are inextricably fused:

> In vain they strove now to unchain. In vain with bitter tears
> To melt the chain of Jealousy. not Enitharmons death
> Nor the Consummation of Los could ever melt the chain
> Nor unroot the infernal fibres from their rocky bed
> Nor all Urthonas strength nor all the power of Luvahs Bulls
> Tho they each morning drag the unwilling Sun out of the
>   deep
> Could uproot the infernal chain. for it had taken root
> Into the iron rock & grew a chain beneath the Earth
> Even to the Center wrapping round the Center & the limbs
> Of Orc entering with fibres. became one with him a living
>   Chain
> Sustained by the Demons life.
>
>   (V 160-70; 62:26-63:4 E335-36)

Among other things, this passage is a variation on the theme of repression recurrent in the *Zoas*, the point here being the difficulty of undoing such repression. Excessively stern parents who try to reclaim an alienated child through belated gentleness are not often successful.

On an allegorical level, we are to understand that jealousy and love, like wheat and tares, are inseparable in the fallen world that the middle triad of the poem describes; they are linked by an inexorable law of experience unalterable by even the most heroic effort. Yet Blake's technique in presenting this hopelessness is a tour de force, an apparent proof that something cannot happen that in fact is to happen. Later in the poem jealousy will indeed be annihilated, just as in Jesus' parable the wheat and tares, which cannot be separated in the normal course of things, are sorted out in the apocalyptic harvest (which for Blake is an overthrow of man's mere "nature").

The tone of intense insistency in the description of Orc's enrooted chain amounts to an unusually strong intrusion of authorial judgment upon Los and Enitharmon;[6] their new motives of love and self-sacrifice are thus, by contrast, thrown into especially strong relief. These impulses require of Los genuine heroism; "parental love returnd' to him "Tho terrible his dread of that infernal chain," and he desires to return Orc to his mother "Even if his own death resulted so much pity him paind" (v 146-54; 62:12-20 E335). Enitharmon too, after the unsuccessful attempt to release Orc, experiences a vast enlargement of her powers of sympathy, not only toward her husband and son but also toward her sister Emanations. Earlier she had shut the gates of her heart against Los out of sexual jealousy (I 564-66; 20:5-7 E308); in the present scene she feels, briefly but piercingly, her essential affinity with other female characters:

Enitharmon on the road of Dranthon felt the inmost gate
Of her bright heart burst open & again close with a deadly
 pain
Within her heart Vala began to reanimate in bursting sobs
And when the Gate was open she beheld that dreary Deep
Where bright Ahania wept.

(V 177-81; 63:11-15 E336)

These are immensely significant changes in Los and Enitharmon. For the first time we see them acting in the spirit of unselfish sacrifice that later, when it is finally tested and then fully confirmed, will set the work of redemption in motion. A seed of the sympathy conditioned by suffering, which George Eliot venerates and which moves Shelley's Prometheus to retract his curse, has been planted in the human imagination. In later Nights the fruits will appear, when Los exhorts Enitharmon to "Tremble not . . . at the awful gates / Of thy poor broken Heart" but rather look within to see the Lamb of God (VIIA 412-15; 87:41-44 E355) and again when Los is able to "enter into Enitharmons bosom . . . now the Obdurate heart was broken" (VIII 32-33; 99:26-27 E358). At this point, on this climactic emotional note, Los and Enitharmon disappear and remain offstage, except for a few fleeting references to them, until their conversion in Night VIIA.

This is a good point from which to examine just what their basic function is—in relation to reason and emotion—in the state of fallenness, and in the middle section of the poem. Earlier we outlined a paradigm of the *Zoas* in which Nights I and IV focus on instinct and imagination, Nights II and V on passion, and Nights III and VI on reason. The parallels are clearly marked. Besides those already mentioned there are many minor or subtle connections. For example, the burning Luvah of Night II, imprisoned in a furnace, provides an emblem of sublimation, while the burning Orc of

Night V

Night V represents, through a variant image of contained combustion, the inverse of sublimation, the implosive conversion of all human faculties into libidinal passion. The parallels and sharp contrasts between Luvah-Orc and Urizen within the middle Nights are even more striking. Los has, in different ways, given a body to Urizen and a body to Orc; each is an utterly physical body, though Urizen's is initially a frozen corpse and Orc's a core of radiating energy. Within the middle Nights too Night V is a clearly contrasting parallel to Night VI. In Night V Orc turns matter into energy; in Night VI Urizen will try to reduce everything vital to something that, in Coleridge's phrase, is "fixed and dead." Many smaller details reinforce the parallel. For example, the wholly organic life-force that is Orc is partially devitalized as he becomes one with his iron chains and rocky bed, while in Night VI the life-denying force that is Urizen is mitigated when a providential "ever pitying one" provides a bed of slime into which Urizen can fall and renew himself like a seed (VI 157-63; 71:25-31 E341).

The result of this strategy of directing the reader's attention to the polarities of Urizen and Orc is that their idiosyncrasies so balance each other that the reader sees beyond them to the essential pattern of their interrelationship and concentrates on the force that created the pattern. That force is easily defined: it owes something to instinct, but it is mainly imagination. It is therefore possible to see the middle Nights as a sustained comment on imagination and how it operates in the state of fallenness. When we look at the middle Nights this way, we see not so much discrete contrasts and parallels but a single act with many implications. The birth of Orc is not merely set against the incarnation of Urizen but is an inevitable outgrowth of it, indeed virtually the same event. Providing Urizen with the organs of sense and the means of emotion inevitably means the eruption and expression of those senses and emotions—in short, the appearance of Orc. That eruption, in turn, demands an equal and opposite reaction in the form of a renewed effort at control by intellect; therefore it is inevitable that Urizen be awakened, as in fact he now is—by the pulsations of Orc. This view of the middle movement of the *Zoas* as a single action at the same time that it is a set of alternatives is strengthened by the fluid connections between Nights IV and V (repeated mention of Los's spasmodic dance) and between Nights V and VI: the words "So Urizen arose" in the first line of Night VI provide an explicit narrative link to Urizen's awakening in Night V; the reference in the same line to exploring "dens" recalls both the "Caves" Urizen mentions in a soliloquy at the end of Night V and the "dens of Urthona" that are the setting for his soliloquy (v 189; 63:23 E336).

The main agent of the middle Nights, then, is Los; the main pattern is incarnation. The body and what it implies are the work of imagination, but it is still fallen imagination. Although Tharmas, instinct, had come to man's rescue at the crisis when total death threatened, the only being who can actually perform work is Urthona-Los. That work—the incarnations of Urizen and Orc—has had to be undertaken by an imagination not yet in full control of its powers; it is compelled by occasion as is the "uncouth swain" who reluctantly plucks his unripe berries in *Lycidas*. And not only has imagination been forced to work prematurely, it has had to create its own tools and raw materials. No art could be produced in a world where neither intellect nor emotion existed, nor can Los make anything entirely good until Urizen and Orc at least exist—and Los has to cause them to exist. He produces fallen and largely evil forms of intellect and emotion, because he is himself fallen. Or one could put this the other way around: he is fallen *because* (especially at the beginning of Night IV) he lives in a world vacated by his brother Zoas of reason and emotion and thus by definition he and his world are less than fully human. (Here as elsewhere in the poem, tenor and vehicle, cause and effect, are often reversible.) Nevertheless, the imaginative faculty called Los has made the necessary beginning: elemental forces of mind and feeling, however inadequate and even nefarious they may be, have been rescued from that paralysis that Blake sometimes calls the indefinite. Analogously, in cases of severe mental derangement, a patient who cannot cope with reality (however one defines it) must first become convinced that there is such a thing as reality—must learn to see a rose or glass of water, however distorted an image they may present, must think actual thoughts, however false they may be, must substitute for a stifled, passionless numbness an emotion real enough at least to cause a pang and find a natural outlet.

It makes sense, then, that the most unnaturally cruel act in the poem is committed by the power of imagination that Blake so highly venerated, and also that the motive for this cruelty is jealousy, which Blake consistently regarded as either the source or main symptom of all evil in human relationships. For this is fallen imagination, which creates because it is imagination but creates evil because it is fallen. Rather than allegory, however, realistic dramatization accounts for the next juxtaposition: Los's most blamable act is followed immediately by his first truly noble behavior. In the act of creating Urizen he had recognized his kinship with him; in the act of binding down his son Orc he has recognized this kinship too. In this second case it is as if Shelley had had Jupiter recognize himself in the suffering Prometheus instead of the other way around. All these examples, hypothetical and not, illustrate the going outside of the self which, for Blake as for Shelley, is the fundamental imaginative act. In the actions taken by the heartbroken and repentant Los and Enitharmon, Blake hints at a point to be developed in

Night VIIA: suffering may be the beginning of imaginative wisdom, the source of creative power—if not for all art, then at least for Romantic art.

It would seem that the poem has turned the corner toward human recovery. In one sense this is very nearly true; the next full-scale scene involving Los and Enitharmon, in VIIA, will dramatize their complete conversion. This event, if we do not concern ourselves with clock time, can be imagined as happening very soon after the parents depart sorrowing in the fifth Night. The line "all their after life was lamentation" (v 175; 63:9 E336) contradicts this notion, but that line is an exaggeration appropriate to their emotional state at the time, for it also contradicts what happens in the great renewal of the last Nights.

The awakening of Urizen, who "shuddring heard" the pulsations of Orc (v 188; 63:22 E336), is another manifestation of sympathy in a physical and almost in an emotional sense. (The intuitive perception of a distant cry or force ties the end of Night V with the end of Night II, when Enion uttered the lament sensed by Ahania, and looks forward to the antiphony between Enion and Ahania at the end of Night VIII.) Urizen's soliloquy after he awakens is astonishingly sane and serene. In the quatrains often used for the poem's arias, Urizen mourns the loss of the blissful past earlier recalled by Ahania, the time when the delights of the mind were sensual in their quality and intensity, and takes his full share of blame for the fall. His frankness and clarity is that of Satan in *Paradise Lost* when he interrupts his machinations against God and man to express clear insight:

> he deserv'd no such return
> From me, whom he created what I was
> In that bright eminence, and with his good
> Upbraided none; nor was his service hard.

(IV 42-45)

Night V

Urizen laments:

> Ah how shall Urizen the King submit to this dark mansion
> Ah how is this! Once on the heights I stretchd my throne
> sublime
>
> .   .   .   .
>
> O Fool to think that I could hide from his all piercing eyes
> The gold & silver & costly stones his holy workmanship
> O Fool could I forget the light that filled my bright spheres
> Was a reflection of his face who calld me from the deep
>
> I well remember for I heard the mild & holy voice
> Saying O light spring up & shine & I sprang up from the deep
> He gave to me a silver scepter & crownd me with a golden
> crown
> & said Go forth & guide my Son who wanders on the ocean
>
> I went not forth.
>
> (V 190-222; 63:24-64:25 E336-37)

Instead, Urizen confesses, he initiated the conspiracy against man, his "Lord," exchanging his steeds of light for Luvah's wine and bringing Luvah to destruction, along with his Emanation Vala and Urthona (see Appendix B). Urizen's generosity toward Luvah, whose "pure feet stepd on the steps divine. too pure for other feet" and whose "fair locks shadowd thine eyes from the divine effulgence" (v 230-31; 65:1-2 E337), is the most surprising of many reversals in Urizen's confession. It seems that in the privacy of his solitary confinement, relieved from the necessity of proving his strength and rectitude to his wife and others, Urizen can admit his errors.

When, looking ahead, we consider how he acts and perceives in the following Night, however, far more rigidly and reductively even than in Nights II and III, the insight and charity attributed here to Urizen seem anomalous. They are

not entirely so. His soft words notwithstanding, he is still
incapable of finding fulfillment in the present moment; his
longing for the past here is the other side of his obsession
with a dread future in Night III. Moreover, his esteem for
Luvah is conditioned by the new and, to Urizen, frightening
form Luvah has assumed in Orc. Compared with this titanic
revolutionary, the unfallen Luvah whom Urizen had opposed
can be seen for what he was, a force of beauty and purity.
Nevertheless, something truly good has happened to Urizen,
in accord with the pattern of imaginative revivifying in the
middle Nights. Though he deals cruelly with the creatures
he encounters in Night VI, he does recognize them as his
children, and however vain his attempts to communicate with
them, he does at least make the attempt. In Nights II and III
he did no such thing; a straining at communication was then
unnecessary, since that earlier world had retained some poetry
and, though it occasioned uneasiness, had stopped short of
total alienation. The Urizen of Night VI is Newtonian rationalism, but he is also the fallen mind of the Romantic
age and after, feeling intensely a need for union with nature
that is all the greater for his recognition of estrangement from
it. Thus Urizen's decision to "arise Explore these dens &
find that deep pulsation / That shakes my caverns with strong
shudders" (v 238-39; 65:9-10 E337) is both a counteroffensive
against Orc and, at a far deeper level, a movement toward
unity with an enemy who is really his counterpart. (The
phrase "strong shudders" is an ambiguous dangling modifier
that could apply equally to Urizen and to Orc.) His specula-
tion that

> perhaps this is the night
> Of Prophecy & Luvah hath burst his way from Enitharmon
> When Thought is closd in Caves. Then Love shall shew its
> root in deepest Hell

(V 239-41; 65:10-12 E337)

describes a situation he had not only foreseen earlier but also decreed (III 18-23; 38:6-11 E320) ; that ambiguity is reflected even more strongly in the tone of his surmise here, which sounds like both trepidation and incipient hope.

Night VI.

Acting on his new resolve, Urizen sets out in Night VI to explore his dens and to find the seismic force whose pulsations he has sensed. After the restraints imposed in the parallel scenes of Los's binding of Urizen and Orc in Nights IV and V, Urizen's renewed activity may almost be welcomed as a positive sign of life, a display of what even the sense-bound and time-bound mind is capable of doing. It almost seems that Blake is trying to elicit sympathy for his most tyrannical character; Urizen's poignant expression of his woes and repentance for his errors at the end of Night V are plausible evidence of a genuine change of heart. His motivation for exploring his dens appears to be a desire to make contact with Luvah in his new form and perhaps even to become reconciled with him. But so long as Albion is fallen and no one is working effectively for his recovery, all four of the Zoas are villains, and the reader is not allowed to forget that Urizen is the most dangerous of the four, because intellectual error is more all-encompassing and insidious than other human failings. Urizen's exploration of his dens in Night VI, his learning how to operate within the physical and temporal limits set by Los—"heroic" though it seems to be—actually contributes to human recovery only insofar as Urizen, by reaching a new depth of folly and evil, exemplifies in his own person a consolidation of error which is completed in Night VIII with his appearance in an unmistakably negative form.

By stylistic signals, Blake continually undercuts the heroism of Urizen's exploits. For example, the landscape of Urizen's journey is sharply contrasted with that of Orc's captivity: Night VI depicts a world of death antithetical to the prolific earth of Night V, in which even the chains around Orc take root and all the elements respond to his needs. In addition, the language and imagery of Night VI point relentlessly to hell in repeated allusions to both Milton and Dante: Urizen's exploration is modeled on the journeys of Satan, Sin, and Death in *Paradise Lost*; his surroundings resemble specific scenes in the *Inferno*.[1] Furthermore, Night VI has a peculiar monotony of tone and plot; though insistently horrific, it lacks rhetorical and dramatic variety, as if tailored to a reductionist world view that cannot distinguish among the minute differentiae to which the other Zoas are sensitive.

Ironically, Urizen's travel and travail describe a circle, resulting in no real progress, for Night VI ends with Urizen in the "dens" or "Vale" of Urthona where in Night V he had been imprisoned before his journey (v 189; 63:23 E336; vi 294; 75:3 E345). Imagistically, this grand circumnavigation is related to Enion's Circle of Destiny in Night I and the Starry Wheels to which Jesus sets a limit in Night IV; thematically, it is the antithesis of Orc's cycles and revolutions. Night VI is much concerned with a mythic geography, including compass directions, though in the end they provide no real orientation. Rather, the circularity is symptomatic of a narrowly rationalistic outlook confined to pointless investigations of meaningless data that can be arranged to yield whatever result the investigator expects.

Before describing Urizen's bewildering journey, Night VI announces its theme in a scene resembling the introductory dumbshows of early Renaissance plays. This structural device, common in Blake's other works, is used nowhere else in *The Four Zoas* in quite the same way.[2] It may be called the epitomizing introduction, or epigraph passage; it is the verbal equivalent of the pictorial frontispieces Blake often uses in the illuminated poems to sum up the central situation, mood, or message of a work. Such epigraph passages include the Introduction lyrics to *Innocence* and to *Experience,* the Motto to *The Book of Thel,* the Argument to *The Marriage of Heaven and Hell,* and the Preludia to *America* and *Europe.*[3] Probably the closest analogue of all with the opening of Night VI is *Visions of the Daughters of Albion,* in which both a separate Argument and a compressed introductory narrative provide a preview and mythic exposition of the main action. Like Night VI of the *Zoas, Visions* expands and explores the implications of a single issue and situation outlined briefly at the beginning. Both Night VI and *Visions* deal with the theme of the soul-killing effect of Urizenic values. The epigraphic passage in the *Zoas* ends with Urizen cursing his daughters. Significantly, that curse includes a quotation from *Visions,* echoing Bromion's boast that he controls slaves whose daughters "worship terrors & obey the violent" (vi 45; 68:26 e339; *Visions* 1:21-23).

Though the opening scene of Night VI is believed by most commentators to have a specific but as yet not well understood allegorical meaning, its purpose as a dramatic prologue seems more important. The episode is like a little folktale characterizing Urizen and dramatizing his relation to others, serving much the same purpose in Night VI as the opening scene of *King Lear* in that play. Having set out to explore his dens—that is, to establish rationalist control of his world as both discoverer and surveyor—Urizen comes to a river and after filling his silver helmet once and drinking from it is barred from the water by three eerie naiads. The eldest is a cloudy rain spirit with a name written on her forehead (like the character called Mystery in Revelation); the middle one is a powerful fountain-spirit clad in blue (who is able to magnetize water); the youngest, in green, divides the water into four rivers (suggestive of the rivers of Eden except that these are "dreadful rivers"). The three women silently deny his requests for water, but when he raises his spear they recognize him as their father, scream, and shrink into their suddenly dried-up channels. Tearfully Urizen retaliates with curses (vi 1-46; 67:1-68:27 e338-39).

The details may be problematical, but the broad significance of this episode is clear. Urizen, though apparently motivated by a benevolent impulse to seek his fellow Zoa, approaches nature with helmet and spear. Rejected, he becomes embittered and furious. Like Milton's Satan he is unable to recognize his own offspring, the appalling results of his own corruption. He would doubtless claim that he is armed only to make his way through hostile terrain; to his daughters, however, his spear reveals his identity and gives away his true purpose. Even the most benevolent rationalism is a form of tyranny if it excludes imagination, passion, and instinct—as is well known by those who reject such diverse utopias as those of Plato, More, Swift's Houyhnhnms, Wells, and Skinner because of the richness and passion they leave out. The resistance of Urizen's daughters represents the resistance of the natural world and the remnants of intellectual beauty to rationalist advances. Their water is both the vital moisture of the natural cycle and the nourishment of the human spirit. The "sighs & care" of the first sister, "frowning" of the second, and "labour & care" of the third suggest also the flow of life and feeling in the postlapsarian world.

At the level of psychological allegory, concerned with divisions within the rational faculty itself, the meaning of the episode is that Ahania's once-gentle daughters, the three Graces of mental pleasure, have become niggardly custodians of the water of life. Their forbidding presence is now suggestive of the Weird Sisters or the three Fates rather than the Graces; when they next appear as drudges under the domination of Urizen in Night VIIA, they are called by the Teutonic-sounding names of Eleth, Uveth, and Ona. To Urizen, his unrecognized daughters are "spirits of darkness"; in his anticreative vision what should be a natural cycle is a progressive devolution: a watercourse that begins in Mystery and ends in the divided rivers of a dreadful Eden cannot possibly be the river of life. Since the daughters represent both nature as perceived by the fallen mind and the once-beautiful thoughts within that mind, their drying up at the sight of Urizen's spear suggests that both nature and mind become barren under the threat of aggressive and exploitative rationalism.

As an epigraph for Night VI, this brief scene makes the point that the present relation between mind and nature has deteriorated from what was once an intimate familial connection. Urizen's recognition of the green and blue and cloudy water spirits as his daughters establishes a context for his addresses to other creatures and phenomena in the rest of Night VI, all of whom he acknowledges as his ruined and estranged children. The pattern of his encounter at the river is followed in most of his dealings with the world. He finds nature inhospitable, then barren, whereupon he makes things worse by corrupting it with his curse. The primal tie between mind and nature is not restored until the reinvigoration of Urizen and the renovation of science in Night IX. Despite the villainy of Urizen during most of the poem, this eventual restoration should be welcomed by the reader as a profoundly desired aspect of the apocalypse, for in "sweet Science" the mind once more participates in a productive interchange with nature through a mode of genuine understanding that cannot be achieved by the other human faculties either separately or in any combination that excludes reason.

The opening episode serves also to provide a transition from Urizen's enlightened soliloquy in Night V to his benighted actions in the rest of Night VI. By the end of the episode Urizen has resumed his characteristically antagonistic attitude toward everyone and everything that falls outside his increasingly narrow definition of himself, except that within his new limitations he is as yet unable to overpower others. His effect on his daughters is like a negative miracle that turns water into rock, but it signifies no mastery of mind over matter. Urizen's other attempts in this Night to master his surroundings end in similar frustration. The element of nostalgia in Urizen's curse is itself part of a transition, helping to smooth the way between the characterization of Urizen in his soliloquy in Night V and his actions during his exploratory journey. Instead of stimulating a tender mood of repentance as in Night V, his memories of the unfallen world are combined in his curse with self-pity and bitterness, emotions that rise to the surface also in his questions to his ruined "children" in the main action of Night VI.

Urizen's fearful curse on his daughters, recalling Lear's imprecations when his paternal will is crossed, blends nostalgic sentimentality with a general complaint against ingratitude:

> those whom I loved best
> On whom I pourd the beauties of my light adorning them
> With jewels & precious ornament labourd with art divine
> Vests of the radiant colours of heaven & crowns of golden fire
> I gave sweet lillies to their breasts & roses to their hair
> I taught them songs of sweet delight
>
> .   .   .   .
>
> Now will I pour my fury on them & I will reverse
> The precious benediction. for their colours of loveliness
> I will give blackness for jewels hoary frost for ornament deformity
> For crowns wreathd Serpents for sweet odors stinking corruptibility
> For voices of delight hoarse croakings inarticulate thro frost
> (VI 25-39; 68:6-20 E338-39)

Instead of invoking the goddess Nature to infect, lame, and deform a daughter's nature, as Lear does (*King Lear,* I.iv;

II.iv), Urizen appeals to no power but his own; his curse will be enforced in his distorted mental representation of nature. What he calls "hoarse croakings" and "stinking corruptibility" are simply his blighting perceptions of the sights, sounds, and odors of nature. Decaying flowers, "hoary frost," and "wreathd Serpents" have become aspects of the fall of man, like Adam's faded garland of roses, the seasonal extremes of earth, and the accursed serpent in *Paradise Lost*. Whatever Urizen's daughters may intend by withholding water from their father, they have become what they are as a result of Urizen's estrangement from Ahania and their subsequent fall. The curse is in fact less a punishment than a formal declaration of an already existing hostility. In cursing his daughters, Urizen willfully forces upon himself a view of nature as inherently vile. In reality, nature to Blake is inherently neutral; it is whatever mind and imagination make it, and to the visionary it can be the paradise celebrated in *Milton* (27:11-29:65).

Presumably because his daughters have appeared in a watery form, Urizen assumes that they are under the influence of Tharmas, and he wishes to punish them in order "That they may curse Tharmas their God & Los his adopted son / That they may curse & worship the obscure Demon of destruction" (vi 43-44; 68:24-25 e339). That is, he is not only rejecting his daughters but also turning them against the other Zoas. (The "obscure Demon" is certainly the young Orc, whom Urizen has not yet seen; Los is called an "adopted son" because, as Urthona, he had originally been a brother, equal in status with Tharmas and the other Zoas.) Urizen's thirst and his reference to Tharmas imply some dim awareness by reason of instinctual needs, though they are less consciously recognized now than in Night III when Ahania was at his side to relay, interpret, and articulate the promptings of Enion. At this point Tharmas, who in Night IV had commissioned the binding of Urizen "Lest he should rise again from death" (IV 121; 51:4 E327), is once more aroused to act. He comes "riding in his fury" in response to the "deadly scream" of the daughters, the "loud sounding voice" of Urizen, and the chilling effect of Urizen on his watery environment, demanding to know "What & who art thou Cold Demon. art thou Urizen / Art thou like me risen again from death or art thou deathless" (VI 47-56; 68:28-69:7 E339).

Urizen's curse and the darkness cast by his cold helmet and spear have plunged the world into a sudden cold so deep that it freezes Tharmas's ocean solid and brakes his furious charge upon Urizen so that the attack turns into a Parthian retreat, as Tharmas "fled & flying fought" (VI 54; 69:5 E339). Tharmas's reaction suggests that the daughters of Urizen, as water spirits, were tributaries of Tharmas's ocean; thus the point at which the youngest daughter divided the river into four must be the delta through which their current emptied into the ocean before they dried up and retreated behind a rocky wall. The "frost' twice called down upon them in their father's curse anticipates what has happened to Tharmas with the failure of Urizen's warmth and light. Thus threatened, Tharmas's death wish returns, now deliberately intended as a means of destroying Urizen, and with him Albion as well.

The scene between Tharmas and Urizen is necessarily absurd, for in the fallen state they have nothing in common—now not even the daughters who might have mediated between reason and instinct by offering Urizen their vital refreshment and by functioning for Tharmas as the intelligences of his waters. Urizen's compulsive need for order and control and Tharmas's chaotic helplessness—potentially of mutual benefit—have become self-contained and self-perpetuating states of being. Tharmas is aware, in his vague way, that his province is the "Body of Man" (VI 60; 69:11 E339) and that the body-consciousness or life-force which is his identity is indestructible and continues to appear in lower forms of life even when it is lost to a fully integrated humanity. He also understands that he and Urizen are part of one another and ultimately of Albion, and that if they continue to deny each other their unique resources Albion will die.

On the basis of his dim certainty that the Zoas are interconnected, Tharmas proposes a plan for mutual destruction: Tharmas will withhold the "food" Urizen needs on condition that Urizen withhold his "light" from Tharmas. In this way instinct would remain dark and stupid and intellect would be cut off from instinctual nourishment so that humanity would die out altogether. Ironically, much of what Tharmas proposes is already taking place. That Tharmas has been weakened by the freeze is evident in the contrast between his plea to Urizen, "give me death" (VI 57; 69:8 E339), and his invigorating challenge to Los: "Death choose or life . . . now choose life / And all the Elements shall serve thee" (IV 152-53; 52:2-3 E328). Urizen, for his part, is entirely indifferent to his fellow Zoa's suffering, merely using Tharmas's frozen waters as a place to walk upon during his journey of exploration.

Despite themselves, the Zoas are inexorably linked. Tharmas's frustration because life still "surges forth in fish & monsters of the deeps" is akin to the distress Urizen suffers as "hideous monsters of the deeps annoyd him sore / Scaled & finnd with iron & brass" (VI 60-76; 69:11-27 E339). Both perceptions are excessive responses to the teeming of oceanic life. To Tharmas, such vitality is the stubborn survival instinct that defeats his will to die; to Urizen it is no more than an inconvenient distraction on his quest for absolute sovereignty over nature. Both the absurdity and the interdependence of their relationship come out clearly in Tharmas's madly illogical threat to kill Urizen if he does not accept his suicide pact—and to kill him by withholding food, exactly the method proposed in the suicide plan. The absurdity is compounded in that if the Zoas were capable of cooperating as Tharmas proposes he would have no need to suggest suicide.

Tharmas's presence during Urizen's travels is henceforth hardly more than an overtone, though his appearance at the end of Night VI is a further indication that Urizen's journeys have brought him back to his starting place. Similarly, the other Zoas are mentioned only obliquely in a few brief references to Luvah, also parent to the "children" of nature (VI 88,237; 70:6,73:25 E340,343), and to Los, who broods menacingly above the dark scene oblivious of Urizen (VI 83; 70:1 E340). Nonetheless, Urizen's sense of his fellow Zoas as rivals to his epistemology and to his hegemony over nature supplies him with a perverse stamina in his tremendous journey. His sick reliance on himself alone grows in proportion to his sense of alienation from the other Zoas. Repeatedly he enters the "world" of one or another of the Zoas, including his own world,[4] without realizing that all such territories are part of the one world of humanity.

To Urizen, the universe seems not only isolated from human intelligence but fragmented within itself, unorganized even by nonhuman laws, a mere dust storm. In contrast, "howlings gnashings groanings shriekings shudderings sobbings burstings" mingle together "to create a world for Los" (VI 81-82; 69:32-33 E340). Such a world is potential raw material for the ordering imagination, a chaos awaiting, as Coleridge says, a repetition in the finite mind of the eternal act of creation, but Los has as yet shown no sign that he is capable of such an act. Fallen reason, for its part, can in isolation do no more than create mechanical patterns, models, laws. In Coleridge's statement that "all objects (*as* objects) are essentially fixed and dead" (*Biographia Literaria*, chap. 13), the weight of meaning is carried in the italics. This dead world of dissociated objects is the result of Urizen's perception, even though in his better moments he abhors and mourns over these products of his mind. Most of the time he

is content with or resigned to a universe of death, so long
as he can measure and reduce it to his liking.

By the light of his "Globe of fire"—common daylight,
which is all that remains of his brilliant intelligence—Urizen
surveys his accursed universe, an "Abyss" of dissociated entities, and he methodically records his observations in "books
of iron & brass" (vi 83-87; 70:1-5 E340). To show the sore
need of discrete objects for a synthesizing and humanizing
transfiguration—from their own point of view—Blake represents each separate item in Urizen's purview as a lost soul,
suffering in a hell of meaninglessness, isolation, and irrele-
vance. Much of the power of the description is drawn from
a complex node of Dantean images:[5]

> Scard at the sound of their own sigh that seems to shake the
> immense
> They wander Moping
>
> .   .   .   .
>
> Beyond the bounds of their own self their senses cannot
> penetrate
> As the tree knows not what is outside of its leaves & bark
> And yet it drinks the summer joy & fears the winter sorrow
> So in the regions of the grave none knows his dark compeer
> Tho he partakes of his dire woes & mutual returns the pang
> The throb the dolor the convulsion in soul sickening woes
>
> The horrid shapes & sights of torment in burning dungeons
> & in
> Fetters of red hot iron some with crowns of serpents & some
> With monsters girding round their bosoms. Some lying on
> beds of sulphur
> On racks & wheels he beheld women marching oer burning
> wastes
> Of Sand in bands of hundreds & of fifties & of thousands
> (VI 89-107; 70:7-22 E340)

Tigers and lions, and by implication all natural beings, are "dishumanizd men" (VI 116; 70:31 E340). Again Blake is describing both mind and object: men dishumanize themselves when they allow a rich perceptual interchange with nature to become truncated by analytic rationalism, and animals are dishumanized *by* men when they are perceived as mere objects to be classified, without regard to man's imaginative and emotional needs.

What is best in Urizen wants to communicate with these objects and creatures who are his children; what is worst in him has cursed them (as in the "hoarse croakings inarticulate" wished upon his daughters) and thus made communication impossible. His is the voice of the unanswered questioner in *The Tyger* rather than that of the child who answers his own question in *The Lamb*:

> His voice to them was but an inarticulate thunder for their
> Ears
> Were heavy & dull & their eyes & nostrils closed up
> Oft he stood by a howling victim Questioning in words
> Soothing or Furious no one answerd every one wrapd up
> In his own sorrow howld regardless of his words, nor voice
> Of sweet response could he obtain tho oft assayd with tears
> He knew they were his Children ruind in his ruind world.
> .   .   .   .
>   then a lion he would Sieze
> By the fierce mane staying his howling course in vain the
> voice
> Of Urizen in vain the Eloquent tongue. A Rock a Cloud a
> Mountain
> Were now not Vocal as in Climes of happy Eternity
> Where the lamb replies to the infant voice & the lion to the
> man of years
> Giving them sweet instructions Where the Cloud the River &
> the Field
> Talk with the husbandman & shepherd. But these attackd
> him sore
>   (VI 124-38; 70:39-71:8 E340-41)

These frustrations directly contrast with the sufferings of Orc in Night V, whom the elements willingly obey and who, for all his pain, lives intensely in the moment of desire. Urizen lives in the future and past, which are all he can imagine; having cast his shadow futureward in his earlier curse, he now looks to the past, repenting his malediction because his children are already "cursd beyond his Curse"; indeed, they are almost personifications of his curses. For all the contrasts between Urizen and Orc, reminders of their affinity are also present. As Orc's body, chains, and rocky bed had become inseparable from one another, so Urizen "could not take [his children's] fetters off for they grew from the soul / Nor could he quench the fires for they flamd out from the heart." This phenomenon is explained in another of Blake's densely compressed puns: Urizen "himself was Subject" (vi 141-45; 70:46-71:13 E341). The statement means both that Urizen is captured by his own system and that he is the mere subject of a master (ideally, he is the subject of Albion the whole man; in his fallen state he is the subject of his own worst self); the statement is also playing on the philosophical duality of subject–object that Blake satirizes throughout the poem but especially in the fifth and sixth Nights. The pun and the passage help explain what Blake means in *London* by "mind-forg'd manacles." The mechanist world view seems to have become an ineluctable premise in human consciousness. Yet the power of rationalism and ma- terialistic duality in Night VI, like the strength of jealousy in Night V, is presented as seemingly invincible precisely so that we may better appreciate its destruction in the human triumph of Night IX.

Arriving at Luvah's East, now vacant and storm-beaten, Urizen finds himself sinking, whirling in bottomless space, a variant of the non-entity toward which Enion and Ahania have drifted. The providential force intervenes once more, however; the "ever pitying one" creates a bosom of slimy clay on which Urizen can rest and begin a cycle of continual life, death, and rebirth (vi 147-66; 71:15-34 e341-42). Fertile clay is the merciful lower limit for Urizen because to the fallen intelligence, uncontrollable organic life—as opposed to fixed and classifiable mineral objects—is of all conditions of being the most repugnant; to be merely a biological creature is the lowliest state to which the proud mind can sink. Urizen's fall into this vitalizing slime "As the seed falls from the sowers hand" (vi 160; 71:28 e341) recalls the wintry plants of Night V, withering and casting their seeds on barren mountain tops (v 9-11; 57:9-11 e332), but it anticipates the hopeful germinating described in the voice of Enion from the grave in Night VIII (viii 558-60; 110:3-5 e370) as well as the gigantic expansion of the metaphor in the agricultural myth of human resurrection in Night IX.

The notion that withering and corruption are part of a life-giving process is sardonically undercut, however, in the description of Urizen's books during his numerous deaths and resurrections. These books—both discursive works and account books that Urizen must "regulate"—are written with iron pen on adamantine leaves, interlined with brass, iron, and gold. Wrapped by Urizen in graveclothes, they lie beside his grave during his deaths, and after his resurrections they remain "unconsumd" though the graveclothes around them are rotten. The deadly records are preserved in an ironic incorruptibility, immune to natural metamorphoses (vi 167-80; 71:35-72:6 e342). This is black humor, a wry or bitter comment on the ability of rationalism to survive any one of its versions; in a more elaborate way, a similar point will be made at the end of Night VIII when rationalist mystery dies phoenixlike only to produce a new version of itself.

Urizen has also begun to create "many a Vortex fixing many a Science in the deep" (vi 187; 72:13 e342). The bent and stretched spaces through which Urizen travels are like problems in topology, a feature of Blake's prefigurative critique of the mathematical vortex in systems of Descartes and Newton.[6] In the psychological allegory, a vortex is a configuration of attitudes and events corresponding to what people mean when they say they are "going through" something. In a broader sense, a vortex is a way of looking at things, an orientation, a pathway through chaos. As reason throws itself into meaninglessness, it both organizes and limits raw experience and data. But at least a sense of direction and equilibrium results from establishing the vortex. Urizen's disorientation between vortexes, with its prospect of laborious ascents, is probably modeled on the moment in the *Inferno* when Dante and Virgil, having reached the center of hell and of the earth, find their descent transformed into an upward climb (*Inferno,* xxxiv 76-120). Blake's inscription on his design illustrating the circles of Dante's hell provides a gloss both on it and on Urizen's version: "This is Upside Down When viewd from Hells Gate But right When Viewd from Purgatory after they have passed the Center." "In Equivocal Worlds Up & Down are Equivocal" (E668, κ785). When Urizen

> came to where a Vortex ceasd to operate
> Nor down nor up remaind then if he turnd & lookd back
> From whence he came twas upward all. & if he turnd and viewd
> The unpassd void upward was still his mighty wandring

Any movement he makes is a struggle in chaos, like that of Milton's Satan. He rejects the one point of equilibrium, a "grey of air serene / Where he might live in peace & where his life might meet repose," which is where he is in the present moment. Discontented with the present, always "labouring up against futurity" as if it were the gravity holding him back, he wants a godlike vantage point above reality, or a foundation point beneath it:

Night VI

> But Urizen said Can I not leave this world of Cumbrous
>   wheels
> Circle oer Circle nor on high attain a void
> Where self sustaining I may view all things beneath my feet
> Or sinking thro these Elemental wonders swift to fall
> I thought perhaps to find an End a world beneath of voidness
> Whence I might travel round the outside of this Dark
>   confusion.
>
> (VI 186-201; 72:12-27 E342)

Either of these positions, above or beneath, would be a void. But that is what Urizen wants, since removing himself from the thick of phenomena would make it easier for him to create and thus control a monomorphic world. The variegated universe praised in Hopkins's *Pied Beauty* can be only a nuisance to him. His effort of reductive domination requires the suppression of three-fourths of the psyche, a task demanding courage and a prowess that, appalling though it is, is nevertheless awesome.

Urizen's misguided heroism is announced in lines that provide one of the few rhetorical climaxes of this Night: "Here will I fix my foot & here rebuild / Here Mountains of Brass promise much riches in their dreadful bosoms" (VI 227-28; 73:14-15 E343). This statement is another dense node of meaning, implication, and allusion. Urizen means both his bodily foot and that of his Newtonian compass—the same pun realized visually in the famous frontispiece to *Europe*. Moreover, the Urizen who has already been cast by Blake as Milton's Satan becomes at this point Milton's Mammon also, the devil who had been an architect in heaven (somewhat like Urizen in Night II) and later in hell, mining precious metals to build Pandemonium. The allusion to Mammon helps mark a broadening of theme and scope in the last Nights; though the psychodrama continues to develop, the poem becomes more explicitly concerned with societal correlatives of human psychic ills. The new economic and commercial system implied in Urizen's anticipation of "much riches" is intimately allied with the new philosophy and science:

> So he began to dig form[ing] of gold silver & iron
> And brass vast instruments to measure out the immense & fix
> The whole into another world better suited to obey
> His will where none should dare oppose his will himself being
> King
> Of All & all futurity be bound in his vast chain
>
> And the Sciences were fixd & the Vortexes began to operate
> On all the sons of men & every human soul terrified
> At the turning wheels of heaven shrunk away inward withring
> away
> Gaining a New Dominion over all his sons & Daughters
>
> (VI 229-37; 73:16-24 E343)

The "turning wheels" of heaven imply those of industry; both are mills that inexorably grind reality, whether nature (as in ears of grain) or humanity, into identical indistinguishable atoms.

It is centrally important that Urizen desires not merely to measure the immense but also to "fix" it, along with his investigative methodologies: "And the Sciences were fixd." In this dismal parody of the "sweet Science" toward which the Urizenic side of human nature must eventually move if man is to be liberated, the only reality is what can be dealt with in terms of one's own discipline. To use a modern analogue: it may be that a psychologist who is a strict behaviorist thinks of rats as similar to people *because* rats are available for experimentation, and hunger and sex may be considered of primary importance *because* food pellets and copulations can be counted. There is an even more dehumanizing corollary: when the sciences are fixed, the vortexes begin "to operate"; in other words, a system that purports to be, or originates as, a description soon turns into a coercive dynamic, not simply a scheme or map but a set of imperatives. The economics of Malthus and Ricardo generate not merely laws in the sense of models but prescriptive laws, dictating as moral obligations the payment of low wages, sexual abstinence for the poor, and the withholding of relief during famines. It is no wonder that "every human soul" is "terrified."

Once this principle of unified theory is accepted, it becomes logically impossible to admit any exceptions to it without cracking the system; every field of human thought and action must be subsumed. Accordingly, as Urizen ages he exudes a "white woof," literally his long white hair, a sign of "aged venerableness" that entraps both him and all his children in the Abyss. In the form of a "dire Web," it trails out from him like a spider's web, "A living Mantle adjoind to his life & growing from his Soul" (VI 239-46; 73: 27-34 E343). The web is identified later in the poem as the "Direful Web of Religion," a "web of deceitful Religion" (VIII 176,415; 103:26,106:18 E361,367); in *The Book of Urizen* (25:22) it is "The Net of Religion." More generally, it is tradition, the increased power that Urizenic systems gain with the passage of time. Its psychological and perceptual correlatives—the cause-and-effect relation, like much in *The Four Zoas,* is a chicken-and-egg problem—are a further blocking of the passageways to unfallen being. The "eyelids expansive as morning & the Ears / As a golden ascent winding round to the heavens of heavens" are impaired, and though "every one" retains an avenue to Eternity within, all ignore it because they have accepted the external material world as the only reality:

> But they refusd because their outward forms were in the Abyss

And the wing like tent of the Universe beautiful surrounding
    all
Or drawn up or let down at the will of the immortal man
Vibrated in such anguish the eyelids quiverd
Weak & Weaker their expansive orbs began shrinking
Pangs smote thro the brain

                (VI 249-58; 73:37-74:7 E343-44)

As the caption to plate 11 of *The Gates of Paradise* reads, "Perceptive Organs closed their Objects close" (E262, K767). The eyelids of Urizen's entrapped children quiver in sympathy with the anguished vibration of the sky (which would correspond to the eyelids of Albion); the sky is no longer recognizable as a "tent," the friendly and complaisant heaven that accompanies a man wherever he moves (*Milton*, 29:4-18).

As Urizen nears the end of his epic journey, the evidence becomes clearer that his juggernaut progress over everything human and organic is slowing or meeting with resistance. One sign is his age itself, his skin "barkd oer with wrinkles." Caverns beneath his feet, presumably the mines he had earlier undertaken to dig, thrust forth "metal rock & stone" but "in ever painful throes of vegetation" (VI 262-64; 74:11-13 E344), the images of birth and of the organic suggesting again the impossibility of totally suppressing the Luvah-principle. Though Tharmas is still withholding food from Urizen, and though he is "beat with Snows," he is no longer frozen but "rolld his billows in ceaseless eddies" (VI 270-71; 74:19-20 E344). As Urizen makes his final approach to the world of Urthona, after standing like Milton's Satan on a peaked rock from which the "howling of red Orc" can be heard, he meets an open challenge in the form of two of the least prepossessing characters in the poem. Tharmas "stayd his flight," no longer attempting to starve Urizen, and "stood in stern defiance" with the Spectre of Urthona as his comrade-in-arms, now no longer in his humble guise as black-

Night VI

smith's apprentice but as a Goliath armed in what is almost a parody of warlike might:

> Striding across the narrow vale the Shadow of Urthona
> A spectre Vast appeard whose feet & legs with iron scaled
> Stampd the hard rocks expectant of the unknown wanderer
> Whom he had seen wandring his nether world when distant far
> . . . .
> Round his loins a girdle glowd with many colourd fires
> In his hand a knotted Club whose knots like mountains frownd
> Desart among the Stars them withering with its ridges cold
> Black scales of iron arm the dread visage iron spikes instead
> Of hair shoot from his orbed scull.[7]
>
> (VI 290-308; 74:39-75:17 E344-45)

An equally inauspicious sign, one not lost on Urizen, is that the "Squadrons of Urthona" are being commanded by four sons of Urizen himself (VI 314-15; 75:23-24 E345).

The first movement of the *Zoas* has ended in Night III with rapid acceleration and a climactic shattering crash as Urizen fell from his throne, his elegant but briefly sustained version of science irreparably demolished. The second movement ends here in Night VI with retardation, as Urizen is bogged down by weakness and challenged by new enemies. The facile systems of organizing reality that have worked briefly during human adolescence and its historical equivalent in the history of science are now far in the past. Urizen is about to learn the answer to his anxious question in Night II when he anticipated the birth of Orc: "what will become of me?" The salvation of reason, and of science, now that they have destroyed man's capacity to humanize his vision of the world, must depend on an apocalyptic change in reason itself. Further Nights of progressive degeneration will be necessary to bring Urizen to such a point of self-transformation that he will be able to allow Orc and the other Zoas to act in their own way without his restraints.

In preparing the reader for Nights of increased suffering
caused by the degradation of the rational faculty, Blake does
not follow Milton's model, in which "the will / And high
permission of all-ruling Heaven" allow Satan freedom to do
evil so that "with reiterated crimes he might / Heap on
himself damnation" (*Paradise Lost,* I 211-15). Instead, Blake
sets up an ambiguous relation between the divine will and
human perversity, one that seems not to implicate God in
the evil he allowed when he might have intervened. Urizen

> came into the Abhorred world of Dark Urthona
> By Providence divine conducted not bent from his own will
> Lest death Eternal should be the result for the Will cannot
> be violated

> (VI 281-83; 74:30-32 E344)

Left to himself, Urizen would have continued to retrace his
circular path: "Endless had been his travel but the Divine
hand him led" (VI 176; 72:2 E342); the guidance of Providence has assuredly brought him to Urthona's world where
Orc lies bound. But the phrase "not bent from his own will,"
though meaning primarily that not the will of Urizen but that
of Providence has brought him here, has a secondary meaning
indicating Urizen's stubbornness: even Providence cannot
bend him from his will, lest free will be negated. The phrase
"the Will cannot be violated" dangles in ambiguity, referring
simultaneously to the inviolable will of Providence and the
stubborn free will of Urizen. The force of the statement is
different from Milton's in that it shifts responsibility from
a God beyond the skies to something closer to home: an
immanent Providence—which has already been identified
with the divine element within Albion himself—or man's
own willful rational faculty, necessarily subjected to some
kind of self-healing dynamic of compensation and balance
operating for the sake of human survival.

Night VI

The battle between Urizen and his two unlikely antagonists seems to be joined. Not so, however; Urizen draws back to reassess the situation. As at the end of a fourth act in Shakespeare, the warring parties hesitate and ponder on the brink of a climactic decision. This postponement of resolution will continue through the high drama of Night VIIA, until near the end of that Night an imaginative leap takes place, making it possible for man to abandon his deadly habit of competitive thinking and feeling, so that in Night IX the apocalypse is inaugurated and all the depressingly familiar patterns of human behavior are discarded like outgrown, constricting garments. Night VI ends on a note of uncertainty that in the context of the dreary middle of *The Four Zoas* ought to be a relief from the apparent certainty of despair and darkness. That pinprick of uncertainty will let the light of hope into the poem; the experience of that same uncertainty in each individual may allow him to undergo a healing struggle for new life, which is the ultimate goal of this epic. A full-page drawing, a visual reminder of the reawakening of Albion promised in the Council of God scenes in Nights I and IV, separates Night VI from Night VII. The subject is an up-springing androgynous figure, its outspread arms and legs in the pose of *Albion rose* (known also as "Glad Day"), its hair streaming and flamelike, its face solemn but serene. This person must be Albion, with his Zoas and Emanations reconciled and reunited, all participating in the resurrection.

Night VII.

The conclusion of Night VI has left us in suspense; surely, we feel, some revelation is at hand. And indeed it is, but not in any looked-for way. Blake's idea of Night VIIB, generally assumed by critics to be an earlier version of the seventh Night,[1] was to gratify our expectations of full-scale warfare with horrendous rhetoric: a scene of loud flyting by the four major powers, a war song howled by the enormous demons who surround Orc, and a series of alternating cries of brutality and lamentation from Vala as she surveys the debased Orc and the war arena. In Night VIIB the only notes of hope are sounded by Enitharmon in her call for Los to awake the "watchman" (VIIB 94-97; 98:3-6 E394), by Tharmas in his lament for Enion and his denunciation of Vala (VIIB 232-58; 93:42-94:26 E397-98), and by the Daughters of Beulah, who sing comforting songs of faith and patience as they await the fulfillment of Jesus' words at the resurrection of Lazarus, "If ye will believe your Brother shall rise again" (VIIB 293; 95:6 E399).

In Night VIIA, the version we shall discuss simply as Night VII, the tableau of confrontation dissolves; in its place appear two sequential scenes. The first is an exchange of insults between Urizen and Orc. The second shows the final splintering and first reintegration of the Urthona-principle of creativity, as the Shadow of Enitharmon splits off and the other divisions of Urthona begin to reunite. The embrace of Los and the Spectre of Urthona and the cooperative labor of Los and Enitharmon are much stronger movements toward man's regeneration than any event in the earlier version of this Night. The turnabout is so abrupt that Night VII seems divided within itself: its opening scene blends into the closing of Night VI; the right-angled turn in the action appears without warning in the middle of its second scene.[2]

Blake's strategy here is to slip in his resolution through a modulation rather than a sharp break. In Beethoven's Fifth Symphony something similar occurs: a groping bridge passage ushers in the major-tonic-chord motif of the last movement. In Wordsworth's Intimations Ode the idea that life barely endures is lamented in an image of frost in strophe viii but triumphantly celebrated immediately afterwards in the image of embers in strophe ix. This strategy of paradox and modulation is appropriate for Blake's idea that the consolidation of error coincides with the revelation of truth. Even a muddle about the axioms of mathematics can be cleared up by a consolidation of error: a denial that two plus three equals three plus two reveals both what the commutative law of addition is and the impossibility of thinking straight without it. At this moment on the verge of man's recovery, definitions—whether they are right or wrong—clarify something: if right, an idea; if wrong, the position of the speaker. The events of Night VII are attempts at delineation, the defining of relationships and identities. Another purpose of the doubling-and-modulation technique in Night VII is to anticipate, by inversion or by mythical alternatives, the events of Night VIII, so that the same incidents appear in both temporal and eternal contexts.

The best example of both the structural device of anticipatory narration and the theme of redefinition of identity is Orc's reptilian ascent of the Tree of Mystery (vii 135-65; 80: 27-81:6 e349). In Night VII the event has historical and psychological implications; its vehicle, however, is myth, a deeply meaningful fiction presented through Blake's own surreal landscape and dramatis personae. In Night VIII this event will be reduplicated in a context that is more commonly ac-

cessible, in a historical vehicle that brings together recognizable secular or biblical images and episodes, with old and new
social, religious, and psychological implications. The significance of images and incidents in Night VII is changed by
the shift in their context in Night VIII: the body on the
tree, when it is identified in Night VIII with Jesus' incarnation and crucifixion, comes to be associated not with debasement but with heroic self-sacrifice. And the internal division
of Orc into a reptilian and a human form takes on new meaning when it is reenacted in Urizen's metamorphosis into
dragon and stone man (VIII 415-66; 106:18-107:20 E367-68):
the reptilian shape reveals the secret similarity between serpents of the mind and those of the loins, and the motif of
self-division is reflected in the schizophrenic social motivations and influences of the historical period of the Enlightenment as well as in the self-contradictions within eighteenth-
century religious thought.

The enrichment and broadening of Blake's strategy in the
last three Nights of *The Four Zoas,* especially his intensive
use of this technique of clustering contradictory implications
around a single potent image, helps him achieve in the last
Nights a synthesis of nearly all aspects of his thought, about
psychology, history, religion, and society, and their relations
to one another.

The opening phrase of Night VII, "Then Urizen arose,"
repeated from Night VI, establishes the continuity of action
across the formal division between the two Nights. Urizen's
ascent at the end of Night VI is a retreat into his web as well
as an advance upon his enemies. The wheels of Urizen's war
machine are the bobbins that weave the web of his religion;
they are also the elliptical orbits of the comets, a more modern view of astronomy than the stellar circles usually associated with Urizen. In Night VI these intertwined systems of
war, industry, cosmology, and state religion turn red with
gore as they move like an armored tank through the massed

Night VII

troops of Urthona and Tharmas (vi 319-25; 75:28-34 e345).
But this same ascent of Urizen meets no resistance at the
beginning of Night VII. The instinctive Tharmas, appalled,
is driven away, and one aspect of the imaginative powers,
the Spectre of Urthona, goes into hiding. Now, true to the
wheellike pattern, the ascent becomes a descent; Urizen enters the caves of Orc at last to find the source of the pulsations that in Night V he had set out to locate. Instead of a
battle scene there is a debate, of titanic proportions (viii 44-
150; 78:17-80:42 e346-49).

This dialogue between closed-mindedness and unthinking
rebelliousness—between age and youth, fascism and anarchy,
superego and libido, visiting bureaucrat and jailed hood-
lum—is a display of antagonism for its own sake. Though it
settles nothing in the plot, it affords exhilarating emotional
relief to readers, who recognize primordial forces in the
psyche as they act in familiar personality types. Yet the
emotional relief of the reader can be a form of self-deception.
Anyone at all in sympathy with Blake's conviction that all
act is virtue, as it appears throughout the body of his work,
will be drawn to side with Orc—partly because he is chained
and the underdog, partly because all of us live in social
worlds and most of us in personal worlds where our Urizenic
tendencies are given more scope than our Orckian ones,
which therefore cry out for at least rhetorical relief. At this
point we should remember what the poem tells us in its
opening lines: that both Luvah and Urizen, as well as the
other two Zoas, are present in every man. It is impossible
to feel superior to Urizen once we admit our complicity in
instances of exactly the same envious and cruel derision of
our own impulses—every time we make ourselves feel foolish
or guilty, or force ourselves into compliance with social or
personal regimentation, out of fear of being considered irresponsible by level-headed onlookers. Conversely, if the
Orc within each of us is to admit its identity with Blake's

Orc, it must recognize the flaws Blake builds into his rebel's counteroffensive against Urizen.

In this confrontation the ironic parallels-by-contrast we have been observing in earlier parts of the poem are brought clearly to the fore. Simple contrasts are immediately apparent: for example, Urizen's hypocrisy (his claim that his visit is motivated by pity, despite evidence of his self-centered purpose) against Orc's shrill outspokenness ("Curse thy hoary brows. What dost thou in this deep / Thy Pity I contemn scatter thy snows elsewhere"). But various ironies mitigate the contrasts and remind us once more of the kinship between the antagonists. For example, the energetic Orc has been immobile since puberty while rigid Urizen has just finished an arduous and far-ranging journey of exploration. Orc's cavern is populated not only with Luvah's bulls but with lions, tigers, and the horses that Luvah had seized from Urizen (or won by persuasion or received as gifts or bargained for, depending on whether one believes Enitharmon, Ahania, Tharmas, Urizen, or the narrator), yet Urizen sees "No other living thing / In all this Chasm" (vii 6-17,45-46; 77:6-17,78:18-19 E346). Each asserts that the other is enslaved but is enjoying his enslavement. The organic chain of Jealousy which binds Orc is nearly identical to Urizen's entwining Tree of Mystery. Even the antagonists' rhetoric, despite the contrasts in the substance of their speeches, can be strikingly similar:

Urizen:

> Above a Shower of fire now beats
> Moulded to globes & arrowy wedges rending thy
>   bleeding limbs
> And now a whirling pillar of burning sands to
>   overwhelm thee
> Steeping thy wounds in salts infernal & in bitter anguish
> And now a rock moves on the surface of this lake of fire
> To bear thee down beneath the waves in stifling despair
>
> (VII 51-56; 78:24-29 E347)

Night VII

Orc:

> Anon a cloud filld with a waste of snows
> Covers thee still obdurate still resolvd & writing still
> Tho rocks roll oer thee tho floods pour tho winds black
>   as the Sea
> Cut thee in gashes tho the blood pours down around
>   thy ankles
> Freezing thy feet to the hard rock
>
> (VII 81-85; 79:11-15 E347)

Urizen:

> Yet thou dost laugh at all these tortures & this horrible place
> Yet throw thy limbs these fires abroad that back return
>   upon thee
> While thou reposest throwing rage on rage feeding thyself
> With visions of sweet bliss far other than this burning clime
> Sure thou art bathd in rivers of delight
>
> (VII 59-63; 78:32-36 E347)

Orc:

> Why shouldst thou sit cold grovelling demon of woe
> In tortures of dire coldness now a Lake of waters deep
> Sweeps over thee freezing to solid still thou sitst closd up
> In that transparent rock as if in joy of thy bright prison
>
> (VII 73-76; 79:3-6 E347)

The drama of this confrontation is heightened by its elements of sheer comedy of a uniquely Blakean sort. Blake's intensity, his tone of contempt, hostility, or outrage, obscures his mastery of a wide range of comic modes: the puckish humor of the scene with the Fairy, which appears as plate iii in some copies of *Europe*; the sardonic intellectual humor in the same poem when the angelic hosts fall from the skies directly Newton sounds his trump and thus presumably invents the law of universal gravitation (*Europe*, 13:4-8) ; the subtle raillery of Satan's impeachment as a mere dunce in the Epilogue to *For the Sexes: The Gates of Paradise* (E266, K771) —atypical because the hostility is muted by the mildly sarcastic tone; the boisterously scatological attack on Klopstock from Blake's outhouse (ε491-92, κ186-87). The drollery and whimsy of *An Island in the Moon* are less common in Blake than the pure, unrelieved, blunt invective of the Notebook epigrams, in which the humor—what there is— is savage, bitter, and even crude. The comedy here in *The Four Zoas* is cosmic, almost Olympian. The closest analogue in Blake's other works is the scene between the speaker and the angel in *The Marriage of Heaven and Hell,* plates 17-20, another passage that might be played on stage or in Bloom's visionary cinema; when each shows the other his eternal lot, our sympathies are with Hell but we conclude that the two "impose on one another." The difference between Olympian humor and the comedy in Night VII is that Blake's humor is filled with sadness and desperate impatience and his tragicomic message is that we lack the perspective to recognize that all such mutual recriminations by head and heart are as pointless as the taunts of children. As Orc begins his vermicular ascent of the Tree of Mystery and identifies himself as Luvah, he asks bitterly, "[I]s this the triumph this the Godlike State / That lies beyond the bounds of Science in the Grey obscure" (νιι 149-50; 80:41-42 ε349). Urizen is less enlightened; he is still aiming at total dictatorship, but we readers are given to understand that the complicated machinations of the conspiracy between Luvah and Urizen in Eternity, their efforts to become more than human by usurping the whole, were acts of sheer and profitless insanity.

This permeating mood of tragicomedy erupts into brilliantly theatrical moments in which the narrative reads like stage directions, as in Urizen's gingerly retreat before the encroachments of the Tree of Mystery and his fussy assumption of a new position, bastioned by his books, like a Victorian old maid moving her beach chair away from the advancing tide. A grimmer aspect of the humor is Urizen's amazement

at the sprouting of the tree (VII 36-41; 78:9-14 E346) ; he is
unaware that it arises wherever his snows fall on Orc's fires.
Each character is in his element but is horrified at the flames
or ice of the other. Orc marvels that "thou dost fixd obdurate
brooding sit / Writing thy books. Anon a cloud filld with
a waste of snows / Covers thee still obdurate still resolvd &
writing still," but he is too exasperated to catch the sad absurdity of Urizen's posture. Urizen's obtuse response to
Orc's insults, his notion of how to deal with a revolutionary,
is to give him a reading list on revolutionary theory: "Read
my books explore my Constellations / Enquire of my Sons &
they shall teach thee how to War" (VII 90-91; 79:20-21 E348) .

Under the pretense of lecturing his daughters—a lecture
read sonorously from the Book of Brass—Urizen tries to inti-
midate Orc with his lesson of satanic sociology, the social
philosophy of Bounderby (VII 109-34; 80:1-26 E348-49) .
The strategy is to destroy the integrity of the poor and wreck
the victim's self-definition—thus, more broadly speaking, to
quench the spirit of threatened revolution by depriving it
of its rationale in poverty and social injustice. The technique is to make the victim feel guilty over the very sufferings imposed on him and grateful for crumbs of charitable
relief: "[R]educe the man to want a gift & then give with
pomp"; "Preach temperance say he is overgorgd & drowns
his wit / In strong drink tho you know that bread & water
are all / He can afford." Fill his mind with the spirit of
capitalism so that he will think his poverty is his own fault;
then kill his spirit with hypocritical and condescending kind-
ness. This despicable counsel is a prime example of Blake's
broadening of the scope of his poem in these later Nights beyond the personal to the social, though the incident can still
be understood psychologically: reason is sowing the kind
of doubt, or "self-contempt," as Shelley will call it, that
paralyzes and neutralizes honest indignation, making us feel
that in indulging it we are going too far. The character Mer-

cury in *Prometheus Unbound* is exactly such a "self-despising slave."

These expressions of class hatred continually reveal a perverse mutual attraction, the fallen form of original brotherhood between the two. Urizen envies Orc his youth, the delightful fantasies that feed his torments, and his unbroken spirit; Orc responds despite himself to Urizen's apparent sagacity. Fearing and scorning everything Orc is, Urizen nevertheless tries to justify himself to his enemy and to use, control, and subvert the inevitable outbreak of Orc's energy. Contemptuous of Urizen's fascination, Orc nevertheless takes the trouble to itemize his enemy's intellectual errors, all the while enacting the part of the anarchist who threatens to assert control even if it means destroying his own territory. The Enlightenment kindles the heat of impending revolution—as in the striking image of the oil spilled from the lamps of mercy which now burns the adamantine scales of justice (VII 10-12; 77:10-12 E346); or, according to Orc, "I well remember how I stole thy light & it became fire / Consuming" (VII 147-48; 80:39-40 E349). Instead of bringing warmth to the proceedings of law, the spirit of compassion overflows in a burning torrent and the plow and harrow of intellectual advancement are mired in the blood of class warfare. Even as he threatens rebellion, Orc comes to hunger for the bread of sorrow kneaded by Urizen's daughters, the water spirits of cloud, fountain, and river encountered in Night VI, who are now hoar frost, torrent rain, and ice (VII 95-107; 79:25-37 E348). Free-flowing intelligence turns ever more chill and inhuman.

Perhaps more cruel than the attack on Orc's class, and more effective in arousing self-doubt, is Urizen's reminder to Orc of his origin as the child of Los and Enitharmon. It was they, after all, who had jealously chained him as a way of dealing with the Oedipal situation; only after ages of frustration has Orc arrived at the point of being able to sublimate

Night VII

his love for his mother as passionate worship at her "shrine" (VII 22; 77:22 E346). As a coda to the lecture from the Book of Brass, Urizen abruptly introduces the subject of Enitharmon's pregnancy:

> Lo how the heart & brain are formed in the breeding womb
> Of Enitharmon how it buds with life & forms the bones
> The little heart the liver & the red blood in its labyrinths
> By gratified desire by strong devouring appetite she fills
> Los with ambitious fury that his race shall all devour.
>
> (VII 130-34; 80:22-26 E348-49)

This non sequitur serves two of Urizen's purposes. It implies that the ultimate drive behind the revolutionary program is psychosexual, the result of Orc's problems in infancy and early childhood when he was a pawn in the power games of his parents. It also allows Urizen to probe Orc's primal identity, to find out whether Orc is the fulfillment of Urizen's own fearful prophecy that Luvah would become "in the loins of Los a dark & furious death." In that case Urizen needs to learn the answer to his old question "what will become of me at that dread time?"

Orc manages to utter a final curse as he begins to separate into two beings, a weakened worm that is Urizen's image of a revolution rendered harmless, and a chained man that is Orc's remaining idea of himself as a human victim of oppression (VII 135-65; 80:27-81:6 E349). Urizen has succeeded in dehumanizing the sexual, revolutionary, and demonic forces in Orc and separating them from righteous indignation, constructive wrath, humanly understandable outrage and violence. He has acted just in time; Orc's struggles against his fetters had strengthened him and developed his aspirations so that he was almost at the point of rending his manacles. But Urizen is not really at ease; he is terrified at Orc's claim that he is Luvah and envious that this serpent can "Flame high in pride & laugh to scorn the source of his deceit."

Urizen is unaware that he is himself deceived in his belief that "weakness stretches out in breadth & length" (VII 138-61; 80:30-81:2 E349) and that Orc is therefore not dangerous in his form as a worm. But this worm soon organizes itself a serpent body and ascends the Tree of Mystery, for in Blake the effect of "morality," what Urizen's lecture calls "Moral Duty," is to instill both individually and socially not only piety but a consequently exacerbated resentment. To debase the energies of healthy human desire and anger is to arouse a correspondent revolutionary desperation.

Orc as the serpent is the erroneous identification of energy with evil that has been perpetrated in so much of religious orthodoxy. Orc as the worm is the "Creeping Jesus" whose image Blake attacks as early as *The Marriage of Heaven and Hell* (plates 23–24) and as late as *The Everlasting Gospel* (line 59, E511, K752); he is not Jesus the scourger of money-changers in the temple, who came not to send peace but a sword (Matt. 10:34). Orc's other aspect, the angry young man whose struggles merely tighten his bondage, is, for Blake, the inevitable companion of excessive piety: he is all the victims of all the physical and psychological tortures of religion—all the blood shed in the Christian centuries by all who practice Blake's Druidism in inquisitions, crusades, witch-burnings, and pogroms.

Orc is not simply a victim, however. Paradoxically, as Frye implies in his account of the "Orc cycle," the zeal of the martyr and rebel provides the energy for acts of persecution and repression, abominations that conceal beneath humble piety a Dionysian blood lust. There are countless illustrations, historical and symbolic, great and trivial: the spiritual progeny of saints slaughtered in the Collosseum were the inquisitors and the Puritans who destroyed new rebels; wars (even bullfights and violent sports of all kinds) are regularly accompanied by prayers of petition and dedication. A corollary of this principle is that both the energetic resistance of the victim and evidences of his vulnerability goad the repressor to redouble his efforts, in accord with the motivations attributed by Shelley to the God of *Paradise Lost.*

Both the image of Orc struggling against his tightening fetters and the image of him as a worm illuminate contemporary analyses of the French Revolution: to English liberals its excesses were the inevitable reactions of a people whose humanity had been brutalized for centuries; to conservatives the threat to order demanded and justified so effective a repression of mild dissent that a first step toward reform in England was delayed for nearly two generations.

Urizen is unaware of the profound ambiguity of the image of the serpent wound round the tree:

> He knew that weakness stretches out in breadth & length he
> knew
> That wisdom reaches high & deep & therefore he made Orc
> In Serpent form compelld stretch out & up the mysterious tree
> He sufferd him to Climb that he might draw all human forms
> Into submission to his will nor knew the dread result.
> (VII 161-65; 81:2-6 E349)

But Christian typology has always recognized the connection between the serpent of Eden and the crucified Christ, a clear example of the way its mythical understanding runs deeper than doctrinal purpose. In John 3:14 Christ chose Moses' brazen serpent as his own emblem. In John 12:32 he used language that Blake echoes in the passage just quoted: "And I, if I be lifted up from the earth, will draw all men unto me." On the cross Jesus quoted the first line of Psalm 22, which a few verses later reads, "But I am a worm, and no man; a reproach of men, and despised of the people." This typology asserts both the doctrine that Jesus reversed the damage done in Eden and the mythical insight that he and the serpent are parallel countertypes: "that whence death came, thence also life might arise again, and that he, who

overcame by the tree, by the tree also might be overcome"
(Preface of the Cross in the Roman Catholic liturgy) .

In the mythical, not the doctrinal, image of Jesus as serpent, Jesus abolishes all forms of Orckian sacrifice made
to any manifestation of the Urizenic accusation of sin. Jesus
is not a Redeemer—in the etymological sense of buying back—
but a Savior; he is not suprahumanity taking on the burden
of sin through a specious human disguise, but full and true
humanity freeing fallen man from enslavement to the guilt
and self-contempt implied in the conventional notion of sin
as the violation of some transempyrean code. Instead of pay-
ing for sin, he "put it off on the Cross," as Blake says in
Milton 5:3, and died "that through death he might destroy
him that had the power of death, that is, the devil; and deliver them who through fear of death were all their lifetime
subject to bondage" (Heb. 2:14-15). In some of Blake's paintings of the Crucifixion, a single nail pierces Christ's feet
and the serpent's head, and the satiric epigram beginning
"Nail his neck to the Cross" (E509, K557) plays upon the
same image, as does the passage in *The Everlasting Gospel*
beginning "And thus with wrath he did subdue / The Serpent Bulk of Natures dross / Till he had naild it to the
Cross" (lines 52-54, E515, K749) .

This saving act, this liberation of men from guilt and the
fear of death, is what Jesus as Luvah will perform in Night
VIII. The parodic prototype of Luvah as the serpentine Orc
is a dramatically and psychologically necessary preparation
for the full magnitude of the later episode. For Urizen, however, there is only ignorance of the "dread result" (VII 165;
81:6 E349) . Blake's laconic phrase here is one of his triumphs
of irony and of densely compressed meaning; though the
result will indeed be dread for the satanic form of Urizen, it
will be ultimately an occasion of joy for the whole human
being, including what is best in Urizen himself.

The remainder of Night VII is devoted to the vicissitudes

of the multiform human imagination in the splintered consciousness of Urthona, with Los as the central character.
He has been present all along at the very edge of the scene
between Urizen and the young rebel. Having shared the
pains of Urizen since the end of Night IV, Los "felt the Envy
in his limbs like to a blighted tree" as Urizen "fixed in Envy
sat brooding" over Orc. Urizen's Tree of Mystery has
branched "into the heaven of Los" (VII 19-33; 77:19-78:6
E346), and after Orc's ascent Los sits "in showers of Urizen
watching cold Enitharmon," his gloomy thoughts hatching
as eggs (like Urizen's "Eggs of unnatural production" in *The
Book of Ahania,* 3:10), while Enitharmon's Shadow is drawn
down the tree to weep over Orc (VII 166-71; 81:7-12 E349).
Clearly, the first part of the plan that Urizen had confided to
his daughters has already succeeded: "To bring the shadow
of Enitharmon beneath our wondrous tree"; now the question for Urizen is whether the second part will work out:
"That Los may Evaporate like smoke & be no more" and the
Spectre of Urthona "have dominion over Los the terrible
shade" (VII 113-16; 80:5-8 E348). As with the opening dialogue between Urizen and Orc, the scene now beginning
between Enitharmon's Shadow and the Spectre is dominated
by the Tree of Mystery; Los's soliloquies are spoken in his
"heaven," off to one side or just above the main action.

With this triangle, Blake returns to his persistent theme
of the torments of love and jealousy. The great lyric lament
of Los over Enitharmon (VII 184-208; 81:23-82:14 E350) emphasizes that she is summery and delectable in his absence but
wintry and forbidding in his presence, when her "Shadow"
or "spirit" (VII 173-75; 81:14-16 E349-50) is off on elusive
wanderings. The seasonal imagery makes clear how utterly
out of phase the lovers are; as with Shelley's "desire of the
night for the morrow," Enitharmon's elusiveness intensifies
Los's longing, while his approach sickens her soul until she
is hardly more than a corpse. To Los, she is unresponsive

and withdrawn; to the Spectre, she is hostile and secretive until she is petted, pitied, and wooed (vii 217-36; 82:23-83:4 E350-51).

All this recalls suspiciously the fickle side of Enitharmon that one thought she had outgrown in Night V—especially after we have read that "Los sat in showers of Urizen watching cold Enitharmon"; even after the embrace she shares with Los and the Spectre, "Enitharmon trembling fled & hid beneath Urizens tree" (vii 372; 87:1 E354). It is sometimes conjectured that Night VII not only describes a critical conversion for humankind but also reflects a breakthrough for Blake the author. The conjecture could be supported by Blake's having written but then deleted the emphatic lines "She Secret joyd to see She fed herself on his Despair / She said I am avengd for all my sufferings of old" (vii 177-78; E755). The speaker of those lines would indeed have been the old Enitharmon. But Blake changed his view of her, choosing instead to see Enitharmon as a victim herself, however tantalizing she may appear from Los's lovesick point of view. She no longer flirts with Urizen; rather, she needs to be redeemed from the Urizenic—a trait in her that Blake tends to dramatize as a kind of status seeking.

Enitharmon in her worst days had behaved toward Los like a haughty belle who had married beneath her; despite the lesson in resignation to her unglamorous lot that she had learned in Night V, she has still not learned to love her husband in either of his essential roles, as creative artist or as craftsman—which is to say that the human imagination has not yet been wholly and healthily energized as a force in harmony with itself. Just as Los will be liberated only by acknowledging the Spectre in himself, the side of himself that serves rather than rules man and is in touch with the darker realities, so Enitharmon too must learn to love the lower side of Los before she can love him at his ultimate best. She too, then, must be tried, by having her best side separated from her worst. Blake allegorizes her trial by introducing a persona whom he calls her Shadow.

Although Los, the Spectre, and Enitharmon are really aspects of the primal Urthona, so long as they conceive of themselves as separate beings they appear as independent characters in the plot. The problematical figure called the Shadow of Enitharmon, however, is not the nonce character she might seem to be, created to play a key role at the threshold of the poem's crisis and then eliminated; rather the Shadow is the familiar Enitharmon as she behaves in certain moods, a manifestation of that element in the female personality that is attracted to selfishness and deadness in the male and repelled by his vitality. The Shadow is the female response to one particular trait of Urthona's Spectre, but she is not a complete counterpart to him nor a fully developed independent character. The specific affinity between the Shadow and the Spectre is seen in their immediately juxtaposed accounts of the fall (VII 236-95; 83:4-84:29 E351-52), significantly introduced as a prelude to the mating scene wherein the "spirit of Enitharmon" fervently embraces the Spectre, "Her once lovd Lord now but a Shade herself also a shade" (VII 311-13; 85:1-3 E353). What the Shadow and the Spectre share, and reveal in their twin accounts of the fall, is an especially acute sense of sexual jealousy and possessiveness coupled with ambivalent obsession-revulsion toward the natural, material world.

There is a parallel between the Shadow's fascination with and envious hatred of Vala as sexual Amazon and the Spectre's sexual rivalry with "that demon Los." Enitharmon's obsession with sexual morality will lead later in Night VII to her Eve-like terror at the approach of the Lamb of God. Here the sexual strife, frustration, and the explicitly sexual reenactment of the fall in Genesis, in addition to the sexual torments of Los, are Blake's development of his mentor Milton's insight in attributing to the newly fallen Adam

and Eve a combination of resentment, lust, and suffering.
(In *Milton* Blake pursues this insight much further by defining the task of Milton's eternal salvation in terms, bio-
graphically, of the six women in his life.) This kind of
psychology has been at work since the beginning of Night I,
when the quarrel and mating of Tharmas and Enion produced the fallen forms of Los and Enitharmon. Now, as
error is consolidated, the most deeply fallen aspects of Urthona and Enitharmon copulate and give birth to the most
dreadful manifestation of Vala in the whole poem, the "wonder horrible" or Shadowy Female whose appearance releases
the full threat of male specterism:

> a Cloud she grew & grew
> Till many of the dead burst forth from the bottoms of their
>   tombs
> In male forms without female counterparts or Emanations
> Cruel and ravening with Enmity & Hatred & War
> In dreams of Ulro dark delusive drawn by the lovely shadow.
> (VII 327-31; 85:17-21 E353)

The moment of the Shadowy Female's birth coincides with
the moment of the astonishing fraternal embrace of Los and
the Spectre of Urthona and the consequent reconciliation of
the two with Enitharmon; yet Blake's only grammatical, temporal, and logical transition between these moments is "But
then." As virtually all students of Blake recognize, this embrace is the crisis of the poem. But some see no reason why
it should occur and regard this apparently arbitrary triumph
of loving forgiveness as a structural or psychological weakness in the work. Does the suddenness of reversal reflect a
mysterious, unfathered conversion of the man Blake, as some
critics have surmised? Or is Blake saying that, however inexplicable they may seem, such apparently unconditioned
recoveries do happen and must happen, through the agency

of imagination, a going out of ourselves into other human beings?

Events and characterizations introduced earlier in the poem, especially in Night IV and earlier in Night VII, seemingly without significance for man's recovery, turn out to have contributed to this surprising break in the pattern of further and further fragmentation. Blake's characterization of the Spectre, who even in Night IV could not be dismissed as an absolute fool or knave, is perhaps the most subtle and interesting. Despite his repellent attributes, he reveals even as he seduces Enitharmon a spiritual and psychological perceptiveness not yet possible for her. It is as if the selfish impediment to creativity is coming to realize that it cannot be overcome by mere repression, enslavement to Los. The obstacle the Spectre represents—the artist's block—must be acknowledged and dealt with honestly, as he insists to Los in the very act of embracing him (vii 336-51; 85:26-39 e353). Although his boast to Enitharmon that he is the creator and superior of Los is unfounded, his memories of the unity and happiness of Eternity are genuine, and he can see the hope of and necessity for the reunion with their Emanations of Tharmas, Luvah, and himself as Urthona. He deplores his own spectrous condition, knowing that spectres as such are insane, brutish, and deformed, and he interprets his longing for Enitharmon as evidence that he is a spectre of the living rather than of the dead (vii 269-310; 84:3-40 e352). Regeneration, he sees, is possible for him because he has a living counterpart, which the spectres of the dead lack. After he is accepted by Los, his sense of responsibility for the creation of spectres, those released by his begetting of the Shadowy Female, is the basis of his urging Los to give form and beauty to these pitiful shapeless abstractions (vii 401-10; 87:30-39 e355); this suggestion inaugurates a great cultural renaissance, a new kind of redemptive artistic activity. Even his terror at Vala's new appearance (vii 332; 85:22 e353) is evidence of his special insight, an insight that can deepen art rather than block it, a recognition of evil and deadness that need not break an artist but can help him become more mature.

One of the most suggestive of the Spectre's ideas is his view of the Tree of Mystery as something "given us for a Shelter from the tempests of Void & Solid / Till once again the morn of ages shall renew upon us" (vii 268-69; 84:2-3 e352). This statement seems a radical distortion of the truth, but it comes very close to the Christian interpretation of the old dispensation, the Law, as a divinely appointed stopgap; indeed in Night VIII the Lamb of God, assuming Luvah's robes of blood, will transfigure the image of the crucifixion on the Tree of Mystery. Here in Night VII the very ascendancy of the tree over both passion and imagination, the very urgency and clarity of the sense of sin however falsely defined, builds up a pressure for imminent liberation. Despair over evil and guilt can be healthy if it awakens an acute and agonizing need for an utterly new state of existence. After the Spectre puts Vala in charge of Orc in the lower world, the topmost branch of the tree sprouts to form roots of the same tree in the upper, conscious, world of Los (vii 332-35; 85:22-25 e353), making the influence of evil and mystery recognizable now on all levels of the human imagination.

When the serpent-wound tree, with its outrageously false Urizenic identification of energy with evil, overshadows Los and he joins Enitharmon in eating its fruit, he too falls into the moral system (vii 395; 87:24 e355); he then experiences a psychic suffocation and a wasteful sense of guilt so terrible that they can only be remedied by a clean break, a free existential act like that of Shelley's Prometheus. On the dramatic level this new direction is possible because Los and Enitharmon have lived and suffered enough to have become different persons; in grief and sorrow they have found a depth of humanity capable of reconciliation and forgiveness. From no other fallen faculty can this act arise; it is truly an imaginative leap. Yet the act is precipitated by the eating of the fruit—through "self accusation" and "Self conviction," through the couple's imposition on themselves of an unbearable burden of guilt and of a false but uncompromising morality, through a despair that would lead to "death Eternal" but for the Spectre's role as comforter and mediator between Los and Enitharmon (vii 385-98; 87:14-27 E354-55). A passage from Hermann Hesse helps clarify Blake's thinking here: "The way to innocence, to the uncreated and to God leads on, not back, not back to the wolf or to the child, but ever further into sin, ever deeper into human life."[3]

Undeniably, though, Blake leaves an area of disjunction between despair and recovery, something not spelled out for us. Far from being a flaw in *The Four Zoas,* this gap reflects Blake's honesty and acumen. If the conversion were totally explainable, the training of psychiatrists could be much abbreviated and all mental illness, perhaps even all social problems related to it, could be cured in one and the same way. Blake's wisdom in leaving this hiatus of explanation is confirmed in other great works that explore the spiritual dark night and recovery from it. The reversal in *Prometheus Unbound* arises from the hero's free, imaginative act of loving forgiveness, but the agency of regeneration is embodied in the enigmatic Demogorgon, who is a personified question mark, the "somehow" in statements like "Somehow we survived." The same arbitrariness of recovery occurs with Wordsworth in *The Prelude* and with the Red Cross Knight in Book I of *The Faerie Queene*; after the protagonists are reduced to something near despair they are rescued through a form of grace, something they cannot fully understand or explain.

Blake takes us further than either Wordsworth or Spenser into the psychology of recovery, regeneration, renewal, but like them he presents only the *experience* of grace, not a formula for obtaining it. If a formula were possible, the concept of grace would not be necessary in theology nor the metaphor of the breakthrough in psychology (or in the physical sciences, for that matter). It happens or it does not happen; if it happens at all, it happens in the midst of despair, because of and in spite of an intolerable sense of sin and need. Blake does not anatomize the moment of relief and reconciliation itself; he concentrates in the remainder of Night VII—and on through the rest of the poem— on the renewal of life as it flows out from that moment.

The surge of new life takes the form of creative activity. The benefits to human nature and to art are reciprocal. Man's spiritual sickness is treated by therapeutic art. At the same time this sickness provides new subjects for a deeper, more troubled, and more complex artistic vision; the pressure of these new and disturbing subjects—shadows from the inner life rather than reflections of the outer world—brings new art forms into being. All this is presented in the new relationship between Los, the Spectre, and Enitharmon. In the unwilling drudgery of their collaboration in Night IV, they had rebuilt the fallen mental and physical world; art in Night IV is the mirror held up to nature as the fallen imagination sees the world once more and organizes its outer forms according to concepts of time and space. But in Night VII the collaboration of the Spectre and Los is willing and mutual, and Enitharmon—though fearful—is cooperative. Instead of working as artisan and apprentice to build a body for Urizen as in Night IV, Los and his Spectre join to build in the "nether heavens" a new and separate world for art, the city of Golgonooza, still built within the merciful limits of Satan and Adam, Opacity and Contraction, discovered in Night IV (vii 379-83; 87:8-12 E354).

In the blended consciousness of Los and his Spectre is "a

Night VII

World within / Opening its gates & in it all the real sub-
stances / Of which these in the outward World are shadows
which pass away" (VII 364-66; 86:7-9 E354). Although the
Spectre's claim to Los, "I am thy real Self," is untrue as a
bald, isolated statement, it is effective as a means of forcing
Los to act on his moment of self-recognition. After his impulsive embrace of the Spectre "first as a brother / Then
as another Self; astonishd humanizing & in tears," Los is
forced to listen to the insistent voice of his repressed negative
and sinister personality:

> I am thy real Self
> Tho thus divided from thee & the Slave of Every passion
> Of thy fierce Soul Unbar the Gates of Memory look upon me
> Not as another but as thy real Self I am thy Spectre
> Tho horrible & Ghastly to thine Eyes tho buried beneath
> The ruins of the Universe.
> (VII 339-52; 85:29-40 E353)

When a new world opens within and Los again embraces
the Spectre as well as Enitharmon, the Spectre also "Wondering beheld the Centre opend by Divine Mercy inspired /
He in his turn Gave Tasks to Los" (VII 374-75; 87:3-4 E354).
The Spectre's claim that he is Los's self is a demand that
Los acknowledge his errors; this claim on Los is entirely
different from Urizen's reductive blasphemy in Night I, the
insistence that "The Spectre is the Man the rest is only
delusion & fancy" (I 341; 12:29 E303). Los directs the continued building of Golgonooza, where "beneath / Was
opend new heavens & a new Earth beneath & within," but
it is the Spectre who proposes the new direction for art, the
creation of forms for man's shadowy hopes, fears, negative
thoughts, desires, failures of nerve, frustrations: "Let us
Create them Counterparts / For without a Created body the
Spectre is Eternal Death" (VII 409-10; 87:38-39 E355).
The Spectre has found his place as a part of the whole

mature artistic consciousness—a dark vision of emptiness and longing, an intimate knowledge of passion, guilt, and sin, the negative and doubting shadow of idealism, which annihilates the ideal if it is disowned and denied but strengthens it if honestly admitted. From Los's acceptance of his Spectre comes the power of Romantic and modern art, which admits its own vulnerability and thus speaks to man's doubts as well as his faith. Acceptance of the Spectre allows Wordsworth apparently to undercut his most affirmative statements with such remarks as "If this be but a vain belief." Just as the artist's admission of his difficulties and his incorporation of negative possibilities into his work may serve to enrich and enliven his efforts, so an acceptance of doubt can strengthen any activity of the human imagination. Thus in the last two stanzas of the Intimations Ode, Wordsworth can affirm the thoughts too deep for tears because he no longer shuts out the dark truths avoided in strophes iii and iv.

Once the Spectre's vision is blended with Los's own and the Spectre no longer serves merely as an apprentice-slave, Los is free to share his creative work with his spouse (vII 439-75; 90:8-43 E356). Their complementary activity in art gives rise to a new intimacy in their male–female relationship. The Enitharmon who calls Los "wonder of Eternity," her "defence & guide," and says, "Thy works are all my joy. & in thy fires my soul delights" does not sound like the same person who evaded her husband's sexual advances or even the one who tearfully and bitterly accepted the shadowy embrace of the Spectre. Alluding broadly to his own graphic art, Blake has Los create celestial murals, with Enitharmon as the colorist. Her bosom is now translucent, not opaque, and her broken heart becomes another open center like that opened within Los by the Spectre (vII 413,437; 87:42,90:6 E355,356). These open centers within contrast with the confining circumferences of the Circle of Destiny in Night I and the various circles Urizen has drawn Night after Night.

Deriving from his own Spectre the idea of forming counterparts for all spectres, Los confides to Enitharmon his "Stern desire / . . . to fabricate embodied semblances in which the dead /May live"; Enitharmon responds that she sighs forth vanishing forms from her bosom, for whom Los should "fabricate forms sublime / Such as the piteous spectres may assimilate themselves into." Symbolically, she is the artist's inspiration; dramatically, she is his helpmeet and best influence. Heeding her plea for "sweet moderated fury," Los, "his hands divine inspired began / To modulate his fires." No longer the dogged blacksmith imposing his will on his Spectre, his Emanation, his material, his technique, and his form, he becomes the genius whom the very elements gladly obey. His flames are "delighted" and the weeping spectres willingly "Assimilating to those forms" become young and lovely.

It is particularly significant that these delightful forms are drawn on the "walls of shining heaven" and are colored "with beams of blushing love." Throughout *The Four Zoas* the sky has been a test of man's ability to humanize his vision. In some respects the sky is the most indefinite thing we are able to think of. To give it definite and humanized form is a supreme triumph for the imagination, whether in specific works of art like poems, paintings, symphonies, or simply in any instance of imaginative vision —as in Blake's famous claim that he once walked to the horizon and touched the sky with his walking stick. In the world of vision shared by artists and imaginative people generally, the sky is nearer than the "dividing and indifferent blue" of Stevens's *Sunday Morning*. The closed dome of the Mundane Shell that Los had built in Night IV is now a backdrop for new forms of art dealing with what goes on inside the dome of the human skull.

Troubled by the sense of sin, Los, the Spectre, and Enitharmon have felt the need for redemption and have planned to use their artistic creations as sacrificial offerings, ransoms for their sins. But the center opened in Enitharmon's broken

heart affords Los a brief glimpse of the possibility of mental
sacrifice, self-annihilation, mutual forgiveness of each vice,
the spirit of Jesus:

> Turn inwardly thine Eyes & there behold the Lamb of God
> Clothed in Luvahs robes of blood descending to redeem
> O Spectre of Urthona take comfort O Enitharmon
> Couldst thou but cease from terror & trembling & affright
> When I appear before thee in forgiveness of ancient injuries
> Why shouldst thou remember & be afraid. I surely have died
>   in pain
> Often enough to convince thy jealousy & fear & terror
> Come hither be patient let us converse together because
> I also tremble at myself & at all my former life.
>
> > (VII 415-23; 87:44-52 E355)

Although Enitharmon resists this vision and persists in seeing
Jesus as punisher, Los has introduced into the poem the spirit
of self-sacrifice and mutual forgiveness that Blake says opens
the gates of Paradise. In his appearance before Enitharmon
"in forgiveness of ancient injuries" Los is an embodiment
of Jesus; in having "died in pain / Often enough to con-
vince thy jealousy & fear & terror" he has enacted what is
meaningful in Jesus' death, the loving gesture of self-annihilation. If this husband and wife could forgive each other,
they would not need a Redeemer, nor would they need to
sacrifice their mutual creations, their children, to an imagined accuser. No more is said in Night VII about Los's
vision of Jesus, but when the moment of sacrifice comes

> Los loved them & refusd to Sacrifice their infant limbs
> And Enitharmons smiles & tears prevaild over self protection
> They rather chose to meet Eternal death than to destroy
> The offspring of their Care & Pity Urthonas spectre was
>   comforted.
>
> > (VII 482-85; 90:50-53 E357)

Night VII

The imaginative act of creating form, of embodying these ghostly negative ideas, has taught Los and Enitharmon how to sacrifice themselves, not their "offspring." No longer are they the selfish parents who sacrificed Orc to their own jealousies in Night V. Through their artistic endeavors they have given living form to the deadly aggressions that fuel the Urizenic wars; they have become able to see their enemies, Urizen and his eldest son Thiriel, as their own children, Rintrah and Palamabron (vii 476-94; 90:44-62 e356-57). The possibility of a reconciliation with Orc is suggested; art reaches even the natural man, according to Bloom's Commentary in the Erdman edition (e879), and the sullen victim begins to take on the traditional role of Christ as elder brother: "Orc was comforted in the deeps his soul revivd in them / As the Eldest brother is the fathers image So Orc became / As Los a father to his brethren." Tharmas, organizing instinct now fallen into shapelessness, is also heartened by the new forms being created, for he hopes to find among them his lost Enion, the hope that had proved vain in the earlier craftsmanlike work of Los in Night IV (iv 32-33; 48:9-10 e325). Even Urizen finds at least a portion of himself in the loving and shaping hands of a Los who now loves him, and who is surprised at his own ability to love (vii 496-99; 90:64-67 e357).

Night VIII.

In this Night sharply delineated extremes of hope and despair, truth and error, life and death, appear almost simultaneously in their most unmistakable manifestations. This is the Night when Jesus and Jerusalem, the heralds of self-fulfillment through self-sacrifice, enter the human heart to illuminate it, and when Satan and mystery reveal themselves as ultimate error. This is the Night when the forges and looms of Los and Enitharmon create and when the mills and wars of Urizen and Rahab destroy. This is the Night when Jesus in Luvah is crucified; yet even when he is dead and buried, new life is imminent. Ahania and Enion, as antiphonal voices of the grave and the plowed field, define death and life in their natural and spiritual forms. The events of Night VIII are redemptive, but as the events unfold, Los and his associates despair, as the disciples despaired just before the first Easter. Night VIII is the time when Jesus is at last recognized on the human plane, but it is also the time—analogous both to the Saturday before Easter and to the two thousand years of Christendom—when he seems indisputably dead, most painfully absent from those who have been working through time for human salvation.

The powerful eighth Night has more obvious points of external reference than do other parts of the poem. An acquaintance with the Gospels and apocalyptic literature, especially Revelation, along with a knowledge of Blake's consistent condemnation of priests and kings, makes much of this Night immediately clear; both the outline and substance of Albion's nightmare are in the public domain. That is, the main events in this section not only happen timelessly but have happened in recorded human history. The episode of the crucifixion, which is generally faithful to biblical detail, is the most historically oriented part of the poem. The indictment of institutions—mainly the church and the military—is, along with Urizen's lecture in Night VII, the most explicitly sociological. We see now what we see continually in the world around us, the satanic outward results of human psychic dislocations in the collective acts of war and false worship, both based on human sacrifice. But the cause and effect, the tenor and vehicle, are also reversible; the collective acts of war and false worship serve as symbols of psychic disorder. For example, in the war scenes it is clear that military violence is a perversion of human energies, especially sexual ones; at the same time these scenes dramatize and clarify the nature of the inner conflict of man with himself. Each arena of reality reflects the other; yet both are fully intelligible only when they are seen as fallen forms of mental warfare, the life-giving clash of ideas. The mythological anticipations in Night VII have prepared us to recognize in the external actions of Night VIII the outlines of their ideal form, the hint of their redemptive power. Then, at the final stage of clarification, what is seen through a glass darkly in Night VIII will be revealed face to face in the apocalyptic Night IX.

The opening image of Night VIII is of the dead Albion framed in a Gothic arch formed by the joined wingtips of protecting spirits from Beulah. Like Jonah during his three days in the belly of the fish (a traditional type of Jesus' days in the tomb—Matt. 12:40) when "the depth closed me round about, the weeds were wrapped about my head" (Jon. 2:5), Albion lies "Washd with the tides Pale overgrown with weeds." But the allusion to Jonah is also a portent of resurrection. Albion's seven sneezes are another sign that like

the Shunammite's son (2 Kings 4:35) he will be raised from
the dead. In Night I he had sunk down from the Savior's
arms (I 465-66; 18:12-13 E306) ; now once more he rests in
the Savior's embrace. Adverbs in the announcement that
the Council of God, or Jesus, "then" meets to create fallen
man and "now" fixes the limit of Contraction as Albion
"again" reposes in the Savior's arms make clear that the
protection of Albion is both eternal and continually renewed
in time (VIII 1-19; 99:1-14 E357). The repetition—with slight
but significant changes—of the scene in Night I when Albion
first sickened is a reminder that any morning in the fallen
state is the dawn of Eternity if man sees that it is; the point
is perhaps clearer in canceled lines describing the Good
Shepherd's creation of man "Morning by Morning" (E757) .[1]

In this Night Jesus appears not only outside time, as in the
Council of God scene, but also within it; the mythically conceived inhabitants of Eden and Beulah are choric spectators
of the time-bound world of Generation. The double perspective is roughly analogous to our own sense of ourselves: our
minds and our very bodies change from year to year, yet our
days are linked each to each by a mysterious constant of
personal identity. Within time, Jesus is present in the new
compassionate and loving relationship of mutual forgiveness
between Los, now integrated with his Spectre, and Enitharmon, whose tender, open heart in her translucent bosom
(she has thrown off her compulsion for secrecy) is the scene
for Jesus' appearance and for the shaping of spectres into
flesh or works of art. Enitharmon's openness to Los and her
tenderness toward the spectres are the manifestation of the
divinity-in-humanity she has achieved. The total form that
Los and Enitharmon create for all the spectres combined
is "a Universal female form," Jerusalem (VIII 182-93; 103:
32-104:4 E361).

The motif of the hard heart and opaque bosom has been
familiar since Night I, when Tharmas hid Jerusalem within

Night VIII

(or lost her to Enion's jealousy) and the Daughters of Beulah wept that Jerusalem was shut out of Enitharmon's heart.[2] In Night VII Los begged Enitharmon to look within her broken heart for "the Lamb of God / Clothed in Luvahs robes of blood descending to redeem," but at that time Enitharmon could only assume that the Lamb would be bent on punitive destruction (VII 415-31; 87:44-60 E355). Now in her kind-hearted activities she, as well as others, can see the Lamb as a redeemer. This vision is received by the Daughters of Beulah with astonishment and "Rapturous Extacy" and by Urizen with perplexed terror over what he sees as a new form of Orc or Luvah, since Jesus is assuming Luvah's robes. The comprehensive and comprehending view of Beulah, not the self-centered perspective of Urizen, is of course the one to be trusted:

> the Divine Countenance shone
> In Golgonooza Looking down the Daughters of Beulah saw
> With joy the bright Light & in it a Human form
>
> .   .   .   .
>
> They saw the Saviour beyond the Pit of death & destruction
> For whether they lookd upward they saw the Divine Vision
> Or whether they lookd downward still they saw the Divine
>   Vision
> Surrounding them on all sides beyond sin & death & hell.
>
> (VIII 41-51; 100:7-16 E358)

Here the divine countenance shines not from above, as in the well-known benediction of Numbers 6:24–26, but from within, as among the early Christians (Rom. 5:5, 2 Cor. 4:6). Throughout the poem the Daughters of Beulah have been looking down into the world of death, appalled; now up and down are unnecessary distinctions because the Presence is everywhere and all places are one, met in the heart of Enitharmon. This new perspective is not to be confused

with the Urizenic disorientation in Night VI where, as in
the note on the Dante illustrations, "In Equivocal Worlds
Up & Down are Equivocal" (E668, K785). Within and
through the compassionate, shaping work of a transformed
human community appears the Divine Vision; in describing
it Blake boldly alludes to the shining countenance of Jesus
in his Transfiguration (Matt. 17:2) and in his appearance
to John on Patmos (Rev. 1:16), two occasions on which
Jesus' divine humanity (what theologians call the hypostatic
union) is most dazzling.

The passion, crucifixion, and burial of Jesus control the
narrative pattern of this Night of suffering and death, but the
extranarrative images of the Savior's protection and the shining of the divine countenance suggest an alternative interpretation of the main events. In the central plot dominated
by Urizen-Satan and Vala-Rahab, the crucifixion can be only
a Druidic death-worship, the sacrifice of man to a cruel natural order ruled by a tyrant. But according to the vision
newly perceived by Los and Enitharmon the crucifixion is a
loving and continually life-giving sacrifice that gives meaning
to corporeal death and the senseless cycle of nature. The account of Jesus' trial, execution, and burial is interwoven
with descriptions of the wars of Urizen, the mills of Satan,
and the looms and altars of Rahab. In the background, like
the insistent bass line of a passacaglia, now assertive and now
only suggested, is the productive work of Los and Enitharmon. (Similarly, although the negative rather than the positive image is in the background, we are half-consciously
aware of the wakeful, shivering beadsman throughout the
scenes of sensual delight in *The Eve of St. Agnes*.) The
reminders of this activity in Golgonooza and Cathedron (the
site of Enitharmon's looms) are necessary, for the war scenes
create such an illusion of documentary realism that they can
engross our attention at that realistic level alone, blocking

our response to their more psychological and personal implications.

Earlier, the mating of the Spectre of Urthona with the Shadow of Enitharmon had produced the shadowy form of Vala who tempts the spectres to descend from Beulah into Ulro (vii 315-31; 85:5-21 E353). Now the regenerated Los and Enitharmon reverse the process initiated by their spectrous mating in Night VII. They attract to Golgonooza the spectres who have entered Urizen's temple and are participants in the wars of Urizen and Tharmas. Although the spectres are unreal under the abstracting influence of religion and warfare, when they descend through the gate of Pity, Enitharmon's broken heart, they begin to take on new forms by means of two distinct but parallel symbols of the creative process. In her role as the artist's inspiration, Enitharmon sighs the spectres forth upon the wind and Los receives them into his hands. In her role as physical mother, Enitharmon clothes the spectres with human flesh (viii 24-38,108-17,182-84; 99:19-100:4,101:39-48,103:32-34 E357–61).

If we think simply of the actual birth process—presumably the basis of Damon's identification of Luban's gate, where Enitharmon's looms operate, with the vagina—the image is clarified. But it is more important to see this kind of procreation as the central symbol of all creative activity in which forms are made and abstractions are embodied. Allusions to biological and artistic creation are fused: in his forges Los draws the "Passions & Affections / Of Spectrous dead" into wires, which are brought to Enitharmon's looms where the silken "ovarium & the integument" are woven into "sweet clothing" that the spectres put on with delight (viii 208-15; 113:7-14 E362). We have now a new way of thinking about the human body—not as a necessary lower limit of Contraction as in Night IV but as the delightful work of an artist who loves his vocation.[3] At the same time we have an organic conception of art: abstract ideas are conceived in heartbreak, shaped with difficulty, woven of the artist's own substance, and at last made flesh, able to sustain independent life apart from the creator. As the incarnation of Jesus will make absolutely clear, generation is an image of regeneration.

But for the present Urizen dominates the foreground (VIII 61-101; 101:1-101:32 E358-59). At his signal the war that seemed about to break out at the end of Night VI now begins. In Night VI Urizen had faced Tharmas and the ferocious Spectre of Urthona on the brink of war; now Tharmas has disappeared and the Spectre is one with the artist Los, who is drawing the embattled spectres *away* from Urizen's armies. In Night VII Urizen's military preparations were set aside for a specious truce and acrimonious diplomatic negotiations with Orc, then weakened and wormlike; now Orc is a gorgeous serpent who is still seemingly subject to Urizen, even a participant in a secret alliance with the tyrant. Who then is left to fight? Where are the lines drawn? What are the issues and objectives?

All that is clear, even to Urizen, is the contents of his arsenal. Urizen's designs have all the specificity of orders given a foundry or munitions plant: "Horrible hooks & nets . . . molten metals cast in hollow globes & bor'd / Tubes in petrific steel & rammd combustibles & wheels / And chains & pullies."[4] Only what to do with the weapons is vague. Urizen sees in the Lamb of God his old enemy Luvah, yet Luvah-as-Orc is his ally; Urizen is "Communing with the Serpent of Orc in dark dissimulation." He wishes "To undermine the World of Los," which is not even bearing arms. He seems unable to keep all his enemies, or his uneasy and distrusted allies, in focus at the same time; his real motivation seems to be to try anything "if perhaps he might avert / His own despair even at the cost of every thing that breathes" (VIII 138-39; 102:21-22 E360) —exactly the motivation for his efforts at the repression and postponement of

violence in Night II. It seems at times that Orc is a rebel
without a cause, Urizen a rationalist without a purpose. Urizen's obsession with order and consistency as ends in themselves has become sheer compulsiveness, indeed neurotic
mania.

Since Urizen has prepared for war in "self deceit" (VIII
86; 101:26 E359), it is not surprising that his creation takes
a form he had not intended, a black and opaque hermaphro-
dite who is Satan himself (VIII 102-06; 101:33-37 E359). The
senseless clash of Urizen's ignorant armies and the hermaphroditic image of war resemble the self-contradictory politics
of all armies and governments in time of war and the self-
defeating pointlessness of warfare itself. The real opposition
to Urizen comes not from an army, for which his military
preparation would be relevant, but from the creative activity
of Los. The only confrontation Urizen is able to precipitate
is not even an overtly hostile one: the Lamb of God "stood
before him opposite" and "stood before Satan opposite" (VIII
64,268; 101:4,105:1 E358,363). The true cause of the Lamb's
appearance is the loving activity of Los and Enitharmon, not
the warlike posturings of Urizen.

The passages on warfare in Night VIII complicate some
judgments about violence and clarify others. The disturbingly clear descriptions of Urizen's military hardware have
a Swiftean flavor, as when Gulliver, unable to fall back on
the euphemistic jargon of military ordnance, has to explain
to the King of Brobdingnag in words of one syllable the
mechanics of weaponry and its precise effect on human
bodies. In contrast to Urizen's precision-made armaments are
the real but confused psychological disorders of his troops
and the nonviolent, indirect method Los uses to draw them
away from the battle, somewhat like that of the inspired
artists Laon and Cythna in Shelley's *Revolt of Islam*. Against
the "work of death" (VIII 107; 101:38 E359) Los builds the
walls of Golgonooza so that only through the gates of death

can the spectres enter to Enitharmon and be humanized. But Blake treats the whole question of what "human" means in a complicated way, one that may seem to jar with his usual view of war as dehumanizing. Although the troops rending one another are "beastial droves," they appear "in human forms" which they retain only so long as they fight:

> They humanize in the fierce battle where in direful pain
> Troop by troop the beastial droves rend one another sounding loud
> The instruments of sound & troop by troop in human forms they urge
> The dire confusion till the battle faints those that remain
> Return in pangs & horrible convulsions to their beastial state
> For the monsters of the Elements Lions or Tygers or Wolves
> Sound loud the howling music Inspird by Los & Enitharmon
> Sounding loud terrific men
> They seem to one another laughing terrible among the banners
> And when the revolution of their day of battles over
> Relapsing in dire torment they return to forms of woe
> To moping visages returning inanimate tho furious
> No more erect tho strong drawn out in length they ravin
> For senseless gratification & their visages thrust forth
> Flatten above & beneath & stretch out into beastial length
> Weakend they stretch beyond their power in dire droves till war begins
> Or Secret religion in their temples before secret shrines.
> (VIII 115-30; 101:46-102:13 E360)

In declaring that the soldiers "humanize" in battle Blake may simply be using the stock device of the satirist: uttering the precise opposite of truth with a completely straight face. From a fallen perspective, of course, peacetime garrison life seems dull; war offers soldiers the opportunity to prove and display their manliness. Analogously, a person at war with himself may experience his inner turmoil as self-enhancing;

to feel existential anguish or to exult Manfred-like in one-self as a chaos of contradictions has its own seductive and narcissistic exhilaration. The task of Los and Enitharmon is to attract such misdirected psychic energy to their world of beauty and brotherhood. The spectres pass through the gates of death and into a new life as members of "a Vast family wondrous in beauty & love" (VIII 187; 103:37 E361); in the aggregate they are Jerusalem herself, the universal Emanation. Those spectres who do not die to their former life ("those that remain") return to their subhuman spec-trous existence; their war in the aggregate is the "dishuman-izd" universal Spectre, Satan, whom Blake glosses as "mul-titudes of tyrant Men in union blasphemous / Against the divine image. Congregated Assemblies of wicked men" (VIII 252-58; 104:24-30 E363). Out of unreal, deathly, antihuman formlessness, Los and Enitharmon work continually to bring into full being whatever is potentially real, alive, and human: Los's transformation of war into love is one of the many points in Night VIII where opposites collide. Before evil, error, and death can be seen clearly as non-entities to be cast off, all that is real under their domination must be remade. What is left after that, since it is only delusion, will disappear in the mental fires of Night IX.

In Blake's bravura use of the imagery of weaving, his principle of structure continues to be a symmetry of can-cellations,[5] in this instance a fourfold symmetry. Blake plays upon the ambiguity inherent in the archetype of clothing— since Genesis, both a concealment and a sign of what is dis-tinctively human. First, Los and Enitharmon weave the human form divine: the lineaments of gratified desire, the sexual clothing of naked human flesh, as well as the beautiful humanized form given to vague fears and frustrations. In opposition, Satan and his assistants "Build Mills of resistless wheels to unwind the soft threads & reveal /Naked of their clothing the poor spectres before the accusing heavens";

this mill of unmaking produces the nakedness that is shame and self-contempt. In a third mill—the "Spindles" of Rahab and Tirzah—the clothing worn in the fallen world is manufactured; these garments, which cover from head to feet, are mantles, girdles, shoes, and veils, of torture, despair, compunction, indolence, and ignorance—desperate symptoms of and quack remedies for false shame, suffocating coverings for the human spirit. In the fourth and ultimate reversal, the Lamb, the "Universal Humanity," receives "the Integuments woven" and puts off "the clothing of blood" (VIII 200-36; 113:1-35 E362) or Luvah's robes—an image perhaps derived through Blakean typology from Jesus' seamless cloak, the scarlet robe of mock-royalty put on him by the soldiers, and the "vesture dipped in blood" that he wears in Revelation 19:13. Jesus' stripping off of the clothing of false religion reestablishes the nakedness of innocence, so that in Night IX even Urizen casts off his mantles and exults "in naked majesty" (IX 188-92; 121:27-31 E376).

Another sort of reversal occurs in the religion of human sacrifice, which in the crucifixion of the Lamb-as-Luvah becomes genuine self-sacrifice separated from its false form as a propitiation of the cruel God of natural religion. The first movement in this reversal is a series of clarifying exposures of the old mystery-religion as a correlate of bloody warfare. Among other things, this is the religion of fear that afflicts modern fundamentalists as well as pious children and adolescents like Stephen Dedalus, the religion to which the free-spirited child is martyred in *A Little Boy Lost* in *Songs of Experience*. Spectres not yet re-formed by Los and Enitharmon find little difference between war and religion: "Weakend they stretch beyond their power in dire droves till war begins / Or Secret religion in their temples before secret shrines" (VIII 129-30; 102:12-13 E360).

Although both war and religion are dehumanizing and require physical or spiritual human sacrifice, the spectres feel beastlike unless they are involved in one or the other. At the apex of both is Urizen, equally in character as high priest or as king and general. After consecrating his books in the temple of the sun (there is not much difference between his natural history and his natural religion) he proselytizes the universe, "reading incessantly / To myriads of perturbed spirits" (VIII 140-42; 102:23-25 E360). The only apparent audience for this warrior-priest (whose preaching is now as ineffectual as his tyranny) is the Shadowy Female Vala, whose behavior parodies the attentiveness of Mary of Bethany at the feet of Jesus and her mild reproaches that Jesus' absence caused her brother's death. The intimacy between Urizen and Vala (as between rationalism and sensuality, conscience and sexuality, tyranny and the Female Will) is to be exposed as the hermaphroditic union of Satan and Rahab, dragon and whore, two aspects of the same life-hating principle. From both sources comes the lust to torment and destroy true humanity.

Even while Vala and Urizen appear as separate beings, they are united by their obsessive memories of Luvah, the supposed enemy-in-hiding of Urizen and the long-lost lover of Vala. Jesus' appearance in Luvah's robes of blood, Blake's main image for his reinterpretation of the Incarnation and Atonement, is described in flashes from various perspectives (like those glimpses caught early in Night VIII by the Daughters of Beulah, Urizen, and Los-Enitharmon) and is interpreted according to the temperament and perceptiveness of the viewer. Only those in Beulah and Eden and those like Los and Enitharmon who have enacted their own self-sacrificial love are able in Night VIII to recognize this image of suffering as redemptive. Although Urizen and Vala see something new and puzzling, they are unable to conceive of any sufferer other than the old Luvah. Urizen knows the bloody stranger is the Lamb, a new Luvah, but he cannot reconcile this knowledge with Luvah's now-familiar appearance as Orc

(VIII 61-65; 101:1-5 E358). Vala has no perception of the Lamb, only of her spouse's murderer, the usurper of his throne and his robes (VIII 153-55; 103:3-5 E360). Her pathetic question, "Where hast thou hid him whom I love," echoes Mary Magdalene's when she sees the empty tomb and mistakes the risen Lord for the gardener. As far back as Night II Vala has looked elsewhere for the Luvah who is actually present or near. Now in his debasement he is Orc on the Tree of Mystery; in his transfiguration he is the crucified Lamb. And both are right beside her.

In Night I Vala and Luvah were able to see Eternity as "One Man infolded / In Luvahs robes of blood & bearing all his afflictions" (I 363-64; 13:8-9 E303). In the fall love has been perverted to Orckian rebellion and hate, but all the while its potential identification with human suffering has been preserved by the divine economy:

> For when Luvah sunk down himself put on the robes of blood
> Lest the state calld Luvah should cease. & the Divine Vision
> Walked in robes of blood till he who slept should awake.
> (II 263-65; 33:13-15 E315)

The same vision, of the human body and of the Savior clothed in Luvah's garments, had been seen in Night IV by the Council of God and Beulah's Daughters (IV 247-48; 55:10-11 E330). Like so many other redemptive possibilities, this one has been present but unrecognized all along.

That fact has great significance for Blake's view of how the individual person can heal himself. In Night VII the turn toward health had been a breakthrough, the work almost of a moment; in Night VIII we are reminded that these spots of redemptive time, what Blake calls last judgments, are scattered everywhere: more exactly, the possibility of regeneration is constantly present in our lives. Most people experience a fall from faith and psychic unity at some point relatively early in their lives; recovery, if it occurs, follows an almost universally shared pattern of life, learning, and aging. But however frequently this pattern is followed in life or in books, it is a generalization from observed experience, not a law of life; the door to our freedom is never locked. Destiny, along with the whole notion of our entrapment in linear time that Blake associates with memory, is for him a delusion. One of the most remarkable things about *The Four Zoas* is that the poem adheres faithfully to the most common rhythm of human growth while intimating that that rhythm need not control us.

Vala's lament that Luvah was "source of every joy that this mysterious tree / Unfolds in Allegoric fruit" (VIII 168-69; 103:18-19 E361) lends itself to ironic reversals in two directions. What Vala probably means is that Luvah's passionate desire was delectable forbidden fruit to her. What she does not mention is that she has been gathering this fruit, measuring it out, and feeding it to the insatiable Orc. The fruit is kneaded into "pestilential" food by Uveth, one of Urizen's three iron-hearted daughters. When Orc devours the food, it breaks out in various gems all over his serpent body; the gems strive in terrific "emulation" (in the old sense of jealous rivalry) for a place on his nonhuman body, giving Orc the sinister beauty of Keats's Lamia or of Ezekiel's Covering Cherub (VIII 73-85; 101:13-25 E359). From the fruit of the tree the Synagogue of Satan creates mystery (VIII 287; 105:20 E364), and later we read that the "Cup / Of fornication food of Orc & Satan [is] pressed from the fruit of Mystery" (VIII 602-03; 111:6-7 E371). Thus the fruit is the source of anything but joy. According to biblical and Blakean typology, however, the image of Adam's fruit prefigures joy. In the Gospels, Jesus is the vine with many branches; in Revelation instead of the forbidden tree man is given the Tree of Life with its abundant fruit and its leaves for the healing of nations. In Blake, the body of Jesus instead of the pestilential fruit hangs on the Tree of Mystery, witnessing to the inhumanity of bloody sacrifice and the divinity of self-sacrifice.

Vala's prayer to Urizen and her lament for Luvah, with her memories and intuitions of a better world, hint at the reversal she herself will experience. In the depths of error her longing for a reunion with Luvah that will liberate "the sons of God / From Bondage of these terrors" sharply contrasts with Luvah's memory in Night II that he "blotted out / That Human delusion to deliver all the sons of God / From bondage of the Human form" (VIII 157-58; 103:7-8 E361; II 106-08; 27:16-18 E311). (Originally Blake repeated verbatim in Night VIII his wording in Night II; then he altered "the human form"—VIII 158; E759—to "these terrors." The revision sharpens the contrasting parallels with Luvah's early soliloquy and, tantalizingly, hints at a radical change in Blake's thinking even after he had written part of, perhaps a whole version of, Night VIII.) Vala longs for nothing short of a return to innocence, when she, Luvah, and humanity had dwelt in unity and love "as those who sinned not." Although she sees no hope of resurrection for Albion, she leaves open the possibility that the murdered Luvah may still be alive: "Can that which has existed cease or can love & life Expire" (VIII 160-70; 103:10-20 E361). The element of protest in her prayer-lament is another sign of the breakup of Urizen's empire, for her outcry is that of nature itself against rationalist tyranny. She is much like Earth in *Prometheus Unbound* or in *Earth's Answer* in *Songs of Experience*. Imagination and instinct have already begun to resist Urizen effectively; now one aspect of passion also shows signs of breaking free. On any level, even in the lowest state of error, Urizen's rule is intolerable to what is healthiest in the other human faculties.

Blake's use of separate names for radically divided states of a single component of consciousness has been helpful in tracing complex movements like Los's domination over and reconciliation with the Spectre of Urthona and the Divine Humanity's preservation of the unfallen aspect of Luvah during Orc's adventures as maltreated child, chained rebel, and mighty serpent. Urizen and Vala have seemed more consistent in character, and more easily identified with their public images of Zeus-Jupiter-Jehovah and Aphrodite-Astarte-Freya. But in order that error be consolidated, these stubbornly persistent character types too must be splintered; their worst aspects must be seen as separate entities, to be cast off in Night IX. Again Blake uses the device of giving separate names to the splinter-personalities; Urizen's new name is Satan and Rahab's is Mystery.

The isolation of the final form of error in Urizen and Vala had already begun in Night VII, when Los's artistic work had attracted a portion of Urizen to Golgonooza in a surprising avatar as Los's own son Rintrah and when the mating of the Spectre of Urthona with the Shadow of Enitharmon had generated Vala as the Shadowy Female. Now in Night VIII Vala utters her last speech as the goddess of sensuality (VIII 145-70; 102:28-103:20 E360-61) and is seen no more in that character until the passions and senses are regenerated in Night IX. Her shadowy self works in Night VIII through half-real ectoplasmic grotesques named Rahab, Tirzah, and the Females of Amalek. Urizen, with all that is most alive in him already drawn by Los into Golgonooza, is something like a spectre of himself in Night VIII; his war, the aggregate of his spectre armies, is Satan, Urizen's unintentionally revealed lower limit (VIII 247-51; 104:19-23 E363). Urizen's role as villain is taken over by this Satan, an unequivocally negative figure who has been an element in the nature of Albion and of the other Zoas as well. In Albion, Satan is the limit of Opacity beyond which Albion cannot go toward further blindness, stubbornness, and self-enclosure. Satan is also the lowest condition of the angry Orc, love perverted into hate—"when Luvah in Orc became a Serpent he descended into / That State calld Satan" (VIII 382-83; 115:26-27 E366). Even Los has generated this Satan; he acknowledges both Satan and Rahab as two of his many children (VIII 359,365; 115:3,9 E365). If the fact that Blake never associates Satan with Tharmas is significant, it corroborates our impression that although human instinct can become chaotic, weak, and misdirected, it is incapable of the absolute error to which more complex faculties are susceptible.

Vala's last action as the Shadowy Female is to spread herself through the Tree of Mystery, as the Shadow of Enitharmon had done a Night earlier. A weeping, shapeless, indefinite cloud of "laws & deceitful religions," she steeps Urizen's web of religion in tears of sorrow until it falls from oversaturation, altering his carefully established vortexes. Urizen's intellectual, political, and religious systems are no longer under his control; the feminine principle begins its rule, "Misplacing every Center" that his rationalism had established. Urizen is tangled in his own web—now a net of sorrow, lust, and repentance—as in the last plate of *The Book of Urizen* (VIII 171-81; 103:21-31 E361). The cosmic architect who had built so grandly and elegantly in Night II and with such iron utility in Night VI has become a spider caught in his own web, a general who, like Richard III and Macbeth, issues orders to disobedient or nonexistent armies.

The composite spectre of Urizen and Vala subdivides into Satan and Rahab, each further divided within and hiding the other in secret parts (VIII 277-93; 105:10-26 E363-64). Blake's hermaphroditic monster is intellectually inconsistent, self-contradictory, and of course sexually ambivalent; in *Milton* 40:20 and *Jerusalem* 75:20 and 89:53 it is said to be religion hidden in war. The figure is Blake's fusion of various kinds of loathesome inconsistencies—the Law enshrined in the Holy of Holies, the concealed pudenda of pretended chastity that teasingly arouses lust, the tabernacles ("little tents") of the Christian churches that secretly foster warfare and punishment, Blake's chapels of gold violated by serpents, the phallic female whose secret delight is the castration of man, the feminized male whose repressed desire erupts in sexual exploitation. Blake's drawing in the *Four Zoas* manuscript (MS page 44, Night III) of a languorous, though spike-crowned, woman with a gothic triptych or altarpiece in place of genitals expresses this same theme, as does one of his separate drawings which shows a Druidical priestess with male genitals.[6] In *The Everlasting Gospel*, the "Tent of Secret Sins & its Golden / cords & Pins" is the "Bloody Shrine of War / Pinnd around from Star to Star" (E794; lines 21-24, K756-57). In *Jerusalem* Los uses this figure for the unimaginative, naturalistic view of Jesus' incarnation: "A Vegetated Christ & a Virgin Eve, are the Hermaphroditic / Blasphemy" (90:34-35). This blasphemy is the "Satanic Body of Holiness" which the Divine Humanity, the imagination, enters into and casts off. The inverse of the secret hermaphroditic relation between Satan and Rahab-Mystery is the revelation of Jesus within the bosom of Jerusalem, who is herself the product of the imaginative work of Los and Enitharmon. In Jesus and Jerusalem the best in male and female are conjoined, occupying the same space, virtually identified with each other.

A surprising feature of Blake's treatment of Jesus in Night VIII is his matter-of-fact fidelity to the Gospel accounts of Jesus' life and death. Like instantaneous flashes of a long-past traumatic scene that interrupt the flow of present action in a film, vignettes from the Gospel break into descriptions of Satan's and Rahab's ritualized cruelties in war and religion. In each flash the Gospel action has moved ahead in time. "Pitying the Lamb of God Descended . . . & as a Man / Is born on Earth so was he born of Fair Jerusalem"; the Sanhedrim meets "To Judge the Lamb of God to Death as a murderer & robber / As it is written he was numberd among the transgressors"; "The Lamb of God descended

thro the twelve portions of Luvah / Bearing his sorrows &
recieving all his cruel wounds"; "Thus was the Lamb of God
condemnd to Death / They naild him upon the tree . . .
mocking & then worshipping calling him Lord & King";
"Jerusalem saw the Body dead upon the Cross"; "Los took
the Body from the Cross Jerusalem weeping over / They bore
it to the Sepulcher which Los had hewn in the rock / Of
Eternity for himself"; the Lamb "died for all / And all in
him died" (viii 260-340, 483-84; 104:32-106:16,107:37-38
E363-65,368). These phrases can be read as simple repetitions from the Evangelists, literal statements of fact—for
example, that Jesus was born in Palestine. Blakean characters
in each flash of this Passion play enact recognizable biblical
roles; Los, for instance, is obviously Joseph of Arimathea.
The biblical paraphrases sound so familiar that the audience
feels like quoting them along with the players. Yet these
unpretentious lines have great climactic power. Blake follows
the same strategy that gives the childlike parting advice by
the Ancient Mariner its sublime force. He has anticipated
the mythic or typological or psychological complexities of
these terse allusions so that they energize by their very understatement emotions that have already been developed and
heightened almost beyond our bearing. These simple
biblical phrases act on us as do the emotionally catalytic
words of Shakespeare's Cordelia: "No cause, no cause," or
the vow Dorothea makes to Ladislaw in *Middlemarch*: "I
will learn what everything costs."

By the same token, the straightforward narration in the
biblical flashes makes horrifically vivid the newly invented
elements in Blake's staging and casting of the Passion story.
Reading this part of Night VIII is like watching a disorderly
combination of a witches' sabbath, a bacchanalia, a star-
chamber trial, a specialty performance by expensive prosti-
tutes, a pagan sacrifice, and a military campaign. Each
activity is fitfully illuminated by split-second flashes of the

most moving, most awesome, and most revered scene in Western culture.

Two songs, one by the Sons of Eden (VIII 194-245; 104:5-104:17 E361-63) and one by the Females of Amalek (VIII 297-321; 105:30-53 E364), provide a parallel to the flashing alternations between scenes of self-sacrifice and torture: the songs interpret a single event in opposite ways. The brute fact in both songs is the birth, suffering, and death of love—of someone in Luvah's robes·of blood. At a choric distance from the suffering, the Sons of Eden who surround the Lamb sing his praises; in the very process of tormenting their victim, the Females of Amalek chant seductive descriptions of their own sadism. Both groups use the imperative of exhortation: "Assume the dark Satanic body . . . it cannot thee annoy"; "Bind him down Sisters bind him down" (VIII 241,315; 104:13,105:47 E363,364).

From the perspective of Amalek shared by Satan and Rahab, the death of the historical Jesus was no more than what the world always has done and therefore should and will continue to do to the loving imaginative human being who chooses freedom over the established good sense of, say, returning blow for blow. In their combination of cruelty with unctuous pseudopity they resemble Dostoevsky's Grand Inquisitor. Conversely, from the perspective of Eden, Beulah, and Golgonooza, even the worst that moral systems and natural limitations can do to humanity is continually redeemed, time after time, as it is entered into and empathically shared by the universal Jesus. This Jesus is the friend of sinners, not their accuser; the celebrator of life, not the prey of death; the symbol of hope, not of fatalism. Blake's Jesus is the spirit of love and self-sacrifice that was fulfilled, temporally, in the personality of the historical Jesus and is continually fulfilled, eternally, whenever the human imagination is able to transform suffering—not by evading but by embracing it. The Females of Amalek see only the "poor human form" they are tormenting. The Sons of Eden comprehend but transcend the Females' naturalist view of suffering and death; when the Sons "look down into Ulro" and "into Beulah," they see the Lamb even though they are aware of the actions of Satan and Rahab as well (VIII 223-46; 113:22-104:18 E362-63).

The images of Jesus' body and clothing, which are so closely fused as to be indissociable, are treated from the same dual perspective. Jesus wears Luvah's robes of blood but is seen by Los and Enitharmon in Jerusalem's veil (VIII 191; 104:2 E361) and in mystery's woven mantle (VIII 259-63; 104:31-35 E363). Repeatedly, Jesus either puts on or takes off something described as a body, an ambiguity that restates the dual points of view on his redemptive function.[7] As he takes on the dark Satanic body (variously identified in these passages as mystery, suffering, vegetation, mortality, eternal death), he also puts it off; in his living and dying he effects a separation between false and true conceptions of divinity and of suffering. The Christian doctrines of Incarnation and Atonement as commonly understood are, to Blake, part of the Satanic body of false holiness, the veil of mystery that the true Jesus tolerates as a garment only until it is destroyed (cut apart by Rahab or discarded by himself), a biding of time illustrated by many passages in the Gospels wherein Jesus guardedly or ironically endorses the letter of the old Law or its customs and rituals in the process of out-witting his challengers and slipping out of their legalistic entrapments.

Separated from the true Jesus, the mystery-Jesus is revealed as Satan and Rahab. Once Luvah's garments are rent, they may be seen as no more than the "body of sin" and "the body of this death" (Rom. 6:6, 7:24) from which humanity is delivered. (The same stripping away of the Satanic from the divine is succinctly described in several passages in *The Everlasting Gospel*—for example, lines 81-96, E514, K755;

lines 32-53, E515, K749). Jesus' life and death, seen imaginatively, make possible an understanding of mortality as the lower limit from which the liberated human spirit springs, instead of the natural upper limit beyond which humanity cannot aspire—the essential message of *To Tirzah* in *Songs of Experience*. Eden sees Luvah's robes of blood as a garment that can be worn and cast aside, a state that can be entered and then left behind, but Amalek does not know the difference between the garment and the man.

Blake is analyzing in these passages actual religious distortions and disorders, but these in turn are metaphors for many types of psychic illness, not necessarily specifically religious, which have to be cut away in pain or bravely thrown off if old neuroses are to be overcome. (We can easily miss this function of religion as metaphor, since many neuroses are in fact rooted in or associated with crippling religious compulsions.) Before they put off their old habits—their old "bodies" or "clothing"—patients under psychotherapy often identify themselves with these habits as though all coherence, survival itself, depended on them. Even a release from emotional illness, when and if it happens, is often characterized by the same combination of exhilaration and pain that the Sons of Eden and the Females of Amalek, respectively, feel toward Jesus' redeeming sacrifice. Most or all of the chief Blakean characters, singly or in pairs, will feel such ambivalence in parts of the poem yet to come. One of the clearest examples comes near the end of Night VIII, when Rahab destroys her harlot robes even as she kisses them and weeps over them (VIII 609-13; 111:13-17 E371). The ambivalence is much like that expressed so poignantly in Eliot's *Ash Wednesday*, where (ironically from a Blakean point of view) the cure for spiritual malaise is orthodox religion itself.

As the image of the crucified Jesus flashes sharply into the poem, the spectrous forms of Satan and Rahab begin to blur and multiply. Satan is compounded into a whole Sanhedrim (Blake prefers this variant to the more familiar spelling) called the Synagogue of Satan (as in Rev. 2:9 and 3:9) and "Twelve rocky unshapd forms terrific forms of torture & woe." Politically they are "multitudes of tyrant Men in union blasphemous / Against the divine image. Congregated Assemblies of wicked men" (VIII 257-76; 104:29-105:9 E363). Within this synagogue is Rahab or Mystery or Babylon, the great whore of Revelation, "Dividing & Uniting at will in the Cruelties of Holiness . . . When viewd remote She is One when viewd near she divides / To multitude" (VIII 279-84; 105:12-17 E364). Her daughters are Tirzah and the other four daughters of Zelophead who won the right of female inheritance, members of the half-tribe of Manasseh descended from Joseph's Egyptian wife.[8] Tirzah's various divisions are the Females of Amalek and of the other heathen kingdoms, Canaan and Moab: "Sometimes as twelve daughters lovely & sometimes as five / They stood in beaming beauty & sometimes as one even Rahab" (VIII 328-29; 106:4-5 E365).

Rahab is mystery understood both sexually and metaphysically. Tirzah in particular typifies both harlotry and sensory repression. Only the repression is suggested in the poem *To Tirzah*; nonetheless, the poem in *Experience* is a good gloss on Tirzah's song (the song also attributed to the Females of Amalek) in Night VIII. The motto of *To Tirzah*, written on the robe of the old man offering water to the fallen man in Blake's design for the poem, is a prophetic commentary on Tirzah's actions described in her song; the motto, "It is Raised a Spiritual Body" (1 Cor. 15:44), evokes also the first half of the biblical quotation, "It is sown a natural body." Tirzah's torture of her victims is an effort to plant man's natural body into his natural environment, to confine man to his merely physical existence.

Tirzah's keening over the sacrificial victims (all the sufferers epitomized in Luvah-Jesus) is a ghastly hymn of the perversion of desire and the destruction of the senses, sung in an earnest tone of concern, pity, and desperation (VIII 298-321; 105:31-53 E364). Her combination of wantonness and repression, sensuality and modesty, is familiar in sexual pathology; it underlies all pornography that produces its effect through teasing and concealment; it explains the deep coldness of the femme fatale and the frantic libertinism that signals unfulfilled desire. Blake's hatred of sexual mystery is akin to his hatred of metaphysical mystery—the tantalizing elusiveness of an unknown deity who creates the senses only to demand that they be mortified and governs a universe intelligible only to mathematicians and puzzle solvers. This principle of mystery is hidden within Satan "as in an ark & veil / Which christ must rend" (VIII 292-93; 105:25-26 E364). (As Yeats's Crazy Jane tells the Bishop, "Nothing can be sole or whole / That has not been rent.") The veil of mystery that Jesus rends at his death is the biblical veil of the temple (on which the name Vala is a pun) and it is the mantle of Luvah that Rahab herself "smites with her knife of flint" (VIII 234; 113:33 E362) and cuts off.

But this rending and revealing appear to the orthodox religious consciousness, which thrives on mystery, to be just the opposite of what they are. To Tirzah and the mentality she represents, the removal of the veil is not the liberation of humanity but its enslavement to destructive libidinous impulses. In the poem, the crucifixion is, for the Females of Amalek, a memento mori; the senses must be denied or else "mercy & truth are fled away" (VIII 320; 105:52 E364); the victim must be bound down for his own good. The denial of the senses is, of course, exactly what Jesus' crucifixion has so often meant historically for Christianity and individually for most Christians. Blake compounds the irony by stationing the Rahab-Tirzah group around the cross—which is also the rock of their sacrificial altar—like the griev-

ing women in the Gospels (VIII 325-30; 106:1-6 E365). Even
Jerusalem and Los share in misinterpreting the crucifixion.
Jerusalem flees in terror from what she calls "Eternal Death,"
Los buries the dead body "despairing of Life Eternal" (VIII
331-40; 106:7-16 E365), and then Jerusalem "wept over the
Sepulcher two thousand Years" (VIII 596; 110:33 E371).

Blake's Jerusalem is the bride of Albion-Jesus and also
humanity's self-fulfillment and spiritual freedom; likewise
the Church calls itself the bride of Christ. These two millenia
of weeping, then, which correspond to the two days when the
scriptural Jesus lies dead and the disciples despair, coincide
with the period of historical institutional Christianity when
freedom succumbs to the worship of death. Jerusalem begs
Los and Urizen to join her in building a sepulcher where
they can

> worship Death in fear while yet we live
> Death! God of All from whom we rise to whom we all return
> And Let all Nations of the Earth worship at the Sepulcher
> With Gifts & Spices with lamps rich embossd jewels & gold.
> (VIII 334-37; 106:10-13 E365)

For orthodox Christianity, Jesus' execution proves that death
is the norm of human existence from which earthly life is
merely a temporary exile and that the duty of individual
Christians is to spend their lives in devout preparation for
a "good death." Jerusalem's proposed Church of the Holy
Sepulchre, gem-adorned, is a literal description of the archi-
tecture of many actual churches—including the one on the
supposed site of Jesus' tomb; Blake frequently associates the
gems and gold with sex seen negatively or with horror, as in
I saw a chapel all of gold and *The Mental Traveller*. Los's
temporary despair suggests the abasement of art throughout
the centuries when it served the false, degraded Christianity
that is state religion. Thus the two most central functions

of the senses—the sexual and the esthetic—are brought together here in the reactions of Jerusalem and Los.

Los's despair, however, does not blot out what he has learned during eight long Nights of human error, as we see in his dialogue with the now unveiled Rahab, who appears in his workshop to question him. To her anger and petulance Los responds with tenderness and love (VIII 341-409; 113: 38-116:2 E365-66). The gist of his reply is an account of his descendants (which include Satan and Rahab, just as the lineage of Jesus in Matthew 1 includes Rahab, as well as other questionable women like Judah's daughter-in-law Tamar and Uriah's wife Bathsheba), a recapitulation of his own story (including a short version of the Bard's Song in *Milton*), a charitable identification of himself with Rahab as one who also has pierced the Lamb of God, an explanation of the crucial Blakean distinction between states and the individuals passing through those states, and a peroration calling for the liberation of Jerusalem.

The main effect of this beautiful and tender passage, a moving expression of the essential Christian maxim to hate the sin but love the sinner, is to illustrate what Blake often says elsewhere and what Shelley affirms in *A Defence of Poetry*: that the creative principle as it should be is inextricably bound up with human compassion, with love. The dogged labor and unflagging energy Blake attributes to Los can sometimes lead us to see him as a daemon or demiurge whose creative activity is independent of moral purpose. But Los's finest period of imaginative achievement is initiated in Night VII by his loving acceptance of his brother and his spouse. Now the consummate artist even interrupts his labors for the sake of one in error:

Los sat upon his anvil stock they sat beside the forge
Los wipd the sweat from his red brow & thus began
To the delusive female forms shining among his furnaces
(VIII 348-50; 113:45-47 E365)

A gentle but tough-minded irony is generated by the fact that Rahab is herself a type of Christianity in its worst guise of inquisitor and accuser, an irony redoubled by the role assigned to her in Christian typology (in Dante, for example—*Paradiso* ix 112-25) as the heathen providentially saved.

Los's severely compressed version of the Bard's Song, Blake's allegorical account in *Milton* of his own vicissitudes as artist, presents a problem. Surely even a poet so little concerned as Blake was with explicitness to what he called the "idiot" could not have expected readers to make sense of this synopsis apart from its fuller treatment in *Milton*. If the passage in *The Four Zoas* was written later than the Bard's Song, Blake may have hoped to jog the memory of readers already acquainted with the fuller story. If the *Zoas* passage was written first, it may be a brief sketch of what Blake was planning for *Milton*—which would indicate that he had abandoned any intention to make the *Zoas* a finished, free-standing work. At any rate, the general tenor of Los's address to Rahab is identical with the Bard's message to Milton: the necessity of annihilating the selfhood.

Although Rahab appears unmoved by Los's speech, her subsequent actions help carry forward the process of her own disintegration and that of Urizen and Satan. "Los dropd a tear at her departure but he wipd it away in hope" (vIII 410-11; 116:3-4 E367). First Rahab appears to Urizen, who is still immobilized in his web of religion. Urizen's earlier dismay at the appearance of Satan, like Dorian Gray's at the portrait representing the worst in himself, has anticipated the self-recognition precipitated by his encounter with Rahab. Urizen failed then to acknowledge the Satanic in himself, but when Rahab appears before him "in pride the Prince of Light beheld / Reveald before the face of heaven his secret holiness" (vIII 412-13; 116:5-6 E367).

Rahab is Satan's false feminine equivalent, exactly antithetical to what Urizen lost when he rejected his true coun-

terpart Ahania. The shadowy embodiment of the feminine
principle as understood in the stereotype of woman as cus-
todian of morality (what George Eliot calls "the world's
wife") produces a numbing stupor in Urizen, felt also by
Tharmas and Urthona. Following a pattern familiar in the
poem by now, Urizen embraces Rahab in pity, again a perversion of his former relation with Ahania. His false holiness has produced concupiscence in accord with two basic
Blakean principles: that repression produces lust ("since
life cannot be quenchd Life exuded") and that opposites
reveal, parody, or condition each other, a more subtle insight that Albion will suggest to Urizen in Night IX (VIII
415-21,467-68; 106:18-24,107:21-22 E367,368).

The result of Rahab's appearance is that Urizen divides
within himself (VIII 422-37; 106:25-40 E367), as Orc did in
Night VII. The contrast-and-parallel is intricate and accurate. What was most characteristic of Orc had remained in
the form of fire; the ultimate reduction of the rigid Urizen
we have known is, appropriately, stone. The separated part
of both Orc and Urizen becomes a serpent or dragon who
bitterly resents his dehumanization and envies the humanity
of the other Zoas. Luvah and Urizen together had been
agents of man's fall because they set themselves up as gods
and allowed the contentions of passion and intellect to obscure the totally human; now both are beginning to see themselves as subhuman, for in attempting to be more than man
they have become less. As the serpent body of Orc resembles
the gem-encrusted exterior of the Covering Cherub, the
dragon body of Urizen resembles the scaly form of Leviathan;
even the detail of Urizen's "Eyelids like the Sun" recalls
Leviathan's "eyelids of the morning" (Job 41:18). Both
these Old Testament monsters are implied in the serpent-
dragon of Revelation.

The deep schism within Urizen has already been externalized in the crumbling of his hegemony over mind and nature,

the disaffection of his enemies and pseudoallies, and the scattered activities of his multiform alter ego Satan-Rahab. But Urizen's self-understanding is still too dim; the hardened, encapsulated personality still called by his name must be broken. Knowledge of what is hideous in himself must be brought home to Urizen as Urizen; the patient must heal himself. Urizen's dragon form contemplates his petrified humanity "& in vain he swam around his stony form"; he recognizes simultaneously his identity as dragon and as stone man. In his humiliating new shape he is able to see "That not of his own power he bore the human form erect / Nor of his own will gave his Laws in times of Everlasting" (VIII 458-59; 107:13-14 E368).

His recognition that he is a finite portion within a larger humanity brings him closer than he has ever been to the wisdom of the Sons of Eden as they contemplate the Lamb: "Now we know that life Eternal / Depends alone upon the Universal hand & not in us / Is aught but death In individual weakness sorrow & pain" (VIII 197-99; 104:8-10 E361-62). Urizen's self-discovery parallels Satan's humiliation in Book X of *Paradise Lost* when he is confined to the serpent's body he had chosen in order to subvert man. Although in Urizen's stony form "His wisdom still remaind & all his memory stord with woe," his dragon form "forgets his wisdom in the abyss" and he sees "that his wisdom servd but to augment the indefinite lust," for Orc has risen furiously into the heavens and now "reignd over all" (VIII 431-66; 106:34-107:20 E367-68). The struggle between Orc and Urizen is not yet resolved in brotherhood, but the balance has been tipped in the direction of passion; the smugness of repressive rationality has been destroyed. As Job learns in Blake's famous series of illustrations, the upright blameless man must recognize his kinship with sinners before he can find in joy the divinity within. Here Urizen takes on the form he has despised in Orc; the Pharisee acknowledges his affinity with publicans

and harlots and thus with all heretofore disdained portions
of the self.

The stony stupor felt by Urizen threatens Tharmas and
Urthona, as well as Los and Enitharmon, but these positive
psychic forces consolidate their remaining energy in the
person of Los:

> And Tharmas gave his Power to Los Urthona gave his
>   strength
> Into the youthful prophet for the Love of Enitharmon
> And of the nameless Shadowy female in the nether deep
> And for the dread of the dark terrors of Orc & Urizen.
>   (VIII 477-80; 107:31-34 E368)

The consolidation of prophecy is exactly balanced by the
consolidation of error, through the "nameless shadow" or
Vala-principle, into a form that Jesus can cast off:

> Thus in a living Death the nameless shadow all things bound
> All mortal things made permanent that they may be put off
> Time after time by the Divine Lamb who died for all
> And all in him died. & he put off all mortality.
>   (VIII 481-84; 107:35-38 E368)

The delegation of power to Los by Tharmas and Urthona is
entirely different from the unhealthy abdications and usurpa-
tions that had wrecked the psyche in earlier Nights; the new
Los is a Cincinnatus who can be trusted not to tyrannize.
Instead, all the human faculties now capable of loving and
awakening humanity and of resisting error work together
as more than brothers, not dominating one another but uniting as one mighty prophet. The lost universal brotherhood
of man that was lamented in the opening lines of the poem
cannot be long to seek.

Before the further dividings and re-formings of Satan
and Rahab that will end Night VIII, Ahania and Enion sing

a strophe and antistrophe recapitulating and intensifying the major thematic contrasts of this Night (VIII 492-584; 108:8-110:29 E368-71). The key structural motif of Night VIII is contrapuntal, as in the interplay between Urizen's soldiers and Los's family, in the different visions of the Lamb by Urizen and Beulah's Daughters, in Vala's reaction to Urizen's lecture, in the juxtaposition of hymns by the Sons of Eden and the Females of Amalek, in the dialogue of Los and Rahab, and perhaps in the opposition between Urizen's stony and dragon forms. This counterpoint, most distinctly heard in the paired songs of Ahania and Enion, brings out thematic contrasts between natural and spiritual, rational and visionary, especially in relation to the problem of suffering and death. At stake is the main premise of Romantic optimism, perhaps of any optimism that does not depend on belief in an afterlife. The issue is the one that haunts many of the most important works of Keats, Byron, and Coleridge, the one that disturbs Wordsworthian peace and Shelleyan ecstasy even at their most affirmative moments: Does imagination save or is it a demonically cruel fraud? In blunter terms, is Blake right or wrong when he says in the letter to Trusler that "the Visions of Fancy are . . . to be found in This World" and that "a Man may be happy in This World" (E676-77, K793)?

In the antiphon of Ahania and Enion we hear the voices of the banished portions of reason and instinct that have been silent since Night III. Their exchange takes the form of a protest and a reply, a lament to the caverns of the grave and an echo of reassurance from them. Ahania is outside of them, and Enion, who has sunk farther into non-entity than any other human element, is within them. These two feminine particles have been paired as the weakest and sickliest of the Emanations since the end of Night II, when the fall of Enion drew Ahania into its wake, leaving only Enitharmon and Vala in action during the central Nights. Ahania and

Night VIII

Enion have fallen into a void, a seemingly bottomless depression so deadening, so all-absorbing, that they are unable to summon up even a faint gleam of mental pleasure or a nurturing droplet of instinctual life. Ahania's intellectual delight has not been missed at all, especially not by Urizen. The only reminder that Enion's instinctual sense of wholeness ever existed has been the occasional wistful hope of Tharmas that she will reappear as one of the creations of Los and Enitharmon. The voices of these two women, then, have the authority of profound and bitter experience; they sound from the terrifying regions of nonentity and beyond, from the horror of exacerbated consciousness as well as the deepest level of unconsciousness, from the lower reaches of Albion's sleep, sickness, fall, or psychosis.

Ahania's cry is sheer despair, an accurate and clear-eyed synopsis, such as any reasonable but uninspired person would agree to, of what the human condition now is. She sees "not as yet the Divine vision," for her eyes are still toward the oblivious Urizen. In her incessant cry to "all the children of Men" (VIII 489-91; 108:5-7 E368), she recognizes life only as it ends in and is conditioned by death; mankind exists on the same plane as other forms of life. The Eternal Man sleeps rotting in the earth, and the grave mocks the plowed field, saying:

> I am the nourisher thou the destroyer in my bosom is milk &
>   wine
> And a fountain from my breasts to me come all multitudes
> To my breath they obey they worship me I am a goddess &
>   queen.
>
> (VIII 500-02; 108:16-18 E369)

In the words of Tennyson's Nature, "I care for nothing, all shall go" (*In Memoriam*, lvi 4). Ahania's perception of the grave as goddess and queen is like that perception of death as "God of All from whom we rise to whom we all return" which has moved Jerusalem to propose a church-sepulcher. Ahania sees the whole world as deathly: the eagle awaits his opportunity to consume what is left of man's corruptible body; beside him maggots feast on the belly of the dead lion; even the "pale horse," death's steed in Revelation, cannot find an unpolluted pool where he may die in peace. Ahania identifies herself as one who, remembering the unfallen state, sees only "the dark body of corruptible death / Looking for Urizen in vain. in vain I seek for morning" (VIII 529,505-06; 109:9,108:21-22 E369). Her allusion to the biblical "body of death" is a reminder to the reader of the "dark Satanic body" that the Savior has put off; the morning Ahania looks for in vain must be, according to the Easter story followed in Night VIII, the morning of the resurrection.

Enion's answer is in clear parallel and direct contrast to Ahania's lament. She too "Once . . . waild desolate" like Ahania, as in the great laments closing the early Nights; she knows all Ahania knows and more besides. Enion has experienced something like actual death, an utter loss of identity, a period of disintegration and estrangement, of wandering blind and age-bent.[9] Her assurances of new life are not empty wishes but direct accounts of what she herself has found in exploring the terrors of the grave. Unlike Thel, who was offered a foretaste of and an escape from the grave, Enion has stayed in her deathly condition long enough to learn its secrets. First there was a stage of Ahania-like distress: "my fallow fields in fear / Cried to the Churchyards & the Earthworm came in dismal state / I found him in my bosom . . ." Next the worm was accepted like a lover and death seemed to be the "time of Love" (VIII 536-38; 109:16-18 E369). But a voice came in the night, announcing the bridegroom's coming, and Enion awakened like one of the wise virgins. Now the grave and the plowed field reverse the roles Ahania had assigned them; the field is the mocker, not the one mocked. The victory of the grave and the sting

of death are not what they seem to an outsider; Enion, who
has fully experienced death in her awakened state, describes
it from within:

> I die a death
> Of bitter hope altho I consume in these raging waters
> The furrowd field replies to the grave I hear her reply to me
> Behold the time approaches fast that thou shalt be as a thing
> Forgotten when one speaks of thee he will not be believd.
>
> (VIII 546-50; 109:26-30 E370)

To the regenerate human being the whole condition of death,
of error, will become an occasion for incredulity like that
felt by the lovers in *A Midsummer Night's Dream*.

Enion's song suggests another meaning of the subtitle of
The Four Zoas: the poem is a "DREAM of Nine Nights"
not only because it is a visionary work organized according to
the logic of dreams, but also because it describes the nightmare of the sleep of death as something from which it is
possible to awaken. This awakening is ironically different
from the insomnia thrust upon Ahania by Enion at the end
of Night II, when Ahania felt the irresistible pull of Enion's
powerful death instinct. It is particularly appropriate that
Enion should now have the role of inspiriting Ahania: instinct's lament over human and animal suffering in Night II
had ruined the mind's delight; now a wiser instinct, deepened
and developed through suffering and death, feels the stirrings
of new life and tries to make them felt in the softer and ten-
derer areas of the mind.

The insight as well as the imagery of Enion's reply to
Ahania is drawn from Paul's brilliant discussion of resurrection in First Corinthians, chapter 15. On a negative note
that voices the doubts of his addressees, Paul declares almost
brutally, "if there be no resurrection of the dead . . . if
Christ be not risen, then is our preaching vain, and your
faith is also vain . . . If in this life only we have hope in

Christ, we are of all men most miserable" (15:13-19). If we understand "this life" and the resurrection in Blake's sense, this hopeless naturalistic vision is exactly what Ahania sees. "But now [that is, "But in fact," as in the Revised Standard Version] is Christ risen from the dead," Paul continues, "and become the firstfruits of them that slept" (15:20). Blake's sleeper is humanity in Albion, and Paul's direct contradiction of error parallels Enion's direct and positive reply to Ahania. This same chapter from Paul is also the one that provides the motto for *To Tirzah*. Paul's counterpoint of sowing and raising, natural and spiritual, corruptible and incorruptible, underlies the debate between the grave and the plowed field. Another biblical allusion, to the disappearance of "former things" (VIII 553; 109:33 E370; cf. Rev. 21:4), strengthens Enion's statement that mortality is an illusion overcome.

Enion apparently extends the metaphor of grave and plowed field to herself and Ahania: her addressee is "thou Corn field O thou Vegetater happy," and she herself is the "watry Grave," the "dark consumer" who is happier than the "Vegetater" (VIII 542-44; 109:22-24 E370). Enion identifies herself with the actual process of death, through which her deathly spectre is continually being drawn away from her living self. Her selfhood, not her humanity, is lost in the grave. For Enion, the grave *is* the plowed field—not a vegetated field but a field where the natural body is sown (in what might be called the soil of the imagination), where nature is humanized and humanity is regenerated:

> Listen I will tell thee what is done in the caverns of the grave
> The Lamb of God has rent the Veil of Mystery soon to return
> In Clouds & Fires around the rock & the Mysterious tree
> As the seed waits Eagerly watching for its flower & fruit
> Anxious its little soul looks out into the clear expanse
> To see if hungry winds are abroad with their invisible army

Night VIII

So Man looks out in tree & herb & fish & bird & beast
Collecting up the scatterd portions of his immortal body
Into the Elemental forms of every thing that grows.
                            (VIII 555-63; 109:35-110:8 E370)

Enion's references to nature should not be taken as an
argument for resurrection on the basis of seasonal renewal—
as in the natural-religionist's sermon about Easter lilies
springing up out of dead bulbs that is sometimes preached
from Christian pulpits. The continually renewed natural
impulse toward rebirth in springtime, which is just as continually frustrated every winter, is not what causes Albion's
rebirth and it is not evidence for life after death. Enion's
Albion is not an Osiris who seasonally reconstructs himself
out of scattered vegetated parts. If that natural cycle were
an adequate exemplum for human fulfillment, there would
be no need to write a poem like *The Four Zoas*; there would
be little tragic in the fall and little to rejoice at in the cyclical
return of happiness. Both would simply be necessary givens
of existence. The logical result of a belief in such premises
ought to be a state of weary stoicism, as in Hemingway's title
and epigraph from Ecclesiastes for *The Sun Also Rises,*
though few people, even in Hemingway, can bring themselves
emotionally to such a state of resigned acceptance. Dylan
Thomas's "wise men," although they "at their end know
dark is right," do not "go gentle into that good night." Nor
does Ahania; the very fact of her anguish indicates that
humanity, even in its rationality, needs more than the wholly
natural vision of life can give. Ahania's trouble is that her
felt need cannot get past the stubborn facts which are all that
she can see. To pass that barrier she must attend to the voice
of instinct and the experience of life and death that comes
from the Enion in herself.

Speaking for what is deepest in us, Enion takes natural
renewal as an inspiration, an occasion, an incentive, and—

above all—a metaphor for human regeneration, for the individual or for mankind. The spiritual awakening of Albion,
the unified human race, is expressed through his reconciliation with external, alienated nature. Instead of constructing
himself out of natural elements, Albion empathizes with all
the goings-on of nature: images of nature are reconstituted
as images in the human mind. As nature blindly renews itself, so blind instinct after long suffering wills life instead
of death, and it senses the transformation of what Hardy calls
"the ancient pulse of germ and birth" from biological regeneration into psychological and spiritual regeneration.

The premises of Ahania's and Enion's songs parallel those
of the Furies and the spirits who comfort Shelley's Prometheus. The dead-end world view that the Furies present
cannot be rationally denied, even by Prometheus. But his
mother Earth, primitive and deficient in ethical science and
other advanced ideas though she is, can nevertheless offer
Enion-like reassurance from still deeper sources in the mind
than the Furies can tap. From the "dim caves of human
thought" she summons spirits of hope who testify to isolated,
exceptional—but undeniable—instances of love and wisdom
in the fallen world. When Prometheus asks these spirits the
basis of their certainty that regeneration will occur, their
answer is filled with images of natural renewal:

> In the atmosphere we breathe,
> As buds grow red, when the snow-storms flee,
> From Spring gathering up beneath,
> Whose mild winds shake the elder brake,
> And the wandering herdsmen know
> That the white-thorn soon will blow:
> Wisdom, Justice, Love, and Peace,
> When they struggle to increase,
> Are to us as soft winds be
> To shepherd boys, the prophecy
> Which begins and ends in thee.
>
> (*Prometheus Unbound,* I 790-800)

Night VIII

Something starts things budding every spring, whether there is any point or not; something deathless stirs in mankind despite the grave, and this stirring promises human resurrection. But nature provides only an analogy, not a proof or a dynamic. The active force in renewal, according to both Shelley's and Blake's vision, is the human will acting on love whose ultimate source is imagination. The seeds of new life in the human world are small acts of goodness struggling, as in Enion's song, to grow; they flourish in spite of natural cycles, not because of them, and in defiance of the limits seemingly imposed by physical death.

Enion acknowledges that regeneration may seem delayed almost indefinitely, that humanity always seems to have to keep starting over again:

> He touches the remotest pole & in the Center weeps
> That Man should Labour & sorrow & learn & forget & return
> To the dark valley whence he came to begin his labours anew
> In pain he sighs in pain he labours in his universe
> Screaming in birds over the deep & howling in the Wolf
> Over the slain & moaning in the cattle & in the winds
> And weeping over Orc & Urizen in clouds & flaming fires
> And in the cries of birth & in the groans of death his voice
> Is heard throughout the Universe whereever a grass grows
> Or a leaf buds The Eternal Man is seen is heard is felt
> And all his Sorrows till he reassumes his ancient bliss.
>
> (VIII 573-83; 110:18-28 E370)

Yet repeated failures like those described here are an indirect reminder that opportunities for regeneration are repeated, in fact are omnipresent. The blindness of instinct may be exactly what allows man to start over after failing again and again. Already—in Blake's vast mythic metaphor—Albion is alive once more in the surging activity of the natural world which, properly perceived, is an intimate part of him. Much of his laborious renewal comes through his identifying himself with the pain as well as the joy of the

universe. Instead of accepting physical suffering as a limit
of the imagination, the very cries of the suffering animals
become the voice of his own sorrow as well as his rebirth.
The irrepressible vitality of nonhuman nature has only to
be humanized and made available to the mind, to the conscious part of nature. Perhaps some understanding of this
process is what prompts mental hospitals to encourage patients to tend gardens. New psychic life rises from an un-
seen subsurface world where Enion has reached out to fundamental laws of growth and primitive sources of strength from
which humanity has long been alienated.

The messages of Ahania and Enion affect their hearers in
different and unexpected ways. Although Los hears both
parts of the antiphon, he, Enitharmon, and Jerusalem seem
to respond only to Ahania and proceed with the despairing
burial of Jesus—described now for the second time (VIII 593-
96; 110:30-33 E371). It is Rahab who takes the words of
Enion to heart. She has taken Jerusalem a willing captive,
but at the peak of her triumph she sees her victory as hollow:

> But when she saw the form of Ahania weeping on the Void
> And heard Enions voice sound from the caverns of the Grave
> No more spirit remaind in her She secretly left the Synagogue
>   of Satan
> She commund with Orc in secret She hid him with the flax
> That Enitharmon had numberd away from the Heavens.
>
> (VIII 604-08; 111:8-12 E371)

In hiding Orc with Enitharmon's flax, Rahab enacts the part
of her biblical namesake who hid the Hebrew spies "with
the stalks of flax, which she had laid in order upon the roof,"
and her loss of spirit is similar to what happens when the
people of Rahab's Jericho hear the wonders of the Exodus:
"our hearts did melt, neither did there remain any more
courage . . ." (Josh. 2:6,11).[10]

Night VIII

The pattern of self-division so firmly established in the poem makes a scene of conflict within Rahab almost obligatory. She vacillates between her prideful allegiance to the Synagogue of Satan and her humble weeping before Orc, between her love for her harlot robes and her repentant desire to consume them in the flax set aside for Enitharmon's merciful looms (VIII 607-13; 111:11-17 E371). Perhaps Blake implies that a delayed response to Los's expostulation and a vestigial sense of kinship with Enion and the other Emanations are drawing out of Rahab those buried characteristics that will emerge as the new Vala in Night IX, while what is left is re-created as deism, yet another false religion. At any rate, the Emanations are drawn together in Night VIII as never before. Enion, the first Emanation to respond to the fall and also the first to sense complete recovery, comes to Ahania's aid and touches the conscience of the villainess Rahab; Rahab's attention to Orc suggests her derivation from Vala, once the feminine side of love; and her use of Enitharmon's flax reminds us of Enitharmon's handiwork.

Conversely, the spectrous elements are disintegrating, in the very performance of their last concerted act:

> The Synagogue of Satan therefore uniting against Mystery
> Satan divided against Satan resolvd in open Sanhedrim
> To burn Mystery with fire & form another from her ashes
> For God put it into their heart to fulfill all his will
> The Ashes of Mystery began to animate they calld it Deism
> And Natural Religion as of old so now anew began
> Babylon again in Infancy Calld Natural Religion.
>
> (VIII 614-20; 111:18-24 E371)

Of all Blake's reworkings of the Book of Revelation, this one is perhaps the most daring.[11] It juggles paradoxes with virtuoso skill (death and resurrection, unifying and dividing, the open Sanhedrim and the mystery it enshrines) ; it is explosive through sardonic understatement; it is almost offhand in tone but as densely packed with meaning as anything Blake ever wrote. It is also a stumbling block for those who see Blake as essentially a secular humanist and are puzzled by his fulminations against what Voltaire, Rousseau, and the whole historical Enlightenment stood for. Politically, Blake is akin to radicals who recognize little or no difference between Establishment parties of the right or left. Psychological analogues are suggested too, like the sudden conversion of pietist to village atheist (or vice versa) which seems to be a reversal but leaves unchanged the ontology of belief.

The historical reference is the one Blake presses. The Enlightenment claims to dissipate the dark night of medieval superstition, but it is creating something at least equally abominable. In *Europe* Blake himself had ridiculed the dark; in *Mock on mock on Voltaire Rousseau* and here at the end of Night VIII he ridicules the light. On the one hand the target of ridicule is a mystery religion that elevates a God like Milton's, "Dark with excessive bright" (*Paradise Lost*, III 380), who demands absolute worship but reveals himself in the world only through hints like those on which St. Thomas builds his proofs. On the other hand, the target of ridicule is a natural religion whose deity is still hidden, one whose arcane laws of gravitation (or relativity or conditioned responses) are accessible only to scientists and philosophes and are utterly irrelevant to human perceptions and needs. Blake sees little difference between the two deities. The only reformation that will re-form mankind takes place in Night IX; the protean metamorphoses of Satan and Rahab are all variants of the same old story.

Blake has paused to present a false salvation that is plausible to many well-meaning people, a seductive side-path that can lead astray even those who have progressed through the insights developed in Night VIII. The real potential of humanity, the real meaning of salvation, will appear in the ninth Night.

Night IX.
Any attempt to understand Blake's idea of salvation presses imagination to its limits: is it even remotely possible to define or describe the Blakean idea of regeneration or the resurrection to unity? If we seize upon "unity" as a key, we find that it means nothing like unanimity, for Edenic harmony is grounded upon intellectual warfare. Understood even in homely terms as a model for community behavior, this ideal of warfare seems preposterous; that people should consistently disagree passionately and at the same time lovingly would seem to be a highly rarefied oxymoron. And the image of a global debating society is inadequate as a literal presentation of regenerate humanity. Intellectual warfare, like most of Night IX, must be at least partly metaphor. The question is, a metaphor for what?

Nights I through VI, difficult though they are in certain ways, depict human situations that we can recognize all too easily by looking within ourselves. The mood of these Nights, the first two movements of the poem, is unhappiness, and most people know what that is. The earlier part of the third movement, Nights VII and VIII, has presented visions of spiritual and psychological healing, and, although such experiences are less frequent than the darker ones of Nights I through VI, most of us know enough about such recuperation to confirm Blake's dramatization of the process. But in Night IX, in the words of Urizen after his conversion: "Where shall we take our stand to view the infinite & unbounded / Or where [our] human feet?"[1] (IX 228-29; 122:

24-25 E377). We lack a common experience of regeneration, and we cannot even be sure that we have reliable private intuitions of what the actual living of a renewed life would be like. Yet only the reader's intuitions can confirm or deny the authority of any vision of a regained paradise in myth or literature. In response to the depiction of apocalyptic joy, the reader draws on his experiences, however transitory, of electric excitement combined with inner peace, of harmony with the world and other human beings seen as fully, intimately, responsively alive, inviolably themselves yet participants in a shared life.

When this transformed world of the ninth Night is explored from within, fresh problems of interpretation emerge. The first is how nature should be understood, the same question posed by the third and fourth acts of *Prometheus Unbound,* the work probably closest in spirit to *The Four Zoas.* There Shelley presents alternative visions of the physical world perfected and of a world of pure spirit; Blake seems to present both at once in Night IX. Throughout his work Blake considered nature, in one sense, satanic, as is especially clear in his annotations to Wordsworth and to Dante; the overthrow of nature seems to be exactly what Los brings about early in the last Night when Samson-like he tears down the heavens. But the evidence, especially from the lyrics, from the lyrical passages in *Poetical Sketches, Songs of Innocence,* and *Milton,* and even from the *Zoas* itself, is that Blake loved deeply what most people mean by "nature." The very annihilation of nature in Night IX is expressed in images of fundamental natural processes and products. In Blake's metaphorical treatment of nature he demonstrates once more his mastery of tenor-vehicle irony, his ability to use a single image for opposites and contrasting images for the same thing. At the same time Blake seems to be straightforwardly showing us our natural world as it should be and might be.

Night IX

Still more difficult than the problem of Blake's view of material nature is whether or not he is a psychological naturalist; that is, does he show the reader a way in which his inner self can be transformed while he remains in the world be physically inhabits? The answer is almost certainly yes; at any rate, the ninth Night, like the others, makes sense most immediately if so understood. Yet in many respects Blake is unquestionably a supernaturalist: he professed a belief in life after death, he claimed to be inspired by his dead brother and sang of eternal life on his deathbed, he prayed for his friends and referred to Jesus as his Savior, and he returns in critical places in *The Four Zoas* to the motif of grace. Blake is no pietist, but even more emphatically he is no secularist or materialist. He is a genuinely religious poet, though his religious synthesis operates on what for most people are inherently and permanently incompatible antitheses. Much of the resistance that influential critics have shown to accepting Blake's own professions of Christianity derives from a nearly universal Western idea—a lingering, perhaps unconscious assumption—that Christianity necessarily demands submission to external authority and the denial of the senses, especially of sex. Blake, as a radical Protestant, considered it his Christian duty to hate authority and repression, but that does not mean he rotated all orthodox tenets precisely one hundred and eighty degrees. The traditional Christian interpretation of the resurrection of the body—an article of faith that dominates Blake's later works—makes more sense as a gloss on his ideas in Night IX than do the tortuous efforts by some exegetes to defuse and neutralize them as ingenious parodies of Christianity.

Certainly *The Four Zoas* is a psychology and a psychiatry, but its terminus is spiritual; the titanic myth of Night IX is diminished if it is read as nothing more than advice on how to be well adjusted or as a cynical spoof of Christian doctrine. Even to understand it solely as an account of regeneration in this world—a psychological revitalization through the liberation of a strengthened imagination—is to deprive the myth of a spiritual and otherworldly dimension by which Blake himself set great store. In Blake's view, unless we can live abundantly within space and time, we shall not develop the capacity to enjoy a spiritual existence free of material limitations. Exaggerated concern with an afterlife is spiritually damaging because it cuts one off from full participation in this life. Yet a pragmatic resignation to mundane limitations, allowing one's infinite mind to accommodate itself to the finite world, is equally damaging to the soul. The resurrection of the body and soul must begin here and now, but it need not be limited to the here-and-now.

Perhaps it is a mistake in reading the *Zoas* to recognize a clear distinction, even conceptually, between this world and an other world. At the very least one ought not to insist on the distinction as a crucial matter of ontology, though to most people that will be a hard statement whether their attitude toward an afterlife is faith, disbelief, or skepticism. Blake may well have regarded this symptom of dualism as he did so many others: as an impediment to human happiness either because it is false or because it is distracting, as something he had to combat in his role as prophet just as he had to combat the false distinction between human and divine.

The Night opens with a desolate Los and Enitharmon who build Jerusalem while grieving over the death of Jesus and feeling terror at "Non Existence." The building of Golgonooza, artistic activity, has become soul building. Los and Enitharmon are giving a new reality to Jerusalem, the universal Emanation or epiphany of human freedom who has appeared as a female character; the city they build is a social and external form for the regenerated human community. This they do in despair, believing Jesus dead; their efforts indicate what man can do even when he believes that he works alone, without divine aid. Although Los and Enitharmon inaugurated the redemptive process in Night VII, their awareness of its results lags behind Enion's at the end of Night VIII. They do not sense as she does that death has already begun to yield new life, that "Jesus stood beside them in the Spirit Separating / Their Spirit from their body." This last phrase is surprising, since Night IX will be devoted in great part to the reuniting of what has been divided; the wording apparently contradicts the assertion of the Devil in *The Marriage of Heaven and Hell* that man has no body distinct from his soul. In the present context Blake probably means that Jesus, through his dimly understood example, is guiding man and woman away from the despair induced by a belief in the finality of bodily death. Although their "Phantom Eyes" in the merely natural plane of vision see the crucified body, their spirits respond at the same time to the Jesus who is always present and alive in the human world (IX 1-6; 117:1-6 E371-72).

Enion and Tharmas, consistent with their role as the instinctive faculty, are sensors and heralds, rather than agents, of the apocalypse; for example, the unnamed trumpeter in the eleventh line of the Night turns out to be Tharmas. But Los is an agent; in his awesome rending of the universe, "cracking the heavens across from immense to immense," he reenacts Jesus' rending of the veil and sets off the apocalypse. In reflex desperation, Los seizes and tears down the sun and moon. His terrified struggle for life could be misunderstood as a sign that he has not absorbed the Blakean meaning of the Crucifixion as the ultimate act of the annihilation of the self. But as Nights VII and VIII have shown, Los has come further than the other Zoas toward understanding. His resistance here to physical death is not an absolute error; it is a sign that he loves and values life and will tolerate no pseudolife. Stretching out and rooting himself into the cosmos with vegetable-like tenacity, he both causes and experiences the annihilation of the material world. Moreover, his violent struggle knocks down the whole world of illusion, the false universe most of humanity participates in and settles for. We are meant to recall Night II in which, in contrast, Urizen uses the power delegated to him by Albion to construct a false order that soon disintegrates from its own weaknesses and inconsistencies.

Acting now with the strength delegated to him by Tharmas and Urthona in Night VIII, Los moves to destroy what is left of the makeshift worlds of all the Zoas; the result is the revelation of truth in an instantaneous spasm of destruction that reunifies the psychic world (IX 6-17; 117:6-17 E372). The shadowy Spectres of Enitharmon and of Urthona, no longer perceived as substantial, disappear and their bodies are buried in the rubble; Rahab and Tirzah are engulfed in the universal conflagration; the serpentine form of Orc is consumed in his alternate form of fire (IX 24-41; 117:24-118:16 E372). These multiple personalities, which were necessary in Blake's earlier anatomy of error, collapse and organicize into unified characters now purged of error, who in turn collapse and organicize into a reunified humanity. This means, if we render Blake's myth psychologically, that the labyrinthine oversubtleties and involuted rationalizations that have upheld the communal illusion of material reality are precipitately and drastically simplified by exposure to the spiritual dimension, the Edenic fire that has been excluded from human life.

The cracking of the heavens breaks up the firmament that had sealed off this world from the "fires of Eternity"; when our world is opened to Eden these fires are admitted. In an extensive wordplay on the account in Revelation 6:14 of the moment when the heavens are rolled back like a scroll, Blake describes the "scrolls of the Enormous volume of Heaven & Earth," the unrolling of the "books of Urizen,"

Night IX

the gathering of Orc's flames "in animating volumes" (IX 10-35; 117:10-118:10 E372) —all episodes in an internal and external apocalypse that is both terrifying and exhilarating for mankind. We experience simultaneously the liberation from psychic enslavement, the breakdown of civilized rules of order, and the disintegration of the familiar natural world in horrendous cataclysms. Instead of the solid universe—the stony earth and almost stony sky of the Mundane Shell, with its confining yet reassuring limits of the starry floor and watery shore—there emerges what at first seems to be an entirely chaotic universe of blood and fire that swallows up the Tree of Mystery and the Synagogue of Satan (IX 67-69; 119:1-3 E373).

Like the startlingly literal descriptions of weaponry in Night VIII, the realistic scenes that immediately follow Los's act, scenes in which the oppressed take vengeance on their dethroned oppressors, carry a conviction of vivid historical and political reference. The emphasis on vengeance and retribution, dramatized even more circumstantially and vividly later in the Night (IX 241-77; 122:37-123:32 E377-78) and different from anything in *Prometheus Unbound,* throws us back to the mood of poems like *America,* which seem to accept physical violence as necessary to social revolution in the fallen world. Politically, this section depicts the beginning of the apocalypse, the rage of the downtrodden, the last phase of history instead of the ideal world order that should emerge when history has served its purpose. Although analogous passages of vengeance occur in Blake's main model, the New Testament—for example, in the parable of Lazarus and Dives and especially in Jesus' description of the Last Judgment (Matt. 25:31ff.) —this motif seems out of keeping with the theme of a spiritual regeneration predicated on forgiveness rather than accusation. But the tyrants who here get their just deserts are also the tyrants within us that inhibit our true humanity and must be cast out through revolutionary acts of vision. It is common for people newly released from neurotic or other destructive inhibitions to feel outraged hostility toward their own false values, as though these were external enemies and not self-generated and self-imposed errors.

Another important image in this early phase of the apocalypse, a recurrent one in Night IX, is the image of the family: "the trembling families / Of women & children throughout every nation under heaven / Cling round the men in bands of twenties & of fifties" (IX 46-48; 118:20-22 E372). Like the image of clothing, the family image is ambiguous: it can suggest both universal unity (the family of man) and its opposite, the clannishness that repels all outsiders, even friendly ones. One of the major functions of Night IX is to educate humanity to the first of these meanings and to annihilate the second. The family image develops from the poem's imagistic starting point: the torments of love and jealousy, shown earlier to be a threat to connubial bliss and now a barrier to world unity. These families gather not in exclusive units of four or five but in bands of twenties and of fifties; the regenerative effects on society of the enlargement of the family parallel the joyful marital reconciliations of the no-longer-jealous Zoas and Emanations later in this Night.

When the wave of destruction has done its work and all tyranny is destroyed, cut off even from the stony and dragon forms of Urizen, the purifying flames—in a passage Yeats might have written—enter the "Holy City":

> the wild flames whirring up
> The Bloody Deluge living flames winged with intellect
> And Reason round the Earth they march in order flame by
> flame.

Then the blood is left behind and, in lines that appear twice,

"From the clotted gore . . . / Start forth the trembling millions into flames of mental fire / Bathing their Limbs in the bright visions of Eternity" (ıx 85-90,43-45; 119:18-23, 118:17-19 e373,372) . The orderly march of these flames of intellect and reason reconciles the imagery and attributes of Orc and Urizen, and the bright visions of Eternity begin to penetrate the sleeping consciousness of Albion himself.

Suddenly Albion cries out from somewhere "Beyond this Universal Confusion"—that is, as the voice of the human genus itself, not as the aggregate of the millions of trembling individuals feeling the pangs of rebirth. Albion moans from his rocky deathbed in the South, originally Urizen's quarter before the fallen realignments and exchanges of roles described variously in almost every Night of the poem.[2] With his head on the rock, he resembles Jacob on his rocky pillow at Bethel, but what Albion is awakening from is a stupendous nightmare instead of an angelic vision. His lament reiterates those of Ahania and, earlier, of Enion: all good things have been perverted to their opposites and in place of abundant life and joy there is only foul and sterile suffering and death. Groggy as he is, he is at last conscious of his terrible illness. Despite his scorn of the war within his own members and his struggles to rouse himself, he is too weak to do more than cry "When shall the Man of future times become as in days of old" and sit upright upon his "Horrible rock" (ıx 91-122; 119:24-120:12 e373-74) . But his will is strong and he tries again to take charge of his own life, not in a vague lament but in a specific and stern challenge to Urizen.

In his original abdication in Night II Albion had blamed both Luvah and Urizen but had considered Urizen a competent vicegerent. Symmetrically, here in Night IX he will chastise Luvah severely (ıx 363-74; 126:6-17 e380) , but he holds Urizen primarily responsible for the fallen world because reason should be capable of more discrimination than passion. Albion's challenge to Urizen echoes both the "Where art thou" of God's question to Adam and Jesus' call "Come forth" in the episode of Lazarus's resurrection often recalled in *The Four Zoas*.

Urizen fails to respond to his original title as "Prince of Light" or even to the sterner epithets "Schoolmaster of souls great opposer of change," "dread form of Certainty." The only recrimination in this last phrase is the word "dread," for certainty is an important attribute of unfallen reason; Albion wants this certainty softened and humanized so that "little children play around thy feet in gentle awe." But such descriptions of former and future bliss are lost in the void; there is no reply.

Albion is gaining strength and alertness the longer he stays awake. Angrily he addresses Urizen's stony and dragon forms, commanding the dragon to lie down and "let Urizen arise." Urizen is ordered to return to his rightful place and function and rebuked for having deformed his original "beautiful proportions / Of life & person." Instead of hopeful promises, which he reserves for a later stage of Urizen's cure, Albion now hurls threats that he will take back the crown and cast Urizen forever into the indefinite (IX 124-46; 120:14-36 E374-75). Albion's tone to Urizen is like Los's to his Spectre in the first chapter of *Jerusalem*, but Albion will win Urizen over, not merely repress him.

Albion does more than simply denounce Urizen and show that he recognizes his mistake in allowing false reason to rule; his ringing speech to Urizen is that of a fully awakened humanity that now understands fundamental psychological and spiritual principles. One of these principles reaffirms the toleration of excess that had been preached in the Proverbs of Hell: if Urizen allows Luvah to rage without feeding that rage by opposing it, it will subside in peace. Urizen also learns that the perverted energy he finds so frightening is a product of his own attributes:

Night IX

My anger against thee is greater than against this Luvah
For war is energy Enslavd but thy religion
The first author of this war & the distracting of honest minds
Into confused perturbation & strife & honour & pride
Is a deceit so detestable that I will cast thee out
If thou repentest not

(IX 151-56; 120:41-46 E375)

An even more liberating insight is that sin (in the person of Rahab, as described in Joshua 2:18-24) is easily redeemed, even from error's power; it is error that is truly dangerous and deserving of ultimate rejection (IX 158-61; 120:48-51 E375). In correcting Urizen, Albion has renounced the major intellectual and moral errors responsible for man's long and desperate illness.

Urizen responds with a palinode, mixed in its tones but accurate in its expression of regained wisdom. Full of both excitement and misgivings yet eager to reassume the human form, Urizen repents having taken the antisacramental bread and wine of mortality, which transubstantiates the divine into the merely natural. He recites a catalog of his errors: his concern with futurity instead of the present; his development of cities and trade routes, which have devastated nature and befouled cities (apparently he now sees a connection between the grasping intellect and an overindustrialized, urbanized, economically predatory society); his seeking happiness in "spaces remote" rather than finding it in "the Eternal which is always present to the wise" and in "pleasure which unsought falls round the infants path"; his unwearied but nonproductive labors as stonecutter and warrior (instead of his proper work as plowman, resumed later in Night IX); and his ordering of the nations by dividing them, "separating family by family." Like Los immediately before his conversion in Night VII, Urizen feels that he alone is miserable; but now instead of trying to avert his own despair at the

cost of everything that breathes, he "Ungratified" gives all his
hoped-for joy to Luvah and Vala. In climactic lines he renounces all his major principles (ix 162-87; 121:1-26 e375-76) .

> Then Go O dark futurity I will cast thee forth from these
> Heavens of my brain nor will I look upon futurity more
> I cast futurity away & turn my back upon that void
> Which I have made for lo futurity is in this moment
> Let Orc consume let Tharmas rage let dark Urthona give
> All strength to Los & Enitharmon & let Los self cursd
> Rend down this fabric as a wall ruind & family extinct
> Rage Orc Rage Tharmas Urizen no longer curbs your rage.

Even in this speech there is something of the old Urizen. The
dominant tone is exhilaration (even the description of Los
as self-cursed is not a petulant wish but a resolve by Urizen
that no longer will he be the author of curses like the one
he had put on Los in Night III) . But there is an undertone
of his old distrust of excesses, as if he were daring his brother
Zoas to do their worst, go to extremes, have their own way
and find out whether they will like the consequences. It is
psychologically right that even in the act of throwing away
his crutches or his life preserver Urizen should have a sense
of reckless abandon as well as of regaining his life.

The undertone of exasperation is faint, however; as Urizen
loosens his hold on the other Zoas he is at last truly liberated.
Shaking off his aged mantles, "glorious bright Exulting in
his joy / He sounding rose into the heavens in naked majesty
/ In radiant Youth," like the magnificent young man in
Blake's print popularly called "Glad Day." Now Ahania,
"dancing from the East," an Aurora to his Apollo, is restored
to her consort. Her reappearance, inevitable at some point
in the process of general renewal, is particularly appropriate
at this moment, when Urizen has just acted on the advice
he had ignored when she offered it in Night III. The narra-

tive comment at this point, "Excess of Joy is worse than grief," sounds like a Proverb of Hell, and certainly Urizen is unused to the road of excess. At the moment of reunion Ahania dies, as Lear dies when (according to some interpretations of the play) he convinces himself that Cordelia is alive after all. Like many a convalescent so encouraged by the first signs of health that he wants to abandon his regimen, Urizen is unprepared for this heartbreaking setback (IX 191-200; 121:30-39 E376). But Albion, once again calling him "Prince of Light," reassures the widower that Ahania will revive when the time is right. Enormous agricultural labors, like the final therapy necessary for complete recovery, await Urizen's attention. Only when they are done will his Persephone be returned to him, after her winter's sleep. That seasonal pattern will in fact be adopted by all the Emanations, who will imitate Ahania's obedience, following their model Jerusalem, "a City yet a Woman" and Bride of the Lamb— the state and condition of perfect human freedom and the spiritual mother of all regenerate and free human beings (IX 204-24; 121:43-122:20 E376).

The emphasis on woman's obedience here is distressing to admirers of Blake who are concerned with full equality for the sexes. In much of this poem and in other works as well, Blake is fairly evenhanded in his treatment of men and women, yet there is no denying that in his symbolic hierarchy the masculine principle of active genius is superior to the feminine principle of comforting tenderness. The customary defense of Blake on this issue is to point out that such sexual metaphors are age-old expressions of the soul's relation to God (female-to-male) and humanity's relation to nature (male-to-female). But even when Blake is not writing metaphorically, as in his comment on Lavater's Aphorism 539 (E585,K82), he envisions women in a subservient role: "let the men do their duty & the women will be such wonders, the female life lives from the light of the male. see a mans female dependants you know the man."[3]

For redeemed humanity, male or female, however, obedience does not mean what it does for fallen man. Men as well as women, all reborn persons, are to "live in Jerusalem" and thus participate in her relationship with the Lamb. Later in Night IX Albion counsels both the male Luvah and the female Vala henceforth to be servants, to "obey & live" (IX 363; 126:6 E380). In Eternity sexuality obeys humanity and obedience means unforced allegiance to our best, truly and fully human, selves. The paradox resembles the incident in *The Divine Comedy* in which Dante, after completing his purgatorial labors, is crowned and mitred his own king and bishop; henceforth, Virgil tells him, it would be wrong for Dante not to do what he wants to do (*Purgatorio,* xxviii 140-142). The distinction between obedience and following one's own desires becomes, for both poets, meaningless.

Though his cure is assured, Urizen is disappointed that it is neither complete nor instantaneous; he regrets that his error is still with him, that the light of his mind is held in by chains and locks, to be released only on schedule, by "measure" and "carefulness" (the "Lock" checking the flow of the river of light plays also on the philosopher's name and the ordinary padlock). In a mood that combines his new rapture with his old rhetoric and imagery, he asks the question we quoted earlier: "Where shall we take our stand to view the infinite & unbounded / Or where [our] human feet for Lo our eyes are in the heavens" (IX 226-29; 122:22-25 E376-77). In Night VI the declaration "Here will I fix my foot" (VI 227; 73:14 E343), implying also the compass foot, had been a stubborn attempt to make permanent the vortexes, the systems. In Night IX a similar idea, significantly changed in form to a question, produces the contrary result: the universe explodes, "All things reversd flew from their centers." As Enion had foreknown, the paroxysms of human beings caught in the process of rebirth are felt in the animal creation as well, in direct contrast with the uncommunicative animals who in Night VI had dramatized the inadequacy of rationalistic reductionism. In Night IX the description of the unbinding of Urizen reverses some details of his binding in Night IV and assimilates them with imagery from Ezekiel's vision of dry bones: the universe is "rivn link from link," "rattling bones / To bones Join, shaking convulsd the shivering clay breathes" (IX 230-32; 122:26-28 E377). Amid numerous verbal echoes of the parable of sheep and goats and the accounts of rectification in Revelation and Isaiah, a judge who abases himself before the now unforgiving prisoner he had judged unjustly is confronted with the universal judge, the Son of Man who appears with his retinue of patriarchs and Zoas. The biblical detail of Jesus' coming in the cloud (here a bloody one, to remind us that this judge knows what it is like to be a victim) fits Blake's larger pattern of imagery in that it echoes and reverses the emergence from clouds of the spurious forms of deity in earlier episodes (IX 235-84; 122:31-123:39 E377-78).

The pace of regeneration in Night IX is not steady; new life develops fitfully, through sudden energetic advances punctuated by halts and sometimes by slight retrogressions which dramatize two points: that salvation demands persistent effort and that it is in itself a transfigured form of strife. Thus both Albion and Urizen are repelled as they try to "Enter the Consummation / Together" (IX 288-90; 124:3-5 E378). Albion's detention in Beulah is an act of divine mercy intended to make permanent his redeemed body (IX 356-57; 125:38-39 E380); the sojourn suggests the inherent purity of the human body, which will need no purgatorial flames when it is accepted as holy and beautiful. For Urizen the rejection by the flames is a signal for him to begin the work of the universal harvest and vintage, which will continue through the remainder of the poem until at its end Ahania is restored to him.

This great metaphor of harvest and vintage is a rich elaboration and synthesis of images appearing all through the Bible—especially in the toil of Adam; the parables of the sower, the laborers in the vineyard, and the wheat and tares; the joyful bringing in of the sheaves in Psalm 126; the beating of swords into plowshares in Isaiah 2 and Micah 4; and the trampling of the grapes in Isaiah 63 and Revelation 14. It is presented as a circumstantial account of how bread and wine, the symbols of truly human communion, are made. The sublimity of this myth is a product of the grandeur and clarity of the images themselves, their contrast with those appearing in the condemnation of nature earlier in the poem, and especially their way of echoing and fusing interrelated archetypal and biblical metaphors, resulting in a texture so dense that a discussion of most of the biblical parallels is impossible. Throughout, the seeds, grains, and grapes are human souls and their cultivation is made possible only by the new cooperativeness among the Zoas and Emanations, with Albion as benevolent overseer and landlord. The division of labor between farmer and vintner expresses the new relation between the poem's two central antagonists Urizen and Luvah. In deriving both types of labor from famous passages in Isaiah, Blake, as much as any traditional Christian typologist, reads Isaiah as a herald of Messiah.

Aesthetically and prophetically, Urizen's repentance in Night IX demands a parallel response from Luvah. By now "fierce Orc had quite consumd himself in Mental flames / Expending all his energy against the fuel of fire." Albion now addresses Luvah and Vala, the "Demon & Demoness of Smoke" (smoke being the literal product of Orc's extinguished fires as well as a variation of the cloud imagery already established); he commands them to return to their

proper place, the place of seed (IX 358-74; 126:1-17 E380).
Albion's lecture sums up the theme of the whole poem:

> If Gods combine against Man Setting their Dominion above
> The Human form Divine. Thrown down from their high
>   Station
> In the Eternal heavens of Human Imagination: buried
>   beneath
> In dark oblivion with incessant pangs ages on ages
> In Enmity & war first weakend then in stern repentance
> They must renew their brightness & their disorganizd
>   functions
> Again reorganize till they resume the image of the human
> Cooperating in the bliss of Man obeying his Will
> Servants to the infinite & Eternal of the Human form.

Albion's appeal to reason had been impassioned; his appeal
to passion is sternly didactic. Urizen's response had been a
conscious, verbal confession and itemizing of his misdeeds.
From Luvah and Vala, instead of a verbal reply there follows
the appropriate equivalent, a beautiful pastoral interlude,
a masque for the last act of the human drama. When Luvah
later does recite Albion's lesson, he epitomizes it in a mere
nine words: "Attempting to be more than Man We become
less" (IX 709; 135:21 E388) —a maxim well stated by one
who had earlier wished to deliver "the sons of God / From
bondage of the Human form" (II 107-08; 27:17-18 E311).

Probably the first thing that strikes readers of the pastoral
section is its anomalous tone, as though the gods had tired
of nectar and decided to try peasants' fare for a change. This
shift of tone, reflected in the smooth and melodious hepta-
meters of the passage, is significant even apart from the content of the masque. Its tenderness, even silliness in both the
modern sense and the archaic sense of unsophistication, provides a rest from the tensions and unremitting excitement
that have built up since Night VII and have been reintensi-

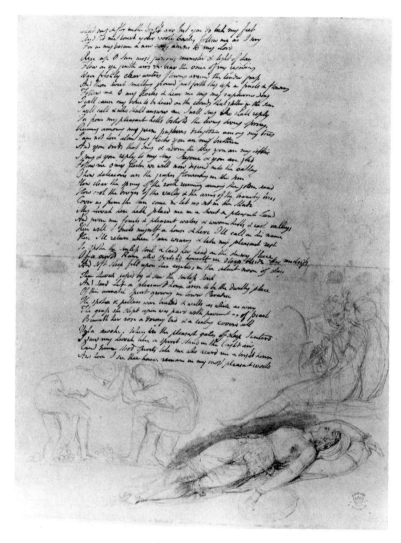

The mood of Vala's idyll: innocent sensuousness. MS page 128 (Night IX). Reproduced by permission of the British Library Board.

fied in the recent transformations. The effect of the dream play is pleasing to anyone who, in a languorous mood, has felt that Blake's Beulah is more attractive than his Eden. In *Milton,* plate 30, the inhabitants of Eden are explicitly stated to have such escapist needs for rest from the exhausting wars of life.

The pastoral interlude is more than escapism, however; it describes a substantive development in man's psychic education and growth. It is presented initially as half-illusory, a dreamy entertainment for the harvest laborers resting from their exertions. But a hint of its more serious thematic function is provided at the outset when Luvah and Vala descend and enter through "the Gates of Dark Urthona" (ix 375-84, 557-58; 126:18-27,131:20-21 E380,385), recalling Thel's admittance to the subterranean world past the "northern bar" lifted by "The eternal gates terrific porter" (*Thel,* 6:1). The pastoral episode of *The Four Zoas* explores some of the central issues posed in *The Book of Thel* and is laden with verbal and visual reminders of it. For Thel the revelation of her sensory potential is horrifying, but in the epic the emotive and passional faculties are learning of their own innocence. Vala's new-found occupation as shepherdess, her rank as mistress of the garden, her lines like "I will call & who shall answer me I will sing who shall reply," and her inclination to "sit me down" and "complain & sigh for immortality" (ix 410-40; 127:16-128:10 E381-82) —all these are strongly reminiscent of Thel's character and situation. But significantly Thel's contrary, Oothoon, is also evoked as Vala gathers "flowers for her bosom" (ix 477; 129:10 E383). The redeemed Vala, sexuality as it should be, is able to reconcile the openness and energy of Oothoon with the delicacy (but not the fearfulness) of Thel.

The pastoral episode has two thematic purposes. One is to show the redeemed view of physical nature, which of course Vala herself personifies. Delighted with her garden, she at first worships the natural sun as the source of her happiness and of her very existence. The Luvah-like error of deifying nature is just as serious as the Urizenic one of elevating its Newtonian laws to the level of ultimate reality. Like a good teacher tolerating a student's fallacious thinking in order to reach a reductio ad absurdum, the now-enlightened Luvah encourages Vala's delusion, telling her that she is no more than grass. Instantly Vala begins, like Thel, to lament her fate "if I am like the grass & so shall pass away." In the same way that Albion has strengthened his Zoas by giving them first hope, then despair, and finally reassurance, Luvah puts Vala through a reversal of feelings: "Yon Sun shall wax old & decay but thou shalt ever flourish." In Vala's new state of wiser joy, she sees the natural sun, the "Guinea" sun of Blake's *Vision of the Last Judgment* (E555, K617), as a mere shadow of the true sun, imaginatively conceived. Her response is a "new song"—as in Psalms 33 and 40, Isaiah 42, and Revelation 5 and 14—of nature made innocent, perceived anew as showing forth the glory of God. Her hymn recalls not only *Spring* in *Songs of Innocence* but also the tenth strophe of the Intimations Ode ("Then sing, ye Birds, sing, sing a joyous song! / And let the young Lambs bound") and Eve's lovely celebration of nature in *Paradise Lost* (IV 635-56) which begins "With thee conversing I forget all time." In Vala's recognition of Luvah as her Lord, Blake may also have had in mind Eve's submissive preface to her anthem: "My Author and Disposer, what thou bidd'st / Unargu'd I obey." Though literally the time is noon, Vala's speech, like Eve's, is a kind of vespers; when "the Sinless Soul" concludes her statement she "laid her head on the downy fleece / Of a curld Ram who stretchd himself in sleep beside his mistress" (IX 455-56; 128:25-26 E382).

Pictorially the mood of this passage is captured perfectly in the definitive scene of innocence on the seventh plate of

Night IX

America. In the rather highly finished drawing here in the *Four Zoas* manuscript (MS page 128), a reclining figure rests her turbaned head on a large pouf and her hand on her tambourine, her transparent Eastern dancing costume revealing her genitals. Above, a girl with bangles on her sleeve (perhaps another harem girl or even a sort of genie) plays a pipe and her companion plays a harp; to the left another girl and a boy hold their downstage arms in hand-wrestling position and play with small round objects with their upstage hands. Perhaps the sleeping tambourine player is dreaming of the musicians and the wrestlers; at any rate the drawing emphasizes the elements of play, fantasy, sensuality, and holiday in this part of the text.

The second purpose of the pastoral interlude is to show the psychic redemption of passion as innocence, which is why Tharmas and Enion enter the masque now in their fundamental character as little children (IX 507-56; 130:4-131:19 E383-85). That passion has now become so nearly identified with instinctual innocence is reflected also in Vala's having become a shepherdess, since in Eternity Tharmas is a shepherd. The terrible quarrel between him and Enion which had opened Night I is now playfully repeated in the courtship spats between these children, easily settled by the now-motherly Vala.

The vehicle of the allegory here, the attempt by Vala to play Pandarus to these two mere children, is startling, though in poems like the manuscript *A cradle song* Blake recognized the complex sexual nature of infants and young children. His allegorical point is a double one, relevant to both passion and instinct. Passion, especially sexuality, is no longer to be considered a hidden activity mysteriously reserved for adults; the very notion that innocence and passion are antithetical has been outgrown, and Vala no longer tries to appropriate for herself the sexual joys of others or to proclaim herself the exclusive deity of sexuality. If wisdom doth live with children round her knees—a Wordsworthian paraphrase for what Albion has taught Urizen earlier—so doth passion.

After all of the parent–child conflicts in the poem, beginning with Los's and Enitharmon's rejection of their parents in Night I, it is significant that Vala takes a nurturing, permissive, and responsible parental role toward the original Parent power Tharmas and his Emanation, who is so closely identified with mother Earth. In this fantasy section, the childlike primeval parents who have been bewildered and hurt by the fall are at last petted and cared for; instinct is valued and protected, not rejected as a despised parent. Blake here makes the allegorical point that instinct must relearn its original trust in itself, the certainty that impulse does not necessarily lead to wickedness as fallen man assumes. Of course if instinct becomes self-conscious it ceases to be instinct; Blake's awareness of this limitation helps explain why the pastoral sequence ends with Tharmas and Enion playing "In infant sorrow & joy alternate." Later the two will be reunited in their adult avatars, where the antithesis between instinct and mature awareness is resolved (ix 613-14; 132:36-37 e386).

After the dream interlude or pastoral masque, we return like Prospero to the world that is still in travail; the revels are over. But dreams and masques are more than mere diversions: dreamer and audience are changed by such interludes and the laborers are ready now to bring in the mature grain and the ripe clusters of grapes. The remainder of the poem, until the last thirty-one lines, alternates between sharply contrasting tones of grief and sorrow, tension and release. This alternation is puzzling; our instincts as readers of epic poetry, as well as our response to the poem's basic movement up to this point, have led us to expect a triumphantly happy ending. The best way to read the last few hundred lines of the poem is not as the conclusion of a temporal sequence, psychological or personal or historical, but as a simultaneous projection of visions of fallen and resurrected man. The river of Lethe, and all that it implies about the forgetfulness of past error, has no positive role in Blake's salvation myth as it has in Dante's. As Demogorgon warns at the end of *Prometheus Unbound,* salvation is not a fixed state that can be achieved once and for all in the human psyche or in the world. Those who have learned to see life imaginatively but who lapse inexplicably into periods of doubt, cynicism, or mere dullness are well aware of this truth.

If *The Four Zoas* did no more than build up to a mere reminder that there are two contrary states of the human soul, or to an observation that time and eternity are coexisting, alternative perspectives on life, the anticlimax would be so disappointing that the work could not seriously demand consideration as an epic. In epic, as Wordsworth says of his experience described in *The Prelude,* all is gratulant if rightly understood. And in Blake's poem the variations of mood in the conclusion are not swings of a pendulum or mere alternations of dissonance and concord. Like all sophisticated epics since Virgil, *The Four Zoas* is more than an attempt just to portray God's ways, it is an attempt to justify them; in the poem each dissonance is resolved, yielding to affirmation. Thus the darkness and storm to which the dreaming laborers awake soon modulates to Urizen's jubilant cry "Times are Ended," whereupon his offspring "exhale the spirits of Luvah & Vala thro the atmosphere" of the thunderstorm (IX 568-70; 131:31-33 E385). The laborers awake from their dream in Beulah to find, like Adam, that the dream is truth; the Zoas really are innocent and regenerate. (Every person who has awakened in heartbreak from a dream in which a great personal grief like that caused by the death of someone loved has been lifted will feel the force of Blake's reversal of this common phenomenon.)

The laborers now join in a joyous harvest feast, a clear

reversal of the ghastly nuptial feast of Night I. The celebration is interrupted by the appearance of Enion in the midst of a whirlwind and a rattling of bones (two major images from Ezekiel). She addresses the guests in imagery of the rotting grave, which soon modulates into that of the emergence of the moth from the cocoon and the renewal of the wasteland; the passage ends in her nourishing the universe with milk and rejoining her husband Tharmas as a guest at the banquet (IX 590-614; 132:13-37 E385-86). But then, as in *The Book of Urizen,*

> Many Eternal Men sat at the golden feast to see
> The female form now separate They shudderd at the horrible thing
> Not born for the sport and amusement of Man but born to drink up all his powers
>
> (IX 621-23; 133:5-7 E386)

One of these guests—who apparently personify a viewpoint above the main action—launches a gloomy indictment of man as a worm and selfish escapist, but this speech too modulates to a description of how human beings, through their very division into families, learn that "Man liveth not by Self alone but in his brothers face / Each shall behold the Eternal Father & love & joy abound" (IX 621-42; 133:5-26 E386-87). A speech by Tharmas begins in vengeful, vituperative glee at the destruction of mystery and kings but is transformed into a generous greeting of newly liberated slaves. This motif is repeated in the touching song composed by an African black, in which he hails his restoration to his native land, his family, and their children, thus sustaining in a context of universal brotherhood the family metaphor used repeatedly in Night IX (IX 657-91; 134:5-135:3 E387-88).

The most striking and challenging of these ambivalent passages begins with the Eternal Man's charge to Luvah to bring in the vintage, which is now ripe. The episode begins auspiciously with Luvah's statement of his new motto, "Attempting to be more than Man we become less," and his willing cooperation with Urizen at shared tasks in both granary and winery. When his crown of thorns falls from his head, Christianity is no longer identified, erroneously, with the worship of suffering. Luvah begins a new song, apparently a work chant, called the Song of Los, and all his sons, his tigers and lions, his villages, even the "Odors of life" released from the winepress, join in. The theme is the joy of resurrection (ix 693-731; 135:5-136:4 e388-89).

Then a situation develops that is not just discordant but appalling. Outside the winepress, where the singing goes on, all is jubilation; after laughing, shouting, and getting drunk on the "odors," many drown in the wine and are placed on skins of wild animals (a contrast to the pastoral slumber of Vala on the fleece of the living ram). This exuberance is appropriate for the regenerated emotions, Luvah, Vala, and the rest. But the souls still within the winepress who have not yet become "Human Odors" are undergoing agony unparalleled even in the blackest Nights of the poem. Those who are suffering are not just the legions of mystery but also "Human Grapes." Like Dante's purgatorians they are willing to endure their torment; they know that the pangs of eternal birth are better than the grief without a pang that is nonexistence. But the victims' willingness to suffer neither explains nor excuses the sadistic glee of their tormentors, the sons and daughters of Luvah who tread the grapes (ix 732-54; 136:5-27 e389). An analogue is the harsh contempt that people who are liberated, or think they are, sometimes show for those more conventional ones who are painfully trying to escape their newly sensed limitations. And within the individual mind the Dionysian feeling of abandon mocks psychic remnants of caution and conservatism. Nevertheless this orgy of violence is hard for the reader to accept at the point in the poem when he longs for misery to be comforted and enmity to be reconciled.

Perhaps a scene of torture and suffering is necessary in the last Night because we need a summation of the interrelated themes of the forgiveness of sin and the uses of suffering. Luvah and Vala sober up from their blood-drunkenness, repent, and are forgiven after a disciplinary banishment .(IX 795-800; 137:28-33 E390). Because the grapes would have simply rotted if they had been left on the vine, the painful crushing of the outlines of their old identity is necessary to preserve their essence and make it potent in the form of new wine. In a new transubstantiation, the blood of human sacrifice becomes the wine of eternal life; no longer will Albion have to lament as at the beginning of Night IX the "sound of rage of Men drinking each others blood / Drunk with the smoking gore & red but not with nourishing wine" (IX 121-22; 120:11-12 E374).

The breadth of Blake's sympathy with different kinds of people and with different portions of the psyche emerges as Albion, man's totality, darkens with sorrow over the sadism of the grape treaders. At the beginning of Night II when he had felt threatened by the Dionysian principle, he had called in a false form of the Apollonian. Now he knows better than to replace one form of psychic tyranny with its opposite; when the associates of Luvah lose consciousness or reach the bellicose stage of drunkenness, Albion does not prescribe austerity but rather sends as his agents a Tharmas and Urthona "satiated / With Mirth & Joy." They are not policemen but imaginative and sensitive helpers, commissioned to finish the work of the great vintage by separating the wine from the lees. Luvah is "put for dung on the ground"; in Psalm 83 and in Jeremiah 16 this is a punishment for the wicked, but in *The Four Zoas* the image suggests a productive, fertilizing use even of the refuse from the wine-making process. When Tharmas, Urthona, and their helpers ceremoniously load the wine on wagons "with solemn songs & joy," the "Human Wine" now liberated through pain from mere natural existence as grapes stand "wondering in all their delightful Expanses," and the music of the spheres is heard (IX 772-800; 137:5-33 E390).

Tharmas and Urthona have another task too: they must complete the corresponding work of breadmaking begun by Urizen's sowing, reaping, and threshing of the grain. The threshing process and especially the winnowing fan or whirlwind used by Tharmas are prophesied by Isaiah (41:15-16) and John the Baptist (Luke 3:17). The mills and ovens, Blakean contributions to the prophetic tradition, are not described in as much detail as the winepress, but the grains suffer no less than the grapes. Yet like its biblical prototypes, this is a harvest that groans to be delivered, and the suffering must be undergone. Since the grain is associated with thought, as grapes are with passion, the suffering symbolized in breadmaking is intellectual: "in their inmost brain / Feeling the crushing Wheels they rise they write the bitter words / Of Stern Philosophy & knead the bread of knowledge with tears & groans." The important contrast here is with the bread of sorrow kneaded in Night VII by Urizen's daughters from a pulp made of the fruit of the Tree of Mystery and fed to Orc. There mystery became sorrow, producing further suffering and mystery. But it is possible for sorrow to become knowledge. Here the final product is the Bread of Life, heaped in gold and silver baskets for the nourishment of eternal humanity (IX 806-24; 138:1-19 E391).

In *Prometheus Unbound* the crucial decision leading to human renewal occurs in the first of the four acts; by Act II the dramatic (though not necessarily the ideological) conflict has been resolved; Act III begins with an overthrow of mental and physical tyranny which is less conflict than ritual; and the rest of the play, more than a third of it, is a celebration of beatitude. In *The Four Zoas* we have to wait until the very last passage, a succinct thirty-one lines, for such a picture of bliss (IX 825-55; 138:20-139:10 E391-92). For the first time in the whole poem the mood is unqualified serenity. Even the gentle pastoral section earlier in Night IX had not sustained this mood firmly; small clouds had appeared in the form of Vala's uncertainties and the small-scale tensions between Tharmas and Enion. In any case, the Arcadian setting there cannot compare in grandeur with the cosmic setting of the poem's conclusion.

That this short final passage sounds unforcedly triumphant, with no suggestion that it has been arbitrarily imposed upon the serious tensions that have persisted to the very threshold of the climax, results from the thematic economy of the last lines. In them Blake again uses the technique used in the Gospel references of Night VIII, the ignition of explosive meanings through sparks of laconic understatement—this time as a coda for the poem as a whole. Motifs that have been progressively developed, refined, and freighted with meaning through thousands of lines are reevoked in rapid succession as straightforward, simple statements. Their tone is an almost enervated sigh of release, but they are also a dense node of themes, a ball formed of myriad golden strings extending far back through the poem's Nights. The sun and moon that had been torn down at the beginning of Night IX are restored in their pristine forms; the stars, seen from a human perspective, rise refreshed from their diurnal bath; plowman, shepherd, blacksmith work in their appointed ways and habitats (Luvah's role and presence are not specified here; perhaps he presides over times of rest); animals converse with man. The Emanations have already joined one another in joyful weaving (IX 778-82; 137:11-15 E390). Stars, formerly conceived as distant fires, are "consumd like a lamp blown out & in their stead behold / The Expanding Eyes of Man behold the depths of wondrous worlds." Instead of starlight, the inner light of human perception illuminates the void and reveals new worlds. All these incidents take their significance from what has gone before. Such density explains how Blake can counterbalance in thirty-one lines the enormous weight the rest of the poem has given to fallenness and struggle.

The conclusion of *The Four Zoas* reaffirms one of Blake's central premises: that fallen reality is a parody of true human happiness, the happiness which, as he told Dr. Trusler, he believed was possible in this world. Ordinary comic parody cannot work unless the parodist and his audience have the authentic original firmly in mind. As Blake knew, it is the sad but important task of every great prophetic artist to construct from its fallen parody an eternal archetype of true life which no one sees steadily and very many do not know at all. Like a paleontologist who envisages the whole and true shape of an organism on the basis of scattered, decayed fragments, the poet-prophet reconstructs from the parodic version of true human fulfillment an outline of its authentic form. Urizen, in the book named for him, had preached with tortured earnestness his perverse notion of unity: "One command, one joy, one desire, / One curse, one weight, one measure / One King, one God, one Law" (4:38-40). That is the parody of unity, though it is far from comic and indeed is taken for truth by much of humanity. *The Four Zoas* is comedy, *commedia* in the best sense, in that it rises from a seemingly real hell to a truly real heaven. Its ending reveals the true meaning of the "Unity" forecast in its opening lines: the "One Earth one sea . . . one Sun" now beheld by newborn man are not those of the fanatic Urizen's revisionism but the divine originals from which parodies like his, with all their power to seduce man from happiness, derive.

The same movement from the parody to the reality dictates the poem's bold last line, which proclaims the supersession of "dark Religions" by "sweet Science." We must face the full implications of the word "science" here, not shy away from them. Blake's presentation of the ideal as the reign of science forces us to recognize not only his energy but his penetrating and graceful intelligence, his respect for science when it is truly that and does not place abstract thought above human values. Blake probably had in mind *scientia* in the medieval sense of knowledge of any kind, and the adjective "sweet" further implies a contrast with the "bitter" variety, presumably the investigation of the purely physical and mechanical that is often thought of as all of science. Tharmas expresses something like this contrast in Night IV when he feels the loss of his humanity: "Is this to be A God far rather would I be a Man / To know sweet Science & to do with simple companions / Sitting beneath a tent & viewing sheepfolds & soft pastures" (IV 146-48; 51:29-31 E328). The false god that is inhuman science is itself one of the "dark Religions" of mystery (as the end of Night VIII makes clear) that "are departed" at the end of time. But the kind of science that meets human needs and desires, that leaves humanity psychologically and spiritually at the center of things and is hailed as eternal by Blake, need not exclude physical science. In the great awakening at the end of *Jerusalem* (98:9) "Bacon & Newton & Locke"—delivered from their satanic roles, the parodies of their best selves and functions—are at the side of "Milton & Shakspear & Chaucer." By implication this is true in the conclusion of *The Four Zoas* also; the day foreseen by Wordsworth in his Preface to *Lyrical Ballads* has at last come, when the "remotest discoveries of the Chemist, the Botanist, or Mineralogist . . . shall be familiar to us . . . as enjoying and suffering beings," and the poet will be at the side of the man of science, "carrying sensation into the midst of the objects of the science itself."

In *The Four Zoas* the fully imaginative life as typified in art has set mankind on the road to fulfillment. But after art has done its work it recedes. It would be wrong to think of Blake's ideal of human existence as synonymous with creativity for its own sake, just as it would be wrong and even ludicrous to think of the redeemed Job and his family, in the 1826 series of engravings of the Book of Job, as spending all their time playing the musical instruments they are holding in the last picture. It is an impressive fact that after Los takes the initiative early in Night IX by tearing down the universe, he is given almost no role in the remainder of the poem. In the final lines Blake writes almost jubilantly that the "Spectre of Prophecy" and the "Spectre Los" have departed. These statements could be taken to mean simply that the Urthona-Los force, creativity, has been purged of the poison that is specterism, but it probably means more: that art itself must avoid setting itself up as a God, that—as the protagonist of *Milton* recognizes when he refuses to let himself or his ideas be apotheosized—the worship of creativity can itself be idolatrous. Art as a specialized, sacral activity must wither away, as in Marxist mythology the state must do when it has helped bring about the millenium of a classless society. We may feel a pang of disappointment at the departure of Los as a dramatic character, though his role is fulfilled and though we know that his primal self Urthona lives and is back at his important work. But in Eternity, when Urthona is restored to his ancient strength, his function is to make the weaponry for intellectual warfare, not to fight these wars himself (IX 853-54; 139:8-9 E392). He is closely identified with Hephaestus; he is not a splendid Apollo, Neptune, or Dionysus like his fellow Zoas. The effect of the conclusion is to reduce the stature of the artist as such in order to place all persons, humanity, humankind, at the acme of reality. Blake's regenerated artist is the servant and not the lord of humanity, not even the first among equals. For a person who was himself a great artist to forswear such elitism is a final indication of Blake's ultimate concern with the resurrection to unity, with the restoration of full humanity to every kind and sort of human being. *The Four Zoas* is, in the end, not a justification of Blake's or the artist's ways but a justification of God's ways—which are the actions in time and eternity of the Eternal Man in all of us.

Appendix A: Night VII B

Night VIIB differs so obviously from VIIA that to describe them as different versions is inaccurate. The most important question is not how the two Nights differ but what, if anything, they have in common. In events, tone, texture, and above all in their ways of resolving the human crisis, A and B seem both to portray and to prescribe totally different worlds. The fundamental difference between A and B cannot be isolated, however, unless both the half-hidden similarities and the pointedness of the contrasts are taken into account. Night VIIB does have links to VIIA, and also to the other climactic Nights of *The Four Zoas*. Version B is tied to the rest of the poem by narrative threads as well as by parallels in theme and imagery. If Blake had retained VIIB as definitive, Nights VIII and IX would have had to be different from what they are, yet much in these Nights could have been used in a different form to follow B instead of A. Even where Blake charts different courses for the poem he seeks a single destination: human happiness through human integration. In both A and B the problem he is trying to solve remains the problem he had dramatized in Nights I through VI.

The joinery of Night VIIB, its articulation with the earlier and later parts of the poem, is in some ways clearer than in the A version. Although it has no verbal echoes of Night VI as close as the words "Then Urizen arose" with which VIIA opens, VIIB fulfills better than VIIA the expectations of frontal warfare raised in Night VI. The major links between the end of VIIB and the later Nights are the emphasis on activity in Beulah, which bridges VIIB and VIII, and the buildup of frustrations, which is released in Los's tearing down of the heavens in Night IX (IX 5-9; 117:5-9 E371-72). Chief among the contrasting parallels between VIIA and VIIB is the presentation of the basic problem of wholeness, of identity. In VIIB this problem is explored through somewhat realistic scenes of mistaken identity and emotional ambivalence; in VIIA these same matters are treated surrealistically.

The most obvious difference between the two versions is in their action, though a common pattern underlies both. Night VIIA deals first with a debate, between Urizen and Orc, and then explores the final splintering and initial step toward re-unification of the creative principle. The B version also divides into two sections, the first an outburst of vengeful warfare among the Zoas, the second a recognition by most of the participants of the futility of the civil war. In broad outline, A and B are basically similar: a movement from conflict to a point of rest.

Another striking difference between VIIA and VIIB is in their tones and textures. Compared with A, Night VIIB is coarsely woven. A is full of subtleties and niceties; even its comedy, as in the insults exchanged by Urizen and Orc, is full of fine-textured sardonic detail. Much of VIIB is so ludicrously bombastic that it seems to mock even the mock-heroic, like Fielding's *Jonathan Wild* or *Tom Thumb the Great*. If the issue were not the all-important one of human psychic survival, one could easily call Night VIIB farce. Unlike the unconscious self-revelations and subtle self-recognitions of VIIA, states of mind in B are relatively uncomplicated. Enmities are downright, strategies are direct, taunts and cruelties are raw. Although the import of a few passages is elusive (for example, the song sung by the "demons of the deep"—VIIB 187-210; 92:34-93:20 E396-97), motivations are generally prosaic: Enitharmon's wish to be protected and Tharmas's desire for retaliation, for example. Even where states of feeling are not so simple, the conflicts or contradictions are often between two feelings that are both simple in themselves, like wanting to eat one's cake and have it too.

As we argued earlier, the last three Nights broaden the poem's canvas to include events in the outer, more objective worlds of politics, sociology, institutional religion. Except for religion, about which VIIB has little to say, this trend is even more recognizable in VIIB than in VIIA and VIII. Urizen's lecture on the degradation of the poor in VIIA is startlingly explicit in its context (VIIA 117-29; 80:9-21 E348); but the two corresponding passages in VIIB are an even more literal documentary on the conditions of labor and industry (VIIB 12-17,170-86; 95: 25-30,92:17-33 E392,396). The lecture in VIIA is a subtle anatomy of ruling-class motives and methods in the use of brainwashing; the comments on commerce, the slave trade, and dehumanizing mechanization in VIIB are a practical handbook on the outward results of capitalist economics.

In sum, then: if VIIA was meant to supersede a Night VIIB written earlier (a theory that is still open to debate), Blake was enacting the Romantic pattern of shifting emphasis from the outer to the inner. Perhaps the best surmise about why Blake abandoned VIIB for VIIA is that, although the solution proposed in the latter remains problematical, it is at least some kind of solution; Night VIIB finds no solution at all. Night VIIB does not flatly equate human happiness and unhappiness with external conditions; like the rest of the poem it too is a psychodrama. But it does explore a solution—the impulse to hit back—which is the psychological equivalent of the overturning of external institutions. The solution is incompatible with one of the most deeply seated Romantic, and indeed Christian, insights, namely, that to overcome the enemy one must transform him by first transforming oneself. Night VIIB is thus a valuable appendage to *The Four Zoas* in that before allowing the poem to define the true, more subtle and difficult method of human regeneration, it explores at some length the alternative that, as history and literature attest, an impatient humanity almost always tries before disillusionment either brings on resigned cynicism or shows man a better way. Even so, Blake (unlike the historical Milton but like Shelley and even Wordsworth) allowed a hope to survive that somehow, perhaps through some loophole of events in the world, the human community and polity would eventually be renovated. That would be a bonus, however—a something added after the true kingdom of God which is within has been sought and found. One must do first things first: start with the inner man and then let Demogorgon, the necessary or at least hoped-for logic of events, work as he will.

Appendix A

The two lines with which Night VIIB opens contain the seed of much of the action in VIIA:

> But in the deeps beneath the Roots of Mystery in darkest
> night
> Where Urizen sat on his rock the Shadow brooded.
> (VIIB 1-2; 95:15-16 E392)

This cryptic anticipation of the later version remains undeveloped here. Instead, the poem moves abruptly to Urizen's self-portrait, the first of several bloated portraits of the Zoas in the tone of braggadocio that runs through much of the Night. Urizen as miles gloriosus is a parody of the Messiah who is portrayed as conquering king in Book V of *Paradise Lost* and identified by Blake in *The Marriage of Heaven and Hell* (plate 5) with "the Governor or Reason":

> The time of Prophecy is now revolvd & all
> This Universal Ornament is mine & in my hands
> The ends of heaven like a Garment will I fold them round me
> Consuming what must be consumd then in power & majesty
> I will walk forth thro those wide fields of endless Eternity
> A God & not a Man a Conqueror in triumphant glory
> And all the Sons of Everlasting shall bow down at my feet.
> (VIIB 4-10; 95:18-24 E392)

The grandiosity hints at some of the grim comic ironies, based on Urizen's failure to understand himself, that Blake multiplies and refines in the later version. If Urizen is the Miltonic Messiah, he is also Satan, as argued in *The Marriage of Heaven and Hell*. Urizen's boasts are absurdly overoptimistic, especially in relation to Satan's fate in *Paradise Lost*:

> with all his host
> Of rebel Angels, by whose aid aspiring
> To set himself in glory above his peers,
> He trusted to have equalled the Most High,
> If he opposed, and with ambitious aim

Appendix A

Against the throne and monarchy of God
Raised impious war in Heaven and battle proud
With vain attempt. Him the Almighty Power
Hurled headlong flaming from the ethereal sky
With hideous ruin and combustion down
(Paradise Lost, I 37-46)

The last lines of this prophecy about Satan are applied to Urizen in a later Night, when his usurpation of the divine humanity of Albion is punished; in VIIB we feel a combination of amusement and contempt at Urizen's absurd posturing. His gross error in believing that "all the Sons of Everlasting shall bow down at my feet" will be belied even within Night VIIB, where all three of the other Zoas will appear early on in the guise of militant opponents. Urizen has done no more than define for them by his example a misguided set of tyrannical, vengeful rules for the war games—rules that they, just as mistakenly, will follow.

There follows a passage in which Urizen establishes another form of the pernicious cosmic polity he had attempted in earlier Nights (vɪɪʙ 12-38; 95:25-96:18 ε392-93). The first article of his new constitution is a set of rules for capitalist commerce, which includes colonialism, child labor, and the slave trade, the whole making up a groaning "Universal Empire." The second article is religious and cosmological. Urizen's sons build a temple for the sun which is also a shrine of religious secrecy and shame; within that temple, significantly, the closer one comes to the innermost sanctum, the greater the mystery and frustration:

They formd the Secret place reversing all the order of delight
That whosoever enterd into the temple might not behold
The hidden wonders allegoric of the Generations
Of secret lust

Urizen's third attempt at constructing the cosmos combines many of the worst features of his earlier attempts in Nights II and VI. This time the referent of the parody is neither Ptolemaic nor Copernican-Newtonian but biblical. In a travesty of the creation of man in God's image, Urizen's sons "Builded a temple in the image of the human heart" and with the aid of the laboring beasts

>   put the Sun
> Into the temple of Urizen to give light to the Abyss
> To light the War by day to hide his secret beams by night
> For he divided day & night in different orderd portions
> The day for war the night for secret religion in his temple.

A deletion of the words "Urizen namd it Pande[monium]" from the next line (VIIB 39; E763) indicates that Blake originally intended to expand the parody both of Genesis and of *Paradise Lost* and to make more explicit the identity of Satan with the God whom most Christians, along with Milton, think of as Satan's antagonist. But Blake changed his mind, leaving unexplored this tempting by-path into mythological satire in order to concentrate on the main dramatic matter of Night VIIB, the confrontation with the other Zoas.

The first to declare war on Urizen are Los and Tharmas. Like Urizen, Los is portrayed (though in the third person) as superhuman, at least in scale; his "mighty stature" towers above the moon, his forehead is encircled with thunders, his naked limbs glitter, his knees are bathed in bloody clouds, his loins are girded with the weapons of war (VIIB 40-44; 96:19-23 E393). Nowhere else in the poem is Los presented in this Homeric or mock-Homeric way, as one of "the silly Greek & Latin slaves of the Sword" (*Milton*, plate 1). His backer and ally is Tharmas, whose attempt at ferocity in his opening words is even less in character. Echoing the parody of Messiah's elevation that a little earlier had given an ironic twist to Urizen's boasts, the Parent power Tharmas commissions his own son:

> But thou O Son whom I have crowned and inthrond thee
>   Strong
> I will preserve tho Enemies arise around thee numberless
>
> .   .   .   .
>
> And I will give thee all the ends of heaven for thy possession

Appendix A

> In war shalt thou bear rule in blood shalt thou triumph
>   for me
> Because in times of Everlasting I was rent in sunder
>   (VIIB 52-58; 96:31-97:4 E393)

This last line, in connection with the preceding lines, is a continuation of the parody, suggesting the begetting of the Son by God the Father. It serves also, however, to trigger the directness and honesty from which Tharmas as instinct can never stray for long; his outcry immediately modulates into a lament over a different, more humanly pathetic kind of sundering, his loss to his enemies of what he "loved best"—his "little daughters" and his "Crystal form that lived in my bosom." (As it will turn out, this modulation epitomizes the movement of the Night as a whole.) A little later the tetrad of titans is completed with the arising of Orc—in the stage-Homeric form that suits him better than it does the other Zoas (VIIB 125-43; 91:2-20 E395). In the meantime, Tharmas has performed for the reader a valuable service by stating in the simple language of instinct, unmodified by subtleties, the principle that structurally and thematically governs the greater part of Night VIIB: "Therefore I will reward them as they have rewarded me" (VIIB 68; 97:14 E393).

As Night VIIA and even the conclusion of VIIB itself will show, this law of retaliation is no solution. That lesson, most of the Romantics came to believe, must be learned by every apostle of violent political revolution, and learned the hard way, through failure. So too the human individual must learn that psychic imbalances cannot be rectified by head-on conflict between the components of the psyche, tempting though that simplistic solution is. Urizenically induced virgin fears and guilt cannot be exorcised by a deliberately chosen regimen of profligacy, irresponsible cutting-loose; nor can libidinous excess be cured by the iron laws of either reason or conscience; nor can good art proceed from a facile anti-intellectualism. These rough-hewn solutions, seen in the coarse-grained characterization and action of Night VIIB, fail for two reasons: first, because they do not recognize the organic interdependence of all mental faculties in the whole person—that is, the essential brotherhood of the

Zoas; second, because they consider the enemy something external—external to the person as he confronts the world and external to any particular component of the psyche as it confronts the other components that are its rivals for power. With Prometheus, man and his individual psychic elements must learn to say "It doth repent me" in order to find in themselves the Satan they had until then regarded, paranoically, as "him" or "them." Night VIIB shows the futility of opposition. But it does no more than that. At the end of VIIB hope and comfort are still distant, in the hands of the providence called Beulah; man is again "Waiting with Patience for the fulfilment of the Promise Divine" (VIIB 295; 95:8 E399) after having temporarily lost that patience.

In the revision, Night VIIA, man learns to find himself in the enemy and the enemy in himself; this is the subtle import of the pseudodebate between Orc and Urizen in that Night, and it is brought out clearly in the recognition scene between Los and his Spectre and their consequent reconciliation with Enitharmon. In VIIB the Zoas, portrayed elsewhere in the poem as having highly distinctive personalities, are almost mirror images of one another through their tacit mutual pledge to abide by the same basic rules of militancy.

Enitharmon, the first of the Emanations to be introduced in the action of Night VIIB, now appears, in a state of mental confusion and dividedness that in this Night will be especially typical of its women: "clouds & tempests / Beat round her head all night all day she riots in Excess." Both drawn toward her lover Los, who is away at war, and removed as far as possible from him, she is a moon in opposition to his sun, reflecting timidly his lurid light. (Blake's astronomy is accurate, incidentally; Los shines in the south while Enitharmon reflects that light in the north, just as for observers in the northern hemisphere the moon rides high in winter while the sun rides low.) She cowers before the scaly warrior, whom she seems to believe is Orc—a not unnatural mistake, since Los is now closely identified with Orc both imagistically (Los is now reptilian) and in textual juxtaposition ("Red rage the furies of fierce Orc black thunders roll round Los"). Los, she claims, is her protector, who has built for her a bower of refuge, though she cannot reach this shelter.

Appendix A

In lines that dimly anticipate Enion's reply to Ahania in their duet in Night VIII, Enitharmon calls on Los to awaken her sleeping "watchman" (VIIB 73-97; 97:19-98:6 E394).

Although her alternations between fear and orgiastic riot indicate that Enitharmon is not above blame, and although her Vala-like inability to identify her lover accurately is a symptom of sore distress, Enitharmon's confusion is at this point a remnant of sanity. The Zoas have tried to make themselves carbon copies of one another. But the Emanations, like Andromache in the *Iliad,* have at least the good sense to be distressed by the spectacle of war as such (though part of them also revels in it). For them there is something suspect about a war in which it is hard to tell one general from another. What Enitharmon wants here in terror is the same thing Ahania wanted more calmly in Night III: she wants her mate to be true to his best self and not to cast himself in an alien role. In her present confusion and fallenness Enitharmon is unable to articulate or even consciously recognize so positive a thesis, and like Vala later in Night VIIB she lacks a coherent vision of what should be, even though her instinct tells her that the specious and dehumanized unity achieved through abandoning one's proper role is calamitous.

In preparation for the entrance of Vala, who also will be portrayed as self-divided, the earth (identified with Vala throughout the poem and providing a "terrible . . . bed" for Enitharmon here) is portrayed ambiguously, as in the Preludium to *Europe.* The oak penetrates through caves of death, but into "Existence"; the beech "advancd / Terrific into the pained heavens" in a struggle for what seems to be both death and life; the fruit trees, though they emulate the warfare going on around them, are described as "humanizing." Animals too are caught up in the battle: the sheep walks through it sullenly; the bull, the lion, and the tiger rage; the serpent and the scorpion "irritate" (VIIB 98-113; 98:7-22 E394-95). There is a rough inversion of our normal image of the chain of being, which ascends from the vegetable to the human: here the vegetable world is most human. In another inversion, evoking the final serpentine degradation of the archangelic Satan in *Paradise Lost,* the Prester Serpent now enters to deliver a message he claims to have received from God. This

Appendix A

is one of the most gothic incidents in Blake's poetry, resembling the ghoulish priests' dispensation of death in Shelley's *Revolt of Islam* and the tomb scene in *Aida*. The mission of the Prester Serpent, the "Priest of God," is to encourage the warriors to propagate the "seven Diseases of Man"; these are the seven sins, here presented as deadly in a literal and concrete way through their identification with war (VIIB 113-18; 98:22-27 E395).

Blake now repeats the incident first related in the Preludia to *America* and *Europe,* Orc's bursting of his chains and his violent sexual union with Vala (the "shadowy Vortex" or Shadowy Female). The *Zoas* version is significantly different from the earlier ones: Blake repeats the line from *America* (2:1) "Silent as despairing love & strong as Jealousy" but specifies the persons who have aroused that jealousy: "Jealous that she was Vala now become Urizens harlot / And the Harlot of Los & the deluded harlot of the Kings of Earth / His soul was gnawn in sunder" (VIIB 124-43; 91:1-20 E395). The naming of names paradoxically obscures rather than clarifies Orc's motives; since he is jealous of all possible rivals, no one of them in particular is Orc's enemy. The simultaneous specifying and generalizing of Orc's enemies is appropriate to VIIB, for in this Night the Zoas are all asserting their own naked egos while at the same time, ironically, acting and feeling almost identically. Blake goes beyond the earlier version of the rape by making Orc a titan like the three Zoas introduced earlier in Night VIIB, inflating him through an elaborate example of the traditional Homeric simile:

> As when the Earthquake rouzes from his den his shoulders huge
> Appear above the crumb[l]ing Mountain. Silence waits around him
> A moment then astounding horror belches from the Center
> The fiery dogs arise the shoulders huge appear
> So Orc rolld round his clouds upon the deeps of dark Urthona
> (VIIB 129-33; 91:6-10 E395)

A similar confusion and inability to differentiate clearly are expressed in the chant that follows (VIIB 146-63; 91:23-92:10 E395-

96), sung by "the Elemental Gods." They seem to be both the elements of earth, a new version of the demons who awakened at the birth of Orc in Night V, and the collective voice of the Zoas, spokesmen for both inner and outer, for natural and psychological, realities. (This double significance is clear from lines that interrupt their song; in the war going on, "blood / From east to west flowd like the human veins in rivers / Of life upon the plains of death & valleys of despair.") They support the dragons of the North, the quadrant that properly belongs to Los or Urthona, and they encourage the "serpents of war," which in this Night are associated explicitly with Los and Orc and indirectly with Urizen. In the end they vote the death of Luvah, but their stated objective is to "Stop . . . the rising of the glorious King," a phrase ordinarily appropriate to Urizen. In this Night the phrase is applicable to any of the four Zoas; all of them have acted in that role and costume during the earlier scenes of the Night. As in Night VIII, the battle lines cannot be clearly drawn, for both in society and within the person there is civil war, fought by guerillas, where fronts cannot be delineated and where ignorant armies clash pointlessly. What we have is, in the external arena, the war of all against all; in the inner arena, the war of each against himself.

Between this chorus and another that follows appears a detailed elaboration of the commercial revolution described near the beginning of the Night. The implements of peaceful trades, "the plow & harrow the loom / The hammer & the Chisel & the rule & compasses" (these last two regarded now not as the symbols of mathematic form but as the mason's practical tools), are converted into weapons. The image of the reversal of Isaiah's millennium is apt, for Blake is portraying futurism in its worst form, the notion that a modern reader would associate with Orwell and the brave new world satirized by Huxley; "And all the arts of life [Urizen's sons] changd into the arts of death." The hourglass is contemned because its simple workmanship is like that of the plowman—that is, of the unfallen Urizen as opposed to the fallen one who has created clock time; the water wheel is contemned as the work of the shepherd, the unfallen

Appendix A

Tharmas who had once controlled those waters that have now become indefinite chaos (viib 170-79; 92:17-26 e396).

This protest by Blake is by no means simple or sentimental primitivism. He is not mourning the hourglass and water wheel because they are picturesque; rather, he is analyzing the psychological motive for considering them obsolete—namely, the fact that they are not machines in the modern sense, "intricate wheels . . . Wheel without wheel." This disease of sensibility is even more familiar today, when, for motives that often seem compulsive, computers are introduced into almost every commercial activity that once depended on the human mind—not necessarily because the computers have greater utility than more old-fashioned ways (the new machines often produce slower results and when inaccurate cannot be corrected) but simply because they are machines. Their fascination is in the very fact that they are not human.

The only functional utility in Urizen's advanced technology is psychological, sociological, ultimately philosophical: it perplexes youth, chains humanity to "sorrowful drudgery," causes it to "view a small portion & think that All" (as in twentieth-century assembly lines), and in general obfuscates, rendering reality more abstract by substituting "Demonstration" for "the simple rules of life" (viib 180-86; 92:27-33 e396). Nor is it coincidence that these laborers are making armaments, for the substitution of dehumanized abstractions for human reality is the very essence of both military discipline and the social psychology that supports war.

Another chant follows (viib 187-210; 92:34-93:20 e396-97), shrill like the earlier one but very different in tone and import. It is sung by "the demons of the deep" to Vala, whom they hail bitterly as the first occasion of the war and the goddess who presides over it in both delight and dismay. The demons are like the "Elemental Gods" in that they voice the cry of outraged nature, the external world; psychologically, they utter the instinctual protest of the Zoas disillusioned with war, and especially of Tharmas, the power who normally rules the "deep." The paradox is that nature and human instinct call for war and yet

Appendix A

bitterly resent it. This paradox is familiar in human experience: reflex violence against the "him" or "them" that threatens is combined with a recognition that such retaliation is ultimately useless—a deeper insight that comes from our need for wholeness and for kinship with other people.

The tone of the demons' song is something of a problem. They impute to Vala a sadistic satisfaction ("Is not the wound of the sword Sweet & the broken bone delightful") but also portray her as a harlot (a "Melancholy Magdalen") whose "feigned terrors" on Albion's couch have produced in her a very real terror she had not anticipated. The song begins with a catalog of sensuous delights—"tender limbs," "blue eyes," "sapphire shoes," "flaming Zone," "golden brow," "silver locks," "white garments"—which recall Blake's delicate lyric *To the Evening Star*. The song to Vala then brutally rubs her nose into the horrors that she, Pandora-like, has loosed upon the world:

> this is no gentle harp
> This is no warbling brook nor Shadow of a Myrtle tree
> But blood & wounds & dismal cries & clarions of war
> And hearts laid open to the light by the broad grizly sword
> And bowels hidden in hammerd steel rippd forth upon the
> Ground
> Call forth thy Smiles of soft deceit call forth thy cloudy tears
> We hear thy sighs in trumpets shrill when Morn shall blood
> renew.

Vala is a Marie Antoinette transported from the world of Fragonard to that of Delacroix and Goya. There may be genuine relish in the demons' catalog of a war-wracked world, but probably it expresses an enraged sarcasm motivated by the same anger that overwhelms Aeneas when amid the flames of Troy he glimpses the cowering Spartan adulteress, or that of the Trojan women as they wait upon the privileged Helen in the ruins of their city.

Like Enitharmon, and like Virgil's Helen, Vala is indeed divided within herself, between lust and excess **on one hand and** pathetic vulnerability on the other. Her rending by Orc has resulted in the loss of his human form and the disintegration of both lovers; in her role as war goddess "She joyd in all the Conflict . . . This was to her Supreme delight." Essentially she is ambivalent: "The Shadowy Female varied in the War in her delight / Howling in discontent . . . making Lamentations / To decieve Tharmas in his rage to soothe his furious soul." The poem has turned rather suddenly, though without any single definable narrative caesura, from almost universally shared blustering confidence to self-doubt, a dawning recognition that war, simple opposition, is futile. The disillusionment is general. The warriors—all the male figures in VIIB are warriors—"mournd disappointed / They go out to war with Strong Shouts & loud Clarions O Pity / They return with lamentations mourning & weeping" (viib 211-21; 93:21-31 e397).

The anticipation here of the more detailed treatment in Night VIII of the warriors' demoralization (viii 107-30; 101:38-102:13 e359-60) is one of many signs that Night VIIB is related not only to VIIA but to parts of the later Nights as well. Another such sign is that from this point on in Night VIIB one can say of Vala and of the other characters what is said of Rahab at the end of Night VIII: "No more spirit remaind" in them (viii 606; 111: 10 e371). The adrenal energy that had kept them going has been drained, their puffed-up personalities have been deflated; now heroes and haughty beauties are seen from the point of view of the proverbial valet or maidservant.

The deflation is marked most clearly in the ensuing dialogue between Vala and Tharmas (viib 228-58; 93:38-94:26 e397-98). Vala has so confused Tharmas that he asks her if she is Enion. Still trying to sustain the tone of cruelty and broad sarcasm that she uses in earlier parts of the Night, Vala taunts Tharmas in baby-talk—the language of Har and Heva in *Tiriel,* the parodic form of the motherly affection she will show for him and Enion when they appear in her garden in Night IX: "Tharmas I am Vala bless thy innocent face / Doth Enion avoid the sight of thy blue watry eyes." In Tharmas there remains scarcely a vestige of his earlier muscle-flexing pretense; now he is unconcealedly wistful and tender, remembering and lamenting the "garden of delight" he had once shared with Enion.

> And she is gone & here alone I war with darkness & death
> I hear thy voice but not thy form see. thou & all delight
> And life appear & vanish mocking me with shadows of false
>   hope.

The confusion of pronouns here ("thy" and "thou" could refer to either Vala or Enion) is significant; the theme of confused or mistaken identity recurs. This time it touches something deep in Vala herself, for she breaks off her sadistic teasing to confess her own kindred loss of her lover and her similar confusion about bodily vehicle and identity:

> Lo him whom I love
> Is hidden from me & I never in all Eternity
> Shall see him Enitharmon & Ahania combind with Enion
> Hid him in that Outrageous form of Orc which torments me
>   for Sin
> For all my Secret faults which he brings forth upon the light
> .   .   .   .
>
> for tho I have the power
> To rise on high Yet love here binds me down & never never
> Will I arise till him I love is loosd from this dark chain.

Tharmas exits cursing, but his very curse of Vala links him with her in what they seek; he vows that "till I can bring love into the light / I never will depart from my great wrath."

Vala too, then, is vulnerable. With Enitharmon and with Tharmas (the least "manly" of the Zoas in their fallen state, especially in the context of this Homeric seventh Night), she has sanity enough to be confused and perturbed, more consciously than the three most pseudoheroic Zoas, though by implication they too have been brought back to earth. The kind of confusion Vala experiences is an especially ironic one; in an unexpected way it illustrates the law of retaliation stated early in the Night by Tharmas: "I will reward them as they have rewarded me." In an attempt to stay Tharmas's rage, Vala disguises herself in various forms of nature—earthquake, cloud, fire, torrent, thunder. But her deception returns upon her poignantly; like Wordsworth, who on the Simplon road crosses the Alps unawares, so Vala moves through a world filled with life, beauty, and delight—everything that her lost Luvah means to her—in complete unconsciousness of its sweetness:

> for the Elements brought forth abundantly
> The living soul in glorious forms & every one came forth
> Walking before her Shadowy face & bowing at her feet
> But in vain delights were poured forth on the howling
>   melancholy.
>
> (VIIB 277-80; 94:45-48 E398)

The sad irony of this climactic instance of mistaken identity, mistaken reality, derives much of its power from Genesis, at the point when Adam has named the animals but has not yet been blessed with a mate for himself. Like Adam, Vala is unfulfilled "Tho all those fair perfections which men know only by name / In beautiful substantial forms appeard & served her" (VIIB 274-75; 94:42-43 E398).

Night VIIB ends, then, in a troubled peace, the obvious but merely extroverted and retaliatory solution for human ills having been tried and rejected. Salvation is back in the hands of the Daughters of Beulah, whose words repeat the persistent promise of resurrection first made after the death of Lazarus (VIIB 290-95; 95:3-8 E399). As the first two lines of Night VIIB epitomize much of the action of VIIA, so the last four epitomize much that is there and in Night VIII as well: in a negative resurrection the dead burst through the bottoms of their tombs to form collectively the Satan who in Night VIII, in a meaningful instead of a mock confrontation, is to be subdued by Jesus, the forgiver of sin rather than the accuser.

Appendix B: Accounts of the Fall of Man in *The Four Zoas*

1. I 260-80; 10:9-11:2 E301. Enitharmon's Song of Death, a Song of Vala: Enitharmon's version, including a projection of herself into Vala's visions.

While Albion and Urizen sleep, Luvah and Vala fly up from the human heart into the brain. Vala slumbers on Albion's pillow and Luvah steals Urizen's horses of light. Albion confesses to Enitharmon that he has refused to look upon the Divine Vision but reproaches Enitharmon for tormenting and dominating Los.

1a. I 282-305; 11:4-18 E302. Los's reply to Enitharmon's Song of Death: A counterstatement, reinterpretation, and sequel to Enitharmon's Song; largely an utterance of prophecy as distinguished from Enitharmon's relation of history.

Albion seeks to comfort Vala, but she refuses to be comforted and seeks Luvah in her garden. Albion sickens, his illness an achievement of Enitharmon's (and all women's?) power. As punishment, Luvah suffers martyrdom under the knife in a shower of blood. Los foresees the swords and spears of futurity. He tells Enitharmon that the two have a world of joy in the human brain, the world of Urizen, but she will never leave the cold world of Tharmas.

2. I 408-21; 15:7-20 E304-05. Part of the song at the marriage feast of Los and Enitharmon, sung by the Demons of the Deep: The point of view of spirits of the natural world.

The first beam of morning, sensing danger at the sound of (Luvah's?) bowstring, tries to warn his father (the sun), but the horse (of light), after being seized and clad in steel, neighs proudly in anticipation of battle. The Mighty Father (the sun? or Tharmas, since he holds the sheephook that is Tharmas's emblem?) brandishes his sheephook and the sun falls. Tharmas flees howling; his chaotic world, a barren waste, crashes down with him. Vala remains in deserts of darkness and solitude. Meanwhile Los and Enitharmon are born.

3. I 484-549; 21:16-19:5 E306-08. Report by the Ambassadors of Beulah to the Council of God in Eternity: A version from the providential point of view, above the fallen world.

Albion weeps and his family slumbers; Urizen and Luvah confer. Urizen suggests that Luvah take over his "wished Kingdom" in the South (Urizen's proper home in Eternity) while Urizen situates himself in the North (Urthona's proper domain). Urizen offers to enfold Albion's tent in opaque clouds while Luvah seizes the chariots of the morning; Urizen, remaining in the porches of the brain, will lay his scepter on Jerusalem the Emanation and on all Urizen's and Luvah's sons; on the following morning he will proclaim his new rule, having been assisted in the coup by accomplices subverted through bribery. Luvah refuses this offer as an insult to his high station, expressing his suspicion that Urizen, in Luvah's absence, will double-cross him and seize his throne and domain (which includes the realm of night). Luvah prefers to smite Albion directly, then to challenge Urizen for primacy. The upshot is that Albion is attacked by Urizen and Luvah simultaneously, each hostile to the other but each using the rival usurper's weapons (Luvah's darkness, Urizen's lances). The outbreak of hostilities interrupts Urthona's peaceful work on agricultural implements in his smithy, attracting all his sons to join the conflict and dividing his Emanation (Enitharmon) and his Spectre (here probably identical with Los) from him; both Enitharmon and the Spectre-Los fall into the world of Tharmas and Enion. Enion murders Enitharmon and embalms her in her bosom. Urizen secretly commands his troops to withdraw, leaving the rage of Luvah to pour itself out upon Luvah himself and upon Albion. All the Zoas fall together into "an unknown Space / Deep horrible without End." Jerusalem is ruined and taken captive.

Appendix B

4. II 1-18; 23:1-24:1 E309. Authorial narration: Albion's commissioning of Urizen.

Albion, turning his eyes away from the Divine Vision and toward himself, asks Urizen to rule while he is incapacitated. The early phase of the fall has already occurred: Luvah has smitten Albion, though Albion implies that Urizen too bears part of the blame. Both Albion and Urizen are partly aware that Enion is in the abyss, blind, aged, and ravening with hunger.

5. III 31-104; 39:2-42:18 E320-22. Ahania's memory and vision: A reproach to Urizen and a warning against his obsession with futurity.

Memory: Luvah persuades Urizen to give him the steeds of light, which now refuse to obey Urizen and require strong restraints and intoxicating food.

Vision: When Urizen sleeps in the porch and Albion is smitten, Albion in a delusive dream-vision walks with Vala. He looks up and sees Urizen, then prostrates himself before a shadowy idol of holiness that has risen from his wearied intellect. When he sees Luvah emerge from the cloud he has been worshiping, Albion feels indignation; he turns his back on Vala. Luvah and Albion wrestle "above the Body where Vala was inclos'd," and Albion's body is left prostrate, covered with boils laid on him by Luvah. Albion then banishes Luvah to a shrunken and constricted sensual existence. Luvah and Vala descend into the human heart, then shrink and fall separately. The vast form of Nature rolls serpentlike between them.

6. IV 79-110; 49:27-50:27 E326-27. Reminiscence by the Spectre of Urthona, addressed to Tharmas: The effect of the fall on the imaginative and instinctual faculties.

Fleeing from the battle on the terrible day of the fall, Tharmas draws all the Sons of Beulah into his vortex; Urthona's sons, standing round him at his anvil, flee from his side when they hear the music of war. Painfully his loins break forth in "veiny pipes" that englobe and bring forth a separated female counterpart whom Urthona embraces and names Enitharmon. Urthona finds himself and Enitharmon together running as bloody rivers through huge caverns, struggling to be delivered from their bonds. She is unsuccessful, but Urthona breaks free as a shadowy blue Spectre through the nostrils of Enion. He beholds Tharmas rotting upon the rocks.

7. IV 111-13; 50:28-30 E327. Tharmas's reminiscence in response to the Spectre: A confirmation of their victimization by Urizen and Luvah.

Tharmas and Urthona lived together happily before the deadly night when Urizen gave the horses of light to Luvah.

8. IV 137-43; 51:20-26 E328. Tharmas's reminiscence, addressed to Los: A further confirmation of the primary guilt of Urizen and Luvah.

Enion once wandered with Tharmas's flocks and rested gently with him at night. She is now vanished like Luvah and Vala because "foul ambition" seized Urizen and Luvah, so that Tharmas is divided from Enion.

9. V 42-65; 58:22-59:20 E333. Song of the Enormous Demons, at the birth of Orc: An indictment and celebration of the Luvah-Vala principle. (Many of the personal references in this account, along with its addressees, are ambiguously identified.)

Luvah, once King of Love, is now King of Rage and Death. At the time of the fall, Urizen casts darkness around Luvah, who hurls Urizen's spears around Albion's tent. Vala's arrows fly as Urthona weeps in secret pain and torment. Someone identified as "he" (Urthona? Albion?) weeps, painfully divides, and lays his head down on the Rock of Eternity. "His" fiery sons are chained down. The "Enormous Spirit" (Orc? Urizen?) is loosed in the deep, along with "his" dark wife, once a fair crystal form (this could be Jerusalem or any of the four lesser Emanations). Someone addressed as "thee" (probably Vala) is soon to be born.

10. V 190-237; 63:24-65:8 E336-37. Urizen's lament, uttered from the dens of Urthona: A confession by Urizen of his primary responsibility for the fall.

Urizen has lived happily and luxuriously in a palace on the heights, enjoying his harpers, gardens, fountains, and banquets of new wine, slumbering at noon in his ivory pavilions and sleeping at night on his silver bed. At the time of the fall he keeps back his horses of light from the Lord of day (Albion), disobeying

Appendix B

the command to guide the Lord's son (the sun), conspiring against his master, and bringing down Urthona, Luvah, and Vala in his fall. Luvah was once cupbearer at the immortal tables and kept, with Urthona, the gates of heaven; at the fall, Luvah exchanges the wine for Urizen's steeds, as a result of which Luvah is bound down. Urizen falls after getting drunk on the stolen wine.

11. VII 147-48; 80:39-40 E349. Orc's recollection, addressed to Urizen: An acknowledgment, or boast, by the fallen Luvah of his responsibility for the fall.

Orc recalls that he, as Luvah, stole Urizen's light, turning it to a consuming fire.

12. VII 236-64; 83:4-32 E351-52. The Shadow of Enitharmon's memory or fantasy, addressed to the Spectre of Urthona: A blend of the seduction and conspiracy theories of the fall and a variant genealogy of the Zoas.

Albion, walking in Beulah, sees Vala and falls in love with her, impregnating her with Urizen. After Vala gives birth to Urizen, she divides into Luvah and Vala. Albion is estranged from heaven and Eternity. Luvah conspires with Urizen to bind Albion and enslave the brethren who are his offspring. Beulah falls; meanwhile, Los and Enitharmon are born, but the Shadow confesses her inability to remember that birth. Luvah has assumed Albion's place and has smitten him.

13. VII 270-95; 84:4-29 E352. The Spectre of Urthona's reminiscence, in reply to Enitharmon: Vala's seduction of Albion and the consequent birth and divisions of Urthona.

The male and female aspects of Urthona once walked in undivided essence, sharing each other's joy, in harmony with Tharmas and Luvah. One dread morning the gentle passions are exhaled through Albion's nostrils as Vala, an "odorous stupefaction." Urthona, standing beside his anvil, suddenly sinks downward to the genitals, where he divides into Los and Enitharmon in Enion's womb. Refusing to be incarnated, the Spectre issues from Enion's brain in a deformed shape and forms Los to be the incarnate counterpart to Enitharmon. The Spectre thus sees Los as his substitute. In due time Los and Enitharmon are born.

Appendix B

14. ɪx 93-96; 119:26-29 ᴇ373-74. Authorial narration: Another reference to Urizen's gift of his horses to Luvah.

When Urizen gives his horses of light to Luvah, a horrible rock far in the South is forsaken. On this rock Albion lies, wrapped in the weeds of death.

Appendix C: Note on Textual References

Quotations from Blake throughout this book are based on the text in *The Poetry and Prose of William Blake,* ed. David V. Erdman, commentary by Harold Bloom; Copyright © 1965 by David V. Erdman and Harold Bloom; reprinted by permission of Doubleday & Company, Inc., We cite the fourth printing (1970), abbreviated as E. Parallel reference is made to *The Complete Writings of William Blake,* ed. Geoffrey Keynes (London and New York: Oxford University Press, 1974), abbreviated as K. References to the manuscript of *The Four Zoas,* especially the drawings, are based on first-hand examination of it and on *William Blake: Vala or The Four Zoas: A Facsimile of the Manuscript, A Transcript of the Poem, and A Study of Its Growth and Significance,* ed. G. E. Bentley, Jr. (Oxford: Clarendon Press, 1963)—identified as Bentley (1963) or simply as the facsimile. A new facsimile is also forthcoming; See Bibliography, under "Magno."

In order to provide full information as succinctly as possible, references to *The Four Zoas* violate logic slightly. Although Erdman's text is the one actually followed, we cite Keynes before Erdman because Keynes numbers the lines (including those Blake deleted) consecutively throughout each Night, though without giving MS page numbers; Erdman begins a new set of line numbers for each MS page. Therefore, we identify the Night first (in roman numerals) and give the *line* number in Keynes; then we cite Erdman by MS page and line numbers followed by E (for Erdman) and the number of the page in his volume on which the passage appears. Thus, for example, VIIB 187-209; 92:34-93: 19 E396-97 refers to the passage from Night VIIB running in

Appendix C

Keynes from line 187 to 209 and running in Erdman from line 34 of MS page 92 to line 19 of MS page 93, printed on pages 396-97 of Erdman's edition. (Occasionally a reference will show a passage beginning on a MS page numbered higher than the one the passage ends on—viii 223-46; 113:22-104:18 e362-63. In such passages an editor is honoring marginal or other instructions by Blake to transfer a passage from the MS page where it appears to a different part of the poem; the orderings in Erdman and Keynes generally agree.) Lines Blake deleted from the manuscript— included within brackets in Keynes's numbered text but isolated by Erdman at the end in his textual notes—are indicated in our usual way except that only the page number of the Erdman volume is given; thus, in the citation i 109; e740 the first of the two arabic numbers is a line number in Keynes, the second a page number in Erdman.

References to Blake's illuminated works cite the plate numbers, followed, for verse passages, by a colon and the line numbers. (Erdman and Keynes almost always agree in their numbering; where they do not, we so indicate.) Thus, *America* 11:4-15 refers to lines 4-15 of plate 11 of that poem, the plate and line numbers being identical in Erdman and Keynes.

Any number that immediately follows the abbreviation E or K indicates a page in the Erdman or Keynes volume. References to prose works, for example, simply give page numbers in the two editions. In the citation *A Vision of The Last Judgment* (e550, k611), the numbers refer to pages in Erdman and Keynes respectively.

Notes

Introduction

1. For the texts used and the method of citing them, see Appendix C.

2. Helen T. McNeil (1970). We are indebted throughout the book to many Blake critics whose ideas have become the common property of Blakeans. The most influential commentators for us have been the following: G. E. Bentley, Jr. (1963), Harold Bloom (1963), S. Foster Damon (1924), Northrop Frye (1947), H. M. Margoliouth (1956), and J. Middleton Murry (1933). Some of our ideas coincide with those of Thomas A. Vogler, *Preludes to Vision: The Epic Venture in Blake, Wordsworth, Keats, and Hart Crane* (Berkeley and Los Angeles: University of California Press, 1971). We recognize that an effort to draw analogies from common experience is central to the approach of Margaret Rudd (1956), but our reading of the poem is plainly different from hers.

3. The drawing is similar to the one Blake engraved for the beginning of Night II of Young's *Night Thoughts* (page 19, a proof page of which is used for MS page 105 of the *Zoas*) and repeated as the title page of Blair's *Grave* (1808).

4. Christ offers rest to those who labor and are heavy laden (Matt. 11:28); Revelation promises that those who die in the Lord may rest from their labor (14:13). See also the exhortation in Hebrews 4:11, "Let us labor therefore to enter into that rest."

5. Bentley (1963, p. 2) points out another ominous detail: the right leg ends in a cloven foot, in contrast to the well-defined five-toed foot on the left. One would like to believe that the right foot is only a rough sketch, but it appears to be as distinctly and purposefully drawn as the normal foot on the left. If Wicksteed's and Damon's left-right distinction is valid and applicable here, the meaning may be that Albion's right, or spiritual, side is

being drawn downward into material reality, or death, as he tosses on his sickbed. He is chained to this world, and the cloven Pan-like or Satanic foot suggests his entrapment through submission to his brute nature. Yet his left side—if the viewer regards him frontally rather than from above—is beginning an upward movement to regain his full life in Eternity. According to Myra Glazer Schotz, "On the Frontispiece of *The Four Zoas*," *Blake Newsletter* 10 (1977), 126-127, the figure is not resting but "rising as he dreams or perhaps even dreaming that he rises."

6. The "Rest" mentioned in the motto can perhaps be understood in the context of hopeful waiting described in Psalms 16: 7-10, quoted by Peter as a prophecy of Christ's resurrection in his sermon at Pentecost (Acts 2:26-27): the Psalmist rejoices that "my reins also instruct me in the night sessions" and proclaims that his "flesh also shall rest in hope," for God will "not leave my soul in hell; neither wilt thou suffer thine Holy One to see corruption."

7. *A Vision of the Last Judgment*, E550, K611.

Night I

1. Erdman (E739) has suggested that the lines should be read as a subtitle, because of the syntax and heavy inking; but the lettering is only slightly larger than elsewhere on the page, and the lines are included among those whose sequence was indicated by Blake in marginal numbers after his tortuous revisions and reordering of the text. Their having been rewritten over a much-erased surface may explain the dark inking and perhaps the syntactic isolation; the verb for "Song" was no doubt lost when the original second and third lines of the poem were erased, after which Blake either overlooked the anomaly or deliberately let it stand to create the effect of dislocation we have mentioned. The first two lines of *Jerusalem,* which announce the theme, are also in slightly larger letters than the other lines on plate 4; see David V. Erdman, ed., *The Illuminated Blake* (Garden City, N. Y.: Anchor-Doubleday, 1974), p. 203.

2. Our argument here is supported by a striking parallel with the beginning of *The Book of Los,* where "Eno aged Mother"

(identified in the first line, by her proper name, as she is in a rejected opening of the *Zoas*—I 1; E739) speaks three verse-paragraphs in her own voice, after which a heavy line across the column of text marks a new beginning by the omniscient narrator.

3. The small figure at the top—similar to the marigold spirit who kisses Oothoon in the "Argument" plate of *Visions of the Daughters of Albion* and the small flying nude who directs the reader into the prophecy on the title page of *America*—lightly springs upward beside the half title, pointing the way into the poem; she personifies that portion of Albion that struggles to rise in the ambiguous frontispiece of *The Four Zoas*. The voluptuous half-reclining female at the bottom of the page, usually identified as Vala, personifies that portion of Albion in the frontispiece that wishes to remain asleep. Her right arm is behind her head, as Albion's left arm is behind his; both her bent right arm and bent right leg are languorous and heavy like Albion's left arm and leg. She seems startled by something that has caught her attention, but her body (redrawn several times) seems too comfortable to move, repeating the combination of vitality and torpor we recognize in Albion on the facing leaf. His eyes are closed, hers are open, possibly to suggest false vision. The "visions of Vala" which will be described several times in the poem are usually false, both in the sense that other characters misunderstand her and give unreliable accounts of her part in the fall and in the sense that she suffers from a perverse blindness to what is immediately in front of or beside her—often her mate Luvah.

4. The metaphor of hearing as an ascent to heaven occurs later in the *Zoas* (VI 249-50; 73:37-38 E343) and also in *Europe* 10:13: our ears are "ever-varying spiral ascents to the heavens of heavens."

5. It is possible that in the revised manuscript the harboring of Enitharmon was really meant to refer to Jerusalem, whose name is substituted for Enitharmon's two lines earlier. See E740 and MS page 4 in the facsimile.

6. Robert F. Gleckner, *Byron and the Ruins of Paradise* (Baltimore: The Johns Hopkins Press, 1967), p. 151.

7. Both MS pages 82 and 104 show a wheel being pushed by a nude woman; on page 82 the wheel is studded with stars and the woman is energetic, on page 104 it is studded with eyes and she seems exhausted.

8. Although in the text the Spectre of Tharmas is called a "shadowy human form winged . . . Glorying in his own eyes Exalted in terrific Pride" (ɪ 127-29; 6:6-8 ᴇ299), in the designs he slumps in despair or inertia and is identifiable only by his wings (MS pages 5, 6)—in contrast to the wingless Zoas who emerge later, in more deeply fallen states.

9. In ᴋ, "Half Woman & half Spectre"; in ᴇ, "Half Woman & half beast," though Erdman has recently accepted a reconstruction of Blake's reworking of this passage (on MS pages 7 and 143) by Andrew Lincoln, which recognizes "Spectre" as the final reading, "beast" as an intermediate reading replacing "Spirit" (forthcoming issue of *Blake: An Illustrated Quarterly*). Keynes (ᴋ381) reads MS page 143 as "desart," not "beast"; see the facsimile of p. 143.

10. The lines cannot be cited in Keynes's version of the intended final text because he follows MS page 7 rather than 143. See note 9, above.

11. This indictment against the arts in our time is well represented in Saul Bellow's acceptance speech for the 1976 Nobel Prize for literature.

12. As a nursing mother (MS page 8) Enion, though described as sorrowful in the text, has indeed become rehumanized, in marked contrast to her monstrously tormented appearance in serpentine coils (which may be part of her own body) with her hair standing on end (MS page 7). But as her children grow older and reject her (Enitharmon holds up and prepares to cut a thread which may be Enion's spectrous life, a detached umbilical cord, or a strand of fate), Enion becomes blind and age-bent, a shadow of her former self (MS page 9).

13. This relation between the One and the many is anticipated in Blake's citation of John 17:21-23 as a marginal gloss on the first MS page of this first Night.

Night II

1. See in the facsimile Blake's incomplete erasure in the heading of MS page 23. Night II is identified as the second Night only at the end, on MS page 36 (see also E747).

2. Lionel Trilling, *Sincerity and Authenticity* (Cambridge: Harvard University Press, 1972), ch. 1, esp. p. 24.

3. For a detailed consideration of Vala in relation to Luvah, in the fallen state, see Jean H. Hagstrum (1973).

4. One might see the Ahania–Urizen division as an example of how the dramatic and mythic thrusts of the poem can occasionally diverge distractingly. On the humanly dramatic level, that Urizen and Ahania should have "Two wills . . . two intellects & not as in times of old" would seem to be a good thing, at least if it means that they both have equal rights to be themselves. But on the mythical level the development would seem a dire one, since it means that reason has become divided against itself. To labor this apparent contradiction as a fault, however, is to miss some of the grim intellectual comedy of the scene. For one thing, Urizen has created, or falsely recognized, the division between himself and Ahania. Furthermore, there is dark comedy in Urizen's characteristic assumption that any departure from single-mindedness must be evil. His obsession with specious unity is the same obsession that had led him to promulgate his laws of uniformity in *Urizen* 4:34-40.

5. The best resolution of the paradox is the poem *Europe* read as a whole. There Enitharmon's sensuous celebration of her triumph is finally revealed as totally self-deceiving.

Night III

1. The point has been made by several writers on Blake, perhaps most incisively by Irene Tayler in *Blake's Illustrations to the Poems of Gray* (Princeton: Princeton University Press, 1971); see, for example, pp. 42-45 and the discussion on pp. 46-55 of Blake's illustrations for Gray's *Ode on the Spring*.

2. In view of Urizen's inveterate antagonism to passion, it seems certain that he is anticipating the rebirth of Luvah as the

boy Orc; that he also has Los in mind is suggested by his use of a phrase applied to Los in Night I: "the fierce prophetic boy" (I 249; 9:35 E301); furthermore, as son of the oceanic Tharmas, Los might be described as "a Boy . . . born of the dark Ocean" (III 14; 38:2 E319).

3. These drawings, much-erased but substantially revealed by infrared photography (see the forthcoming Magno facsimile), make up what is "undoubtedly the most extravagantly erotic sequence of designs Blake is known to have made," according to John E. Grant (1973, p. 182); see Grant's entire discussion of this sequence, pp. 182-194. His remarks (pp. 183-185) on the sinister implications of the design on MS page 37 (see p. 67 above), which depicts Ahania's self-abasement before Urizen, bear on our observation that Ahania is distorting the account of the fall in an effort to vindicate her husband. Grant also points out that the opening scene between Ahania and Urizen on MS page 37 and the concluding scene between Tharmas and Enion on MS page 46, by framing the erotic sequence, establish the designs in Night III as a thematic unit anatomizing the antagonisms between the sexes (p. 185).

4. In both scenes pathological pseudomasculinity is exposed for what it is, through similar images and diction. Both the golden Shadow of Holiness in Night III and the golden form of the Spectre of Tharmas in Night I are narcissistic idols, glorified self-images that spring from radical doubt by the male of his own value and potency. The antifeminine psychology in the two episodes is so nearly identical that in canceled lines that Blake probably reinstated (see Andrew Lincoln's proposal in a forthcoming issue of *Blake: An Illustrated Quarterly*) he gave Tharmas almost the same phrase for Enion that Urizen uses against Ahania: "Diminutive husk & shell" (I 149, E741).

Night IV

1. The three parts of *The Four Zoas,* describing the fall, fallenness, and recovery, correspond respectively to Wordsworth's statement of the loss of celestial light in strophes i-iv, his anatomy of the almost totally killing dominion of custom and the merely

natural in strophes v-viii, and the resurrection of hope in strophes ix-xi. (The sources of hope, discovered by the poets in their "recovery" sections, are of course very different.) The images of entropy, death, sleep, and amnesia are used by both poets to mark the transitions between successive movements.

2. viib 5-10,50-57; 95:19-24,96:29-97:3 e392,393.

3. The last two of the lines quoted also find an echo in *The Four Zoas* in the unnatural forms of nature encountered by Urizen when he explores his "dens" in Night VI. Milton's lines are part of his description of Hell's geography, as discovered by the bands of fallen angels who undertake to explore Hell after Satan's departure for Earth.

4. The appeal to Christ by female figures, usually symbolic of the Church or the human soul, is of course ancient in Christian liturgy and iconography. Although the erotic tone of such appeals or dialogues is also ancient, a particularly tender tone of wistful and weak dependency, exemplified in the plea by the Daughters of Beulah here, seems characteristic of certain eighteenth-century treatments of the motif. Bach's cantatas, in both their texts and musical moods, provide several good examples—consider the duet for female voices that constitutes the second section of the Cantata No. 78, *Jesu Der Du Meine Seele.*

5. Before the line beginning "Spasms siezd" Blake wrote in, either as an afterthought or in order to save time before re-copying the passage in its final form, "Bring in here the Globe of Blood as in the B of Urizen." See MS page 55 in the facsimile. If Blake had gone on to add this passage, he would have provided a third account of the formation of Enitharmon (see Appendix B), and would have strengthened the impression that Los in torturing Enitharmon is torturing the tenderest part of himself.

Night V

1. The musical contrast anticipates a similar effect in Night VIII when the saving work of Los and Enitharmon, associated with "lulling cadences on the wind," is in counterpoint with the warfare directed by Urizen, which includes "harsh instruments of sound / To grate the soul into destruction or to in-

flame with fury / The spirits of life" (VIII 114,135-37; 101:45,102: 18-20 E360).

2. The whole passage should be compared with *To Winter* in *Poetical Sketches* and with the opening stanzas of Milton's Nativity Ode, echoed in *Europe*, plates 3-4.

3. The hymn is strikingly similar to the one, also sung by demons and presenting the same savagely taunting picture of Vala's two faces, in Night VIIB 187-209; 92:34-93:19 E396-97.

4. Los in a later poem discovers, however, that "there is no Limit of Expansion! there is no Limit of Translucence" (*Jerusalem* 42:35).

5. See VIIA 5-150; 77:5-80:42 E346-49; and *America*, plates 7-8.

6. The passage quoted is followed immediately by an even rarer first-person authorial intrusion: "all their lamentations / I write not here" (V 174-75; 63:8-9 E336).

Night VI

1. According to Keynes (K906) Blake probably received the copy of Boyd's translation of the *Inferno*, which Blake annotated, as a gift from William Hayley in about 1800. Blake knew Dante much earlier, though; in *The Marriage of Heaven and Hell*, plate 22, he wrote: "Any man of mechanical talents may from the writings of Paracelsus or Jacob Behmen, produce ten thousand volumes of equal value with Swedenborg's. and from those of Dante or Shakespear, an infinite number."

2. Something like this technique is used, on a much grander scale, for the poem as a whole, the first sixteen lines of Night I serving as a brief description of the entire work. In a less formal way, Tharmas's soliloquy at the beginning of Night IV epitomizes the state of fallenness faced by man in the middle Nights.

3. The Preludium to *The Book of Urizen* has a different purpose; it is literally a prelude, a preparation, rather than an epitome. Neither can the addresses to the Public, the Jews, the Deists, and the Christians, which introduce the four parts of *Jerusalem*, or the Preface and curtain-raising lyric for *Milton*, be called epitomes, being rather authorial exhortation and edi-

torializing. In Blake's epigraph passages there is normally more aesthetic distancing.

4. See IV 47, 78, 82, 156, 179, 278, 281; 68:28, 69:29,33, 71:24, 72:5, 74:27,30 E339-44.

5. The sighing and moping recall the trimmers in the vestibule of Hell (*Inferno,* iii 22-25) and the dwellers in Limbo (iv 25-27); those locked in their senses as within trees recall the suicides who have been transformed into trees and who can speak only if painfully rended (xiii 22-108); the ignorance of one's compeer in regions of the grave recalls the social snobbery of the ensepulchered heretics and their ignorance of present time (x); the serpentine crowns and girdles formed of monsters recall the serpentine bonds and reptilian transformations of the thieves (xxiv 79-105; xxv 46-144); the procession over burning wastes recalls the procession of the sodomites under falling flakes of fire (xv 13-21).

6. For a thorough discussion of these and related matters, see Donald D. Ault *Visionary Physics: Blake's Response to Newton* (Chicago and London: University of Chicago Press, 1974).

7. The imagery and mood of these lines provide a link with the inflated mock-epic tone of Night VIIB (discussed in Appendix A). Some of the details, especially the scales and the iron spikes on the head, also suggest the picture of the mailed crusader on plate 5 of *Europe* in David V. Erdman, ed., *The Illuminated Blake* (Garden City: Anchor/Doubleday, 1974); numbered 6 in E, 5 in K.

Night VII

1. Textual scholars, working with a bewildering mass of primary evidence, are less in accord on this matter than critics who base their interpretations on any one edition. The problem is that Blake left two versions of Night VII without canceling either; both versions have thematic and narrative links with Nights VI and VIII. Each of the versions of Night VII is made up of two subsections, reflecting different stages of composition and plans for integrating the Night into the whole poem. The first four leaves of Night VIIA (MS pages 77-84) were written smoothly in Blake's normal handwriting and at one time were stitched to

MS pages 43-76, a unit containing the last part of Night III and all of Nights IV, V, and VI, all of this unit written with few corrections in Blake's normal hand. The last part of VIIA (MS pages 85-90) was left unstitched, and the handwriting from 85:32 to the end of page 90 is uniformly smaller than that used in the stitched segment. This second section of Night VIIA also makes use of paper unrelated to the *Night Thoughts* project, sheets made by cutting apart one of Blake's other prints. Night VIIB, showing signs of much revision, was once intended to proceed from Vala's appearance through the Prester Serpent's preparations for Urizen's war (from MS page 91 to page 98); in marginal directions, however, Blake indicated that VIIB should be split in two and the order of the two halves reversed, so that the revised Night opens at 95:15, with Urizen's temple-building, and ends with 91-95:14, the appearance of Vala and her dialogue with Tharmas. According to Margoliouth (1956, p. xiii), Bentley (1963, p. 167), and Keynes (κ902), Night VIIB is the later version; according to Erdman (ε755), Night VIIA is "most probably the later, meant at one time to replace the other." W. H. Stevenson (1971, p. 371) states that VIIB as a whole "was undoubtedly written earlier" and "remains in a distinctly earlier state," but since Blake "did not finally reject either" he follows Keynes in printing VIIA and VIIB in sequence.

A special issue of *Blake: An Illustrated Quarterly*, being prepared as this book goes to the press, will present conflicting arguments on the problem by some or all of the following authorities: Andrew Lincoln, Mark S. Lefebvre, and David V. Erdman. On grounds too complicated to summarize here, Lincoln suggests that revisions in VIIB link this Night with the end of VI and the beginning of VIII, and that the insertion of VIIA between the two sections of VIIB makes a satisfactory textual arrangement. Lefebvre, however, suggests that the whole of Night VIIB, in its modified order, should be inserted between the two parts of Night VIIA, so that the physical and thematic connection between the first part of Night VIIA and Night VI can be retained and negative and destructive actions by Los and his compeers can be brought together to precede Los's acceptance of his

Spectre and his cooperative efforts with both Spectre and Emanation. Since neither Lincoln nor Lefebvre can demonstrate that Blake himself ever solved the problem of what to do with his two seventh Nights, Erdman maintains that his own solution in his edition, to relegate VIIB to an appendix, is the only way to avoid severing Blake's careful connections of Night VIIA to both VI and VIII—thus bypassing VIIB. Nevertheless, Erdman notes that both Lincoln and Lefebvre have shown that a simple sequence of VIIA + VIIB has no justification, and that the presumption that VIIB was composed or copied out later than *both* parts of VIIA cannot be substantiated.

It seems likely that Blake himself was considering solutions similar to those advanced by both Lincoln and Lefebvre, and perhaps other solutions as well. A serious reader of *The Four Zoas* would do well to try all five possible sequences (VI + VIIA + VIII; VI + VIIB + VIII; VI + VIIA + VIIB + VIII; VI + $VIIA_1$ + VIIB + $VIIA_2$ + VIII; VI + $VIIB_1$ + VIIA + $VIIB_2$ + VIII) and consider the various thematic and narrative patterns that result.

2. M. H. Abrams, *Natural Supernaturalism: Tradition and Revolution in Romantic Literature* (New York: Norton, 1971), pp. 36, 300, discusses this sort of reversal as one of the features of biblical design adopted by the Romantics. For further discussion of the movement of Night VII, in both versions, and its relation to what precedes and follows, see Appendix A; compare also note 1, above.

3. Hermann Hesse, *Steppenwolf*, trans. Basil Creighton (New York: Henry Holt and Co., 1929), p. 86.

Night VIII

1. In Night I (I 475; 21:7 E306) the Council of God meets on Snowdon; in Night VIII (VIII 2; 99:2 E357) it meets on Gilead and Hermon, boundaries of Israel. Gilead is associated with the balm that Jeremiah called for (Jer. 8:22). Hermon, another name for Sion, is associated with the dew of blessing of eternal life, a symbol of the unity among brethren (Deut. 4:48, Ps. 133:

1,3). By identifying Snowdon with these biblical mountains symbolizing healing and eternal life in brotherly unity, Blake introduces Eternity into time and space through the technique he
worked out most fully in *Jerusalem.*

2. Enitharmon's changes of heart are described in I 560-68;
20:1-9 E308; v 177-81; 63:11-15 E336; VIIA 323-25; 85:13-15 E353;
VIII 27-33; 99:22-27 E358. Compare the "broken heart" of Psalms
34:18 and the "new heart" of Ezekiel 18:31.

3. The development of Blake's symbolic use of the human body
(along with related images like those of clothing and nudity) is
explored at length by Anne Kostelanetz Mellor (1974).

4. David V. Erdman (1969, pp. 398-399) has found in Urizen's
inventions the "hollow globes" of Henry Shrapnel's explosive
shells, the "hooks & boring screws" of Robert Fulton's diving
boat, the "linked chains" of cruelly efficient chain shot (VIII 92-
93,132-33; 100:28-29,102:15-16 E359,360).

5. James C. Evans (1972, p. 315*n*) observes that the poem "is
not linearly but symmetrically organized so that one sees obverse
images of a single event which, depending upon the perceiver's
viewpoint, is either part of the fallen world or part of the divine
image' "—the symmetry between the Council of God and the
Synagogue of Satan, for example, or between Satan's hiding
Rahab within himself and Jerusalem's revealing Jesus in her
bosom.

6. Sir Geoffrey Keynes, ed., *Drawings of William Blake: 92
Pencil Studies* (New York: Dover, 1970), no. 85. In the context of Blake's total thought and *oeuvre,* the drawing on MS page
44 of the *Zoas* is rich in ironies and allusions. The parody of
false religion (each of the three panels of the triptych contains
a lightly sketched figure, as of a saint) and of false human values
is intensified in that for Blake the gothic was in many ways the
ideal of art. The loins-concealing altarpiece is shaped somewhat
like the bats' wings that Blake often associated with mystery.
Such mystery is banished in the batlike creature near the feet
of the exuberant young man in the engraving "Albion rose"
(Rosenwald Collection version). The enshrined worship of mystery is symbolized (as in the *Zoas* drawing) in plate 11 of *Europe,*

where the illumination shows the Pope wearing both bats' wings and a tiara that blends compositionally with a gothic facade. On MS page 44 the motif of teasing is reflected in the woman's ambiguously wispy attire, and sexual ambivalence is possibly suggested by the lowermost triangle of the central panel, beneath her groin, which can be seen as either male or female genitals.

7. For a discussion of related matters, see Jean H. Hagstrum, "Christ's Body," in *William Blake: Essays in Honour of Sir Geoffrey Keynes,* ed. Morton' D. Paley and Michael Phillips (Oxford: Clarendon Press, 1973), pp. 129-56.

8. Josh. 17:3-4. Blake closely associates Ephraim and Manasseh, the half-tribes of Egyptian descent, with the heathen lands surrounding Israel. Tirzah is of course a city as well as a woman, the capital in Manasseh of the Northern Kingdom, the antitype of Jerusalem. Biblical landmarks for the scene of human sacrifice Tirzah presides over are located in or near Manasseh: Kanah is the river between Ephraim and Manasseh (Josh. 17:9-10); Ebal is the mount of cursing, opposed to Gerizim, mount of blessing (Deut. 11:29), and is the place where Joshua built a sacrificial altar and installed an engraved copy of the Commandments (Josh. 8:30-33); Shechem is a central city in Manasseh in the mountain pass between Ebal and Gerizim; Mount Gilead probably refers to the highlands in the half of the land of Gilead given to Manasseh (Josh. 13:31).

9. Our thinking on the psychological death and rebirth of Enion as the instinctive element of the personality has been clarified by an unpublished paper, "Ahania, Enion, and Non Entity in *The Four Zoas,*" by Marilyn Williamson, a graduate student at Georgia State University.

10. W. H. Stevenson (1971, p. 427), using biblical identifications furnished by Michael J. Tolley, notes also that when Sheba sees the glory and wisdom of Solomon, "there was no more spirit in her" (1 Kings 10:5). Many or most of the biblical allusions we discuss may be found in standard commentaries on Blake; our identifications are confined to central allusions we find especially illuminating. A book-length study of Blake's biblical references has been undertaken by Tolley.

11. Blake adapts the episode in Revelation of the internal division within the forces of evil that occurs when the beast attacks the whore. The "ten kings," the ten horns of the great whore's beast, "have one mind, and shall give their power and strength unto the beast"—an act opposite to the delegation of power and strength to Los by Tharmas and Urthona. "And the ten horns . . . shall hate the whore, and shall . . . burn her with fire. For God hath put it in their hearts to fulfill his will" (Rev. 17:12-17). In Revelation the smoke of the whore's burning arises for ever and ever (19:3), but in Blake the horror is merely given a new form, only superficially different. There may also be a parody in Blake's passage of the mythical identification of Christ and the Phoenix common in emblem literature and Renaissance poetry.

Night IX

1. The "are human feet" in the MS seems to be a slip of the pen.

2. See I 260-64; 10:9-13 E301; I 488-99; 21:20-31 E307; II 5-8; 23:5-8 E309; III 30-33; 39:1-4 E320; IV 111-13; 50:28-30 E327; IV 141-42; 51:24-25 E328; V 42-45; 58:22-25 E333; V 208-11; 64:11-14 E337; VI 265-80; 74:14-29 E344; VIIA 147-48; 80:39-40 E349; VIIB 201-02; 93:11-12 E397; IX 93-94; 119:26-27 E373.

3. Irene Tayler (1973) offers help with this troublesome matter.

Bibliography

The following is a selected list of books and essays that are concerned mainly with *The Four Zoas* or include lengthy discussions of it.

Beer, John. 1969. *Blake's Visionary Universe.* Manchester: Manchester University Press. New York: Barnes & Noble.

Bentley, G. E., Jr. 1963. *William Blake: "Vala" or "The Four Zoas": A Facsimile of the Manuscript, a Transcript of the Poem, and a Study of Its Growth and Significance.* Oxford: Clarendon Press.

Blackstone, Bernard. 1949. *English Blake.* Cambridge: Cambridge University Press.

Bloom, Harold. 1963. *Blake's Apocalypse: A Study in Poetic Argument.* New York: Doubleday & Company.

Curran, Stuart, and Joseph Anthony Wittreich, Jr., eds. 1973. *Blake's Sublime Allegory.* Madison: University of Wisconsin Press.

Damon, S. Foster. 1965. *A Blake Dictionary: The Ideas and Symbols of William Blake.* Providence: Brown University Press.

Damon, S. Foster. 1924. *William Blake: His Philosophy and Symbols.* Boston: Houghton Mifflin.

Erdman, David V. 1969. *Blake: Prophet against Empire.* Revised edition. Princeton: Princeton University Press.

Erdman, David V., ed., with commentary by Harold Bloom. 1970. *The Poetry and Prose of William Blake.* Fourth printing, with revisions. Garden City, N.Y.: Doubleday & Company.

Erdman, David V., and John E. Grant, eds. 1970. *Blake's Visionary Forms Dramatic.* Princeton: Princeton University Press.

Bibliography

Evans, James C. 1972. "The Apocalypse As Contrary Vision: Prolegomena to an Analogical Reading of *The Four Zoas,*" in *Texas Studies in Literature and Language* 14, 313-328.

Frye, Northrop. 1947. *Fearful Symmetry: A Study of William Blake.* Princeton: Princeton University Press.

Grant, John E. 1973. "Visions in *Vala*: A Consideration of Some Pictures in the Manuscript," in Stuart Curran and Joseph Anthony Wittreich, Jr., eds. 1973. *Blake's Sublime Allegory,* pp. 141-202. Madison: University of Wisconsin Press.

Hagstrum, Jean H. 1973. "Babylon Revisited, or the Story of Luvah and Vala," in Stuart Curran and Joseph Anthony Wittreich, Jr., eds. 1973. *Blake's Sublime Allegory,* pp. 101-118. Madison: University of Wisconsin Press.

Harper, George Mills. 1965. "Apocalyptic Vision and Pastoral Dream in Blake's *Four Zoas,*" in *South Atlantic Quarterly* 64, 110-124.

Hirsch, E. D., Jr. 1964. *Innocence and Experience: An Introduction to Blake.* New Haven and London: Yale University Press.

Keynes, Sir Geoffrey, ed. 1974. *The Complete Writings of William Blake.* London and New York: Oxford University Press.

Magno, Cettina. A facsimile of *The Four Zoas,* based on infrared photography and including extensive notes on the pictures, has been announced.

Margoliouth, H. M. 1956. *"Vala": Blake's Numbered Text.* Oxford: Clarendon Press.

Margoliouth, H. M. 1951. *William Blake.* London, New York, and Toronto: Geoffrey Cumberlege, Oxford University Press.

McNeil, Helen T. 1970. "The Formal Art of *The Four Zoas,*" in David V. Erdman and John E. Grant, eds. 1970. *Blake's Visionary Forms Dramatic,* pp. 373-390. Princeton: Princeton University Press.

Mellor, Anne Kostelanetz. 1974. *Blake's Human Form Divine.* Berkeley: University of California Press.

Murry, J. Middleton. 1933. *William Blake.* London and Toronto: Jonathan Cape.

Paley, Morton D. 1970. *Energy and the Imagination: A Study of the Development of Blake's Thought.* Oxford: Clarendon Press.

Paley, Morton D. 1973. "The Figure of the Garment in *The Four Zoas, Milton,* and *Jerusalem,*" in Stuart Curran and Joseph Anthony Wittreich, Jr., eds. 1973. *Blake's Sublime Allegory,* pp. 119-139. Madison: University of Wisconsin Press.

Rose, Edward J. 1970. "'Forms Eternal Exist For-ever': The Covenant of the Harvest in Blake's Prophetic Poems," in David V. Erdman and John E. Grant, eds. 1970. *Blake's Visionary Forms Dramatic,* pp. 443-462. Princeton: Princeton University Press.

Rudd, Margaret. 1956. *Organiz'd Innocence: The Story of Blake's Prophetic Books.* London: Routledge & Kegan Paul.

Schorer, Mark. 1946. *William Blake: The Politics of Vision.* New York: Henry Holt and Company.

Sloss, D. J., and J. P. R. Wallis, eds. 1926. *William Blake's Prophetic Writings.* 2 vols. Oxford: Clarendon Press.

Stevenson, W. H., ed., text by David V. Erdman. 1971. *The Poems of William Blake.* London: Longman.

Stevenson, Warren. 1972. *Divine Analogy: A Study of the Creation Motif in Blake and Coleridge.* Salzburg Studies in English Literature. Salzburg: Institut für Englische Sprache und Literatur, Universität Salzburg.

Tayler, Irene. 1973. "The Woman Scaly," in *Bulletin of the Midwest Modern Language Association* 6, 74-87.

Wagenknecht, David. 1973. *Blake's Night: William Blake and the Idea of Pastoral.* Cambridge: Belknap Press of Harvard University Press.

Index

Index

Index

Index

Zelophead, 188

Zeus, 181

Zoas: developed as characters, 2; roles in fall, 16, 118, 255-260 *passim*; essential unity of, 22, 126, 127, 139, 245-246; treated as two pairs, 38; remember fall as conspiracy, 70; and pattern of projection, 97; regeneration of, 195, 214, 229, 234; and geographical quadrants, 215, 249, 256; specious similarity of, 242-248 *passim,* 252, 253; mentioned *passim. See also* Los; Luvah; Orc; Tharmas; Urizen; Urthona